D0867440

PERMISSION

PERMISSION

a novel

MARC KRISTAL

atmosphere press

for Anne

We're not all born good. But we're all born with essential human needs. And the methods that we choose to pursue those needs—you know, to scratch those wounds—are the things that make for drama.

- Waldo Salt

ONE

I have an overwhelming need to confess.

Some time ago, in the last decade of the last century, I moved from New York City to Los Angeles, to do a few years of work—not more than that, two years, come what might—in a state of extravagant, nearly bulletproof optimism: employed in my chosen profession, and with the guarded yet giddy certainty that the time of my life was at hand. Some four years later, I found myself at the desk in my home office—*still* in Los Angeles—prodding the blue bottleneck of veins in my wrist with the point of a buck knife blade: panicked, weepily incensed, most of all hopeless, in the way of one who has seen that his worst fears are true, he is the thing he hates, and there is nothing, nothing he can do.

Los Angeles had been my idea. I'd lived there for a year, then another, after college, but neither time nor familiarity could erode my hatred of the place; I packed up my marbles and decamped. Yet I remained a screenwriter, and after years of dedication, the dynamite of my career had been gathered and arranged, and all that was left to do was to light the fuse. I was on the verge, unexpectedly, of making it.

I say unexpectedly because—taking my first steps, as a writer, as a man—I had refused to frame the argument in terms of success or failure. Life, rather, was an adventure, and the aspect that dictated my moves was the process: how one chose to play it. Sitting around LA, wondering what to make of myself, I read an interview with a director, who declared that all artists could be characterized as finders or seekers. He, unquestionably, was the latter: his films remained imperfect, yet filled with scenes, passages, of originality and truth. This, I decided, was the best kind of genius to be. I liked the idea of making things that didn't quite work: it signified that *doing*, the shock of discovery, mattered more than arriving, with no broken bones, at a predetermined destination. You worked your own way, rashly heedless of failure. Whatever the result, you got better.

This was the identity I chose, at the start of my career, to put on; leaving LA, I committed myself. To those who implied that I lacked the nerve to gut it out in Hollywood, I countered that, by abandoning the marketplace, I was taking a greater risk. If I would find my subject and create a style, matters must turn, not on outcomes, but the quest.

And I *was* a success, immediately upon my eastern arrival. Articles for trade magazines, brochures for industries, public service announcements: I just fell into it, and the ease with which I found I could write in different styles, absorb dreary information and speak it back suavely in the voices of disparate clients, caused me a delight akin to what I'd felt in college, upon discovering that I was attractive to girls. I never considered a steady job (which would have left me no writing time), nor was one proffered: my periodic in-person engagements, copy in hand, served the more profitable purpose of entertainment. Producers, editors, ran to get me the burnt dregs of the day's coffee, they clucked with interest over my nocturnal adventures and literary travails.

Sometimes, I admit, I envied the actors and painters with traditional rent-paying gigs, and not just for the camaraderie, the exchange of ideas after hours. Their stakes were higher: one devoted one's entire creative life to a calling, or one was, truly, a waiter. But if it sapped more of my energies than I could absolutely afford, wordsmithing-for-hire repaid the most precious of dividends: it led me to my subject.

My favorite filmmakers didn't approach their craft conventionally, and it was not my plan to do so, either. Rather, I sought inspiration in what was emerging in me, at the start of the Reagan regime, as a choking anger at the culture: its harsh, glittering hedonism, contempt for need and embrace of avarice, most of all the way it had consigned a generation of social revolution to the trash, keeping only the sex, the drugs, and the rock 'n' roll.

I felt profoundly alienated from this world. But I had a privileged view of it: my clients. My friends were seldom writers or artists, but rather a phylum of those I worked for: commodities traders, junk bond dealers, all of them arrogant, brainless, materialistic. Here, I recognized, was my opportunity: Sipping Jack Daniel's, surveying the metropolis from my Greenwich Village aerie, I knew that I, uniquely, could capture this generation, in acerbic, sharply-etched works that might stand as testaments to a time and place.

Nor need I conceal my intentions: they *loved* it, these weasels, that I wanted to write about them, they were only too happy to gold-card my end of the bill for the noisily extravagant life we led. I even sort of liked them, liked the way they put me on their shoulders and cheered me on. I was aware, of course, that in the city's hipper precincts, the East Village and Triangle Below Canal, there was a transformative scene with which I, going about in limos and sipping Cristal, was not on speaking terms. Yet I was stimulated and challenged by my corrida with my subjects. Like Marquez with Castro, Graham Greene with Torrijos, I was dancing with dictators, and it was a high-wire version of performance art to see how far I could take it.

Plus, I got laid. High-strung girls, ferocious drinkers, all with hard, tiring jobs that owned a weird insubstantiality: focus group leaders, time buyers, food stylists. Generally these women preferred the free-spending bond traders with moussed hair and Basile suits, guys given to making flat pronouncements about market trends in loud, nasal tones. I, in my decomposing high-school tweeds, couldn't compete; instead, I worked my artist-in-residence status. In the course of an evening I built my own brand of intrigue, with an enigmatic manner that seemed to editorialize upon the big doings coming my way. Then, finding myself with this or that one at the bar, I'd confide my perceptions, about the situation, about her; the both of us in the moment at hand.

After eight or ten cocktails, when all kisses seem to have

been joined in progress and to end, somehow, in a platform bed in an L-shaped apartment with a hangover like an axe in the brain, these girls were easy to seduce. I got as many as I could. Relationships belonged to finders; I preferred to pursue a transitory intimacy that bestowed knowledge and didn't prevent the acquisition of more. Women showed up at all hours, drank and confided (and sometimes cried), and then—once they'd begun to express shy pleasure at being at least the part-time (but, surely, the *all*-time) favorite of a hard-drinking Greenwich Village writer-cocksman who saw things other, more financially solvent men failed to perceive (which would compel me to explain that my work must always come first)—went away.

At least I spoke the truth. It was all about the work for me. I stuck with it, expecting no reward greater than what the day's labors had to teach.

In nine years I wrote as many screenplays. All went unsold, but one was admired by a producer I'd been cultivating, who passed it on to a director who needed a rewrite, a man who'd once had a name but now was on the brink of obscurity, so that he couldn't do better than myself, but working for him, for me, was a step up. I rewrote his script, he never got it going, but the job became a calling card: I gave it to the agent I'd managed to acquire, and he laid it before a legendary Hollywood producer, at precisely the moment the man was looking for someone young, unknown and promising. And he *liked* it: The producer hired me, for real money—not by Hollywood standards, but certainly more than I had ever made—to write a screenplay.

And because I had been supported, for those many years, by encouragement and success, because I'd made my way on a philosophy comprised of humility in the face of my task and the conviction that I had a right to do it, I did not see my big chance as a Big Chance, and everything fell into place. For the first and only time, the script wrote itself, and when I turned it in, the producer loved it. At long last, I had arrived.

All that remained to solidify my success was that small

matter, the making of the picture. In the teeth of this, I thought: *Go for it.* I decided to return to LA. Two years, that's all. Two years, come what might.

"I'm not going," said my wife.

I know. I haven't mentioned my wife. More to the point, the picture I've drawn would seem to exclude that kind of connection. I was not, however, opposed to the idea. It was always my assumption that, when I was established, I'd find the right person and settle down. In fact, my generically positive feelings about matrimony often led the parade of my seduction stratagems. If I wanted to go to bed with a woman, and thought that was what she needed to hear—that I was prepared to get serious—I'd say it. For my response to bear the weight of conviction, of course, I had to believe in it, and after uttering it several hundred times, I did indeed, on some level, think that what I was doing on all those dates was trying to find a mate. This quality of conviction, in fact, enabled me to bed my wife. Careful to avoid belligerence, she told me within an hour of our meeting that she wanted to have a child, and soon—not only to beat the clock, but also a certain fate: to put behind her the negative familial associations with which her upbringing had irradiated her.

"I want to have children, too," I said. It was not, given my predilection for promiscuity and retreat, a statement I expected to have to answer for.

Perhaps my wife, for a while, was not entirely real to me either. When we met, I had been in New York for six years, in which I'd lived in my head, in a world of my own construction. Increasingly, after five o'clock, I had come as well to live in drink. My nights were predictable. At first, of an evening, I'd enjoy the clarity a single bourbon can provide, wander down St. Mark's Place and marvel at how my mind seemed to photograph iconic images, click, click: the Vietnamese who sold sunglasses off a pegboard, sighing over a photo of an ormolu clock, or the LP, floating through the air with the ease of a hawk riding a thermal, flung by an experimentally in-your-face, pubescent runaway boy. From there, I'd go on to drinks with friends, the Lion's Head or One University, the bourbon releasing my reflexive wit; in this passage of the night I'd sit in the moment and apart from it, taking a spectator's pleasure in my cleverness even as that cleverness unspooled. Finally, in the dim hour before sleep, my consciousness would become like a mirror hung beside a road, reflecting the headlights of passing thoughts but resisting their penetration. Slumped on the couch after my seventh or eighth, I would lapse into entombment, and revel, safe and uncensored, in my self-fantasy. It is not hard to imagine that, for a man in this zone, the reality of another might remain somewhat at bay.

Thus it was some months—a year, even—before my wife's absolute factuality asserted itself. I liked her, of course, liked her immediately. Ironically, I was not her type: we met on a blind date, and when she saw my face, her disappointment was so palpable, I almost laughed. Yet the lack of promise actually helped, it removed a need to perform, and there arose, in its stead, a simpatico so comprehensive, it bordered on the supernatural. We understood the nuances of each other's histories, cherished the same artistic touchstones, embraced complementary social values, and if it sounds like we only ratified each other's opinions, it is because I lack the powers to describe a transforming experience: that of being known, at last, by an equal. And it was all mercifully lacking in mannered expressions of fascination, in that fruity air of forced delight that can perfume a first date into silliness. She was strictly down-to-earth, my wife, she chomped tortilla chips and made strange faces, volleys of profanity snapped through her arias like grapeshot. Neither of us left the restaurant thinking, This is it, yet the connection was so strong, and such a pleasure, we could not walk away from it.

The impulse to do so was born of a lack of heat. Yet finding myself, on our second date, not so much bothered by the absence of an erotic pull as curious about it, I noticed that she could, at least, capture a man's imagination. She had a ripe Mediterranean body, my wife, a quarter-century of ballet had left her graceful and firm, her proportions ideal. The face completed the picture, a bright-eyed open face, an olive complexion beneath a spill of unmanageable curls. Glimpsing her reflection as we walked, my wife pronounced herself funny-looking, but it would be more accurate to say that her face owned an exaggerated emotional mobility, and this sad or happy or pensive silent-film expressiveness, her elaborate gestures in conversation, served as spark to a certain fantasy. In her neo-Beatnik outfits, my wife reminded me of those innocent, dangerous women in films of the 1950s, free spirits of vaguely Gypsy provenance, who end up dead at the hands of the playboys they sexually enslave, then toss over the gunwales of their lives like so much stale bait. Watching my wife disport above her plate, I reflected that one didn't see many Barefoot Contessas nowadays. Sipping my drink, enjoying its clarity, I warmed to the potential of this retro-chic appeal; to the ego fillip of squiring so much innocence and danger.

The squalor of her existence nearly killed us before we began. Such was the disorder of her Chelsea studio, which I described as being decorated in Early Hideout, that traversing its twenty feet could take half as many minutes: I eased around shadeless lamps with bent harps, stacks of Louis Sherry candy tins and souvenir pen-and-pencil sets, my toe nudged a disemboweled tube radio and snagged on the headrest of an absent barber's chair. "How can you *live* like this?" I blurted, and my wife rolled her eyes and gestured, overwhelmed. I was on the edge of bolting—truly—when I saw what that gesture might mean. While she rummaged through the single, crammed closet in search of a coat, I spotted little notes—"get an agent," "get in a play," and my favorite, "do better"—that suggested a life like my own, a work in progress with an anticipated happy end. In the kitchen, I spied a pad in the shape of a pig, on which my wife had scrawled a grocery list—cranberry juice, condensed milk—and it won me back decisively, I could imagine her seeing it and being enchanted, bringing it home and writing something in her blocky, childlike hand. She was not a slattern, I decided, or clinically depressed, but a cheerful soul who'd become snowed in by the demands of creation. My heart went out to her, my messy contessa. I could, I would, help her.

It was not a sense of duty, however, but this cheerfulness that sealed the deal. My wife arrived for our evenings overbrimming with eagerness to, as she put it, "tell you some things"; every anecdote was not fascinating, every insight not worthy of the name, but what never missed was my wife's enthusiasm, the joy in her eyes as she testified to the wonder and glory of our little world. She was funny, too, especially about herself, and if you teased her, she didn't get pissy, she laughed at the distraction that caused her to take three hours to make her bed. My wife wasn't easily offended like so many women I'd known, she hadn't rushed through her early experience merely to put it all behind her, she didn't have a dreary pile of attitudes that passed for a human nature. She was alive, and eager, for experience, for the indelible, internal bell-note that signals life's beauty, most of all for connection, connection above all. She was real.

We went to bed on our third date. Stripped, my wife proved to be perfection, reminding me of Edward Weston's nudes of Tina Modotti, sunbathing on the azotea. In a first for me, she came and I didn't: my wife's physiognomy kept her from arriving at her destination in any position save one; and the contortions this required caused enough discomfort to keep me firmly off the train. Oddly, I found this helpful: the combination of her limitations (about which I reassured her) and my enhanced longevity (with which she was impressed) relaxed me and granted me power. I was content to lie back and contemplate this sublime photograph, one which, drifting into sleep, murmured, "Thank you."

Not end of story. It has been my observation that the best in people only emerges when their flaws are welcomed into the alchemy of their nature. Perhaps, given my predilection for the imperfect artist, I am simply attracted to those in whom the good depends upon the bad. God knows this was true of my wife. If I respected her struggle, found myself drawn instinctively to the drama of a nature engaged in self-combat, its reality sat heavily upon our relationship—which is to say, it sat upon me.

She was terribly blocked in her work, a condition that evolved from primordial insult. The child of an eminent professor, a wealthy, well-born man who rejected his own father's arrogant certainty and then replicated it, and a modern dancer who, after a night disporting as a faun, a leaf, sat down and never stood up again, and spent the balance of her days in a wheelchair, blaming her daughter for giving her the polio that put her there, my wife had been inoculated from childhood with a Catch-22: The only thing worth being is a successful artist; and no artist could or should be successful, success being the sine qua non of mediocrity. This fiat, reinforced by years of emotional abuse, had fixed my wife in an unbreakable amber of stasis. She could never quit the compulsion to make it "creatively," yet sneered at any sort of strategizing or self-promotion; meanwhile, beneath the bluster, her sense of inadequacy ran deep as a religious conviction. As first a dancer, then a painter, finally an actress, my wife showed a nuanced understanding of quality; she showed ability at each. But marination in this witches' brew of ambition, contempt and self-hatred had left her incapable of seeing what she did as a job, from which magic was released via the humdrum daily business of solving problems.

To be at the center of this, I knew, was agonizing. But it was not the whole story. My wife, it emerged, had money, an inherited blue-chip portfolio that paid enough in dividends to float a vie de la bohème; and the lack of a need to work had leached into the groundwater of her emotional conflict and contaminated its purity, turning it from an obstacle into a catch-all, one that excused an ever more unproductive life.

It had progressed, like all such poisonings, by degrees. My wife had studied, and with some of the century's great teachers, when she came to New York to act; but in the teeth of serial rejection her enthusiasm ebbed, and it became extremely challenging to soldier on. With the prospect of yet another failure too painful to consider—what, after all, was left?—she had retreated into a holding pattern, supplementing her inheritance with chump change earned as a movie extra, and attending cattle-call auditions gleaned from the theatrical trades.

Seldom did this add up to a full day, and so my wife filled the hours, not just with Stanislavski, but dance classes, bargain shopping, the *New York Times* crossword puzzle, and therapy. When questioned about her situation, she trotted out the Catch-22 and sobbed over it, genuinely; yet painful as her life was, in a way, it worked. With no financial incentive to change, it became ever easier for her simply not to try.

Avoiding her larger reality led my wife to avoid its particulars. She blurred, gradually, the difference between blockage and a refusal to play the game, integrity and an unwillingness to earn a real living, and the figure that emerged from this snarl of truth, half-truth and semi-fiction owned a faint but unmistakable arrogance. She never said it aloud, but, on some level, my wife believed the money was her due. She was a "good" person, doing the "right" thing, living "poorly" enough to demonstrate "proper values." Why *shouldn't* she receive this all-but-useless stipend? Given what she'd suffered, did it not amount to a version of reparations? Wasn't she still—in an ironic change on the psychological debt each generation owes the previous— paralyzed?

This self-serving interpretation of therapy-derived insight was, I felt, the most pernicious of my wife's evasions. I didn't doubt that the decades of sessions with one or another talking doctor had been beneficial: from the wretched kid she assured me she had been, my wife had evolved into a happy, sweet-natured, emotionally available grownup. The problem was that she'd had every insight there was to have, there was nothing to do but, as the saying goes, own it: act on her discoveries, and change. My wife dodged this transit with a neat semantic veronica: since she *hadn't* changed, *true* insight, ipso facto, continued to elude her. And so on she slogged, waiting for the letters in the alphabet soup of her psyche to form themselves into a message she was prepared to read. I did not think this would happen. But when I'd suggest as much, my wife would throw it back at me, blaming hostility, on my part, toward self-knowledge.

Here was the nexus at which her miseries became mine. My wife had constructed a complex emotional hothouse on a highly unstable foundation. Anything that kicked too hard at it, she vaporized. Her weapon of choice was the counter-punch. What about *your* blah-blah-blah, she would demand in response to even the mildest criticism. We are all susceptible to this, but my wife took it to extremes. Cross the faintest of lines, and she would ransack the argument for any failing of your character, no matter how whimsical its relevance, and bludgeon you bloody with it.

Great rows could erupt from trivialities. Not surprisingly, my wife pinched the eagle, a trait which appeared most embarrassingly when she picked up a check and left the waiter ten percent. *Fifteen* was standard, I would smolder, twenty ideal. Instantly, my wife would attack: I overtipped because I wanted to be liked, it was insecurity, not a response to service—why didn't I *deal* with it? At least *my* inadequacies got me friends, I would counter. Get a job, you wouldn't have to make excuses for being cheap. Fuck you, would be the reply.

My wife inflicted more lasting damage: her fits drove off my friends. If a social situation made her uncomfortable, she would take control by, in the name of honesty, prising off its lid. "Why are you pushing liquor on him?" she would snap at some hapless copywriter and his middle-management wife as they poured the Jack Damage, eager for the latest bulletin from the front lines of my life. "You *know* he's an alcoholic. You get a kick out of his lifestyle, but *you* don't have to eat it." So personal—and, often, so true—were these outbursts that they poisoned the grace by which such friendships proceeded. When people I'd known for years stopped calling, and I'd complain that my wife had ruined things out of insecurity, she would counter that it was the inability of a bunch of weak, pathetic nobodies to handle a little truth for a change. If I went to therapy, she'd rail, and quit drinking, I'd see it.

This denial mechanism—there is no other term for it—drove me into thermonuclear rages Ralph Kramden would have envied. But there was a reason for it, simple and profound: my wife was a survivor. She had survived her childhood, years so desolating that she'd erased them, save for small, desaturated fragments: her frazzled father, single-parenting while his wife struggled in an iron lung, blaming the burnt macaroni on his daughter's recitation of a rhyme; her returned mother's radioactive outbursts, excused by disability, from which no venomous flourish could be censored. To get through it, my wife, that child, had to unplug: to become dead to the humanity of others if it hurt or threatened or interfered with her. Without that ability, I am certain, there would have been no eagerness, no sweetness. But like so much in my wife's lexicon, the mechanism of self-preservation had metastasized into a way of avoiding change. If I asked her to do something she opposed, she subtracted its validity; if I criticized her, she attacked my character; if I lost my temper, she shut down. These responses were as deeply ingrained as the will to live. They were not going away for me.

Given what I knew, the most remarkable fact of our disputes was their outcome: my wife began staying over seven nights a week, and marriage and parenthood became onrushing inevitabilities. The reason was that our arguments, so apparently petty, in fact amounted to a furious struggle: a fight for the rights to my reality.

As she was at root attacking, not my tipping habits or my friends, but my self-fantasy—that character I'd put on upon leaving LA—I was defending, not a way of life, but that character's right to exist. In practical terms, this meant that I was, over and again, insisting to my wife upon my fitness to be with her. Of *course* I could be "myself" *and* the father of her child, I would say, *certainly* they're not incompatible. It never occurred to me to consider whether or not this was something I *wanted* to be. Just as my wife moved in without officially "moving in," I went straight to assuring our family's success without pondering the larger question of its suitability.

My wife's cause was supported, it must be said, by the fact that, the more she recast my behavior, the more it resembled her description of it. This was particularly true of my drinking. It was, of course, *her fault*. Since most of my buddies had fled the acid rain of my wife's hostility, I was unable to space out my rounds with the usual conversation, I had to put away my quota alone, at home, and out of my wife's sight, and so I became that worst of all things, a secret drinker. If I appeared to nurse one for an hour, I would also sneak glugs from the bottle whenever my wife left the room, or else quickly top myself off; sometimes, my drink sitting on the coffee table, I would actually go *out* for a drink: claim a forgotten errand, then bolt a triple at the always-sympathetic Lesbian bar at the corner ("send 'er over, *we'll* straighten 'er out"), before returning, with a shit-eating grin, bearing the latest issue of *Film Comment*. What had begun as a case of Hemingway-esque brio had devolved into something out of Cheever.

Nightly I felt worse and enjoyed it less, yet I protested, dishonestly, that I'd cut my consumption, if my wife fixed her own life she'd be less obsessed with mine. Alas, I undercut my arguments by going on binges. I would be good for two months, sometimes three, at which point the effort of suppression would become too great, and I'd disappear until dawn, and often later, much later. These episodes were excruciating for my wife, who would collapse into pitiable sobs when, reeking of hooch and b.o., I'd finally make it home. There would ensue a day or so of Hickey-esque avowals of temperance; in a gesture to my wife's vegetarianism, I would eat salad, in lieu of crow. Then the pattern would reassert itself, the denials and accusations would heave themselves up and go through the motions, as joylessly as a team of pensioners at a dance on the old town square.

If it seems incredible that I did not see what the fights were about, or understand the effect they were having—if it is amazing that we continued to go on—consider that I was still riding my wave of encouragement and success, I remained a man engaged in a serious creative mission. Indeed, I had begun to view the elemental nature of our battle through the objectifying microscope of drama.

Considering our relations, I asked myself: Mightn't there be a story in my emotional oscillation, my susceptibility to my wife's arguments, combined with a profound suspicion of her motives? Immediately there arrived the offer of the rewrite job, from the once-famous director who could afford no better than the likes of me. His piece of shit—let us not mince words—was a film noir in the *Double Indemnity* mode: an insurance investigator, a dead husband, a femme fatale. Was I interested? You betcha. In my version, the investigator, as per usual, distrusts the evil temptress; every time he confronts her with an inconvenient fact, however, she turns it around, suggesting that it's his own emotional limitations that cause him to hide behind his professional façade, to view life's ambiguities as proof of someone's guilt. If he'd just let go, she says, and embrace the love (and the $7 million insurance settlement) she's offering, his suspicions would evaporate along with the worst aspects of his personality. The investigator waffles around for thirty pages, throws himself into an affair—and his newfound openness enables him to find a previously unseen clue, one that proves that he'd been right about the bitch all along.

My take enabled me to have it both ways, writing it amused me greatly, and my wife, after reading the script (and making a few pissy faces), approved. Never mind us: It was my crafty spin on a tired genre that got me noticed— got me the job that led back to LA. The influence of the relationship on the work had enabled my first big win.

Things, definitively, had changed. I had entered my thirties, and the days in which I could pass out at three, rise at seven and function lucidly had long since passed. The years had yielded a style and a voice, I had been paid to do what I loved and succeeded at it, my writing had crossed the line from intangible aspiration to something approaching a career. Somewhat to my surprise, I had become a professional. It was now, of course, that marriage, which had gone from being a distant ripple on the horizon to a terrifying tsunami that threatened to obliterate the atoll of my liberty, chose to crash down. My wife was nearing forty, she wanted to have a child. If I wasn't ready, she had to move on.

My position was clear: *no way*. Not because of the financial demands, the ideas that would go unpursued because baby needs new shoes. More than this, I feared the consumptive lunacy a child would bring. I needed order, cleanliness, they were essential if I expected to think. When I considered the synergy that would emerge from my wife's personality mixed with an infant's torrid ways, I groaned aloud.

In truth, my wife's disorder worried me more than any baby's. Her slovenly unconcern, the dirty laundry and open closet doors and uncapped pens she left in her wake were, I had learned, the outward manifestations of her inability to get it together. This, thank God, was not my problem. Whatever my failings, I lived a focused life, a *private* life; letting someone into it required that she feed my clarity and order, not the opposite.

Yet viewed from this perspective, our potential union took on the appealing aspect of risk. Like moving to New York, marriage was a gamble. I had been attracted to making things that didn't quite work precisely because, rather than in spite, of their unresolvable disorders. One knew the ecstasy of touching the stars even if one crashed to earth. I also found it reassuring that, biological imperatives aside, my wife didn't want this any more than I did. "Marriage," she'd say, "AKA, When Bad Things Happen to Good People." Regarding our future, it seemed, the only thing we had in common was ambivalence.

I was flooded, moreover, with a sense of responsibility. I had known from the opening salvos that this baby deadline was looming. I could not abandon a woman whom I'd selfishly kept out of the marriage market at the beginning of the end of her child-bearing years. I could not bring myself to hurt her. One night, as I stared at the television, agonizing over which course of action would ruin my life the least, my wife, her hopeless hair askew and gnarled dancer's feet exposed, put her arms around me and said, in a small voice, "I'll be a good wife. Please don't leave me."

I faced it: it was no longer just me; it was us. Flaubert's maxim about being regular in one's habits like a bourgeois so that one can be bold and wild in one's art would have to be put in play. On a suitably stifling summer day, at City Hall, we tied the knot.

After all the operatic hand-wringing, nothing changed. Early in our relationship, I'd moved into an illegal sublet in the West Village, overrun with mice, redeemed by the pleasures of the neighborhood; at some point, my wife had joined me, and there, post-maritum, we remained, in a condition of impermanence heightened by the fact that she'd not given up her own dump: the rent being negligible, I cleaned it up and began using it as an office. This arrangement worked smoothly; we saw no reason to change it. We had married to legitimize an anticipated child. Beyond that, our lives remained our own.

Shortly thereafter, I got that first Hollywood job; it was on the plane back to New York that I conceived of going west. Apart from making professional sense, the prospect of a few years on the coast suggested a certain amount of pleasure. Rents were cheap and space was plentiful; I'd get a vintage convertible and buzz around beneath the smog-tinted Santa Monica sky. By the time the plane touched down, my idle notion had cemented into certainty: within twelve months, we would be short-time Angelenos.

"I'm not going," said my wife.

She dug in her heels, and over the following months, as I completed two drafts of the script, hammered ferociously at my anxieties: endless meetings would sunder my discipline, I'd become obsessed with the business and two years would be twenty, I'd lose my way. Her own terrors, too, did laps: she had no friends, she'd get no work, she dreaded driving. I reassured her: some pals of mine she actually liked had moved west; Hollywood offered her a larger professional pond in which to fish; I'd play chauffeur until she felt ready to take the wheel. I would—this was a given, but had to be stated—pay for everything. Nothing made a dent.

But my luck held, that great wave I'd ridden for so many years: from my illegal sublet, we were evicted, and my wife failed to produce a child.

To remove the odor from what I have just related, I must explain it. After trying and not succeeding the old-fashioned way, my wife began to see a fertility doctor (a Castilian whose accent caused her to lisp so violently on words such as *szthperm* that it was as though Sylvester the Cat were pondering my wife's uterine mysteries). The move was postponed, and for months she stoically went off to Dr. Maribel carrying cup after cup of my seed, I injected her with hormones and took her temperature, our sex life cratered beneath the strain of calendared fucking, and she endured it all, every humiliation and misfire, with grace and elegance, with nothing short of courage. The closest we came was a fetus that died after six weeks, necessitating another set of horrors, an "abortion" to save the tissue that required running a gauntlet of pro-lifers chanting—this, after nearly two years of trying—"Don't kill your baby."

Following the clinic procedure, I felt deeply ashamed; my ambivalence, I was certain, had driven away the baby's waiting soul. But just as I had gained new respect for my wife, she too had turned a corner in response to my ministrations. As we walked down Park Avenue South, sorrowfully holding hands beneath a foggy drizzle, my wife gave in. "Okay," she said, "okay. You didn't want kids and you made a sacrifice for me. We'll move."

Then the landlord got wise, eviction notices were duct-taped to the door, and the last reason to delay disappeared.

I assured my weepy wife that we would keep her studio, she could visit as often as she pleased. She voiced a sudden, plaintive request: Might we move to Paris when the two years were up? By all means, I said slyly—if *she* planned *that* trip.

With that, the first act of my adult life drew to a close. I had gotten an education, made a grownup of myself; I'd done it my way, and from that immutable fact, drew strength. I had come to the city with nothing but a fantasy. I was departing with a talent, a career, and a marriage.

And: sober. I had my final binge before the fetus terminated, when we were freaked out by the realization that a process the failure of which we'd begun to take for granted had abruptly produced stupendous results. Staggering home, finding the apartment deserted—my wife having decamped in a rage—I experienced a moment of clarity. Perhaps she was wrong to have compelled me to have my fun in the margins; perhaps I had not wanted any of this. But I had it now, and what I was doing was unfair. So I quit, cold. For a few weeks, it was like someone had let the air out of me, and then I bounced off the walls for a bit. But by the time we were ready to leave, it felt easier.

We moved. And I let myself in for all the bad karma in this life, and all the lives preceding; for a universe of bitter shit.

XXXX

What can I add to the literature of Los Angeles? Only the personal.

It has been said of the city that it has no edges and no center; and if, after a time, I recognized that there was indeed a grid there, this absence of boundaries was at first so overwhelming that it seemed to seep into my self-perception and leave me utterly undefended. Looking for a place, a part of town in which to settle, we drove, endlessly, mile after mile, through Hollywood, West Hollywood, Westwood, Woodland Hills, Beverly Hills, Beverlywood—names that flowed into each other with the same lack of difference as the identically landscaped, perfectly deserted streets—but remained unable to gain a purchase: we stared, helpless, as the changeless cityscape washed past our eyes, too dazed even to slow down long enough to make decisions.

So unconvincing were these districts—the ersatz folksiness, stucco bungalows like boxes on concrete slabs—that they seemed to comprise the set design of an elaborate drama, one in which everyone was in on the plot but us. I sensed it in people's behavior: transacting even mundane business, Angelenos struck me as elaborately "on," and they in turn expressed a cool disdain, as though for my own inability to play, or even know, my part. Buying groceries for the friends with whom we crashed, gassing up the car, I felt exposed, and judged; driving, I'd force myself to slow, to get the details off a FOR RENT sign, and instantly I would hear a horn, the impatience of the car behind me. You couldn't see them, but they saw you. And simply by being human, you'd offended them.

It was easy, under these circumstances, to begin judging myself on other people's terms, a tendency exacerbated by the isolating nature of the city, the way it entombed you in a car. The agent of my distress was talk radio, with which I'd had no experience but came to exert a creepy fascination. The callers were monstrous. Nakedly racist, they thought Mexicans were dumb, Jews greedy, blacks dangerous, and Asians bad drivers. Equally were they obsessed with gossip, vetting the boob jobs of the rich and famous, outing movie stars, shooting the breeze about whether so-and-so was bulimic or just had AIDS.

I was contemptuous, repelled; but what held me as I'd sit there, waiting through my third red light to make a left, was the callers' sense of entitlement, their conviction that, if they felt it, it was good. I realized that, like myself, these people were isolated, and this—the essential condition of Los Angeles—had stripped them of humanity. Without the civilizing effects of in-person relations, they never had to pay for their words, and thus were free to unleash an unconscious, assumptive barbarism.

Pelted relentlessly by this storm, my repellence began to give way, first to fear, then awe, then to a kind of sympathy. Certainly I, with my questioning sensibility, did not feel that kind of assurance about anything. And the things the callers ridiculed—morality, art, the life of the mind—were precisely those in which I had invested so much personal capital. What I was hearing, all day, every day, was that the notions I'd cultivated regarding life and self were, really, bullshit, little more than airs, and entombed and unboundaried as I was, I found it difficult not to respect that point of view. It was my personal variant of Stockholm Syndrome: the callers' entitlement became something I began to believe in.

I needed, I knew, to walk. But it was impossible. Nobody walked in LA—nothing drew you forward. No, the mall was your destination, one of the multi-block, multi-story monoliths that sat like ocean liners on the city's major thoroughfares. These were the true town squares of Los Angeles, and it was to them that we gravitated, to the food courts, multiplexes, chain stores (in an ironic flourish, one even found department stores—malls within malls, mall matryoshka). As with traditional town squares, one came not merely to make purchases, but to absorb the community's values. And since there was nothing to do there—nothing— but spend money, I realized that the purchases *were* the values, and this helped me start to decode the city, to get my arms around what was happening to me. I'd become overwhelmed by how desperately wrong LA seemed, in every detail of planning and execution; but now, driven into the malls by a cabin fever induced by an inability to walk, I perceived a powerful intention: the entire Los Angeles experience was contrived to ensure that your needs, fantasies and motivations were determined by what was for sale. The endless diet of driving and talk radio, which seemed so hideously inexplicable, amounted to a kind of deprogramming: you were trussed up in a rolling straitjacket and subjected to unseen myriad brainwashers, who pummeled you with their narcissism until you released your individuality. Then the malls gave you something with which to replace it: a few mass-market goods, and an addiction to the mass sensibility they signified. Then, and only then, were you granted validation—for parking. You got your ticket punched; and, to the barbaric yawps of your fellow citizens, drove home.

What was interesting—ominous—was that being aware of the addiction didn't release you from it. Quite the opposite, if you were in The Business. I was not a kid, I had a classy project going with a major producer, I had spent years cultivating an identity separate from Hollywood. Yet I was not even remotely prepared for the extent to which the city and its most famous industry, with their shared devotion to generic cultural iconography, the canned feelings it inspired, and the money to be made from both, fed off of and reflected each other, until they sucked out your center and replaced it with an all but uncontrollable need to belong. The consuming reality of Hollywood, the place and the mindset, was being accepted, and the feverishness of this vibe vaporized one's independent spirit as cleanly as an ultrasound wave demolished a gallstone. *Everything had to sell.* And if people weren't buying your thing, you bloody well fixed it until they did. It was why Angelenos were so prone to radical, even disfiguring, plastic surgery: so potent was the town's sensibility that it divorced you from the reality of your flesh.

This put me in a rough position. I already felt judged, as though I were offending people, that the values to which I subscribed were of questionable merit. Now I wanted to fit in. But that meant snipping off, not my big nose, but a piece of my talent.

I'd once known a barber, whose right hand, after years of cutting hair, was as textured as the most lived-in of faces. One day he had an accident, the tendons were severed, and he lost the use of it. Within two weeks, it had become as smooth and lifeless as a rubber glove—a representation of a hand, but without the animating essence. I thought of that when, meeting with a producer, he blew off one of my ideas by saying, "You don't *need* it, man. The audience *gets it.*" That meant we didn't need to individualize our characters, because we weren't creating individuals; rather, we were replicating popular-entertainment archetypes that everyone agreed should be in the movies. You gave the audience Barbie or Ken, and a cue, the movie equivalent of a doll outfit—nerd glasses, an empty whiskey bottle—and Mr. and Mrs. America filled in the rest. People *got it*, Hollywood believed, not because they were inured to clichés, but because they'd become them.

God knows I wanted to make it—I was dying to see a hideous flash picture of myself, snapped at an opening, on the back page of *Variety*. But that would mean sawing through the tendons of my scripts and leaving them as proximate—as dead—as my friend's Playtex hand. Thus was an extra layer of anxiety added to my days: the conflict between achieving a profound artistic success, and an overwhelming desire to sell out.

It was not an existence that delivered peace. Distanced as you were from your feelings, you didn't realize it, but you were stoking a murderous resentment at being a kind of double slave, compelled both to make shit and to eat it. And now and then it would become just too much. I felt it soon enough; my guts would begin to shift, and I saw how the effect could be equal to the shifting of those tectonic plates that would, from time to time, respond to their own intolerable pressures and rip the city up. They seemed to work in secret sympathy, the seismic and the existential, and it explained, I thought, why LA was so prone to abrupt acts of convulsive violence, natural and man-made. While I was in residence, there were riots, earthquakes, celebrity murders, parricides. The ground opened up and fire rained down from the skies. The city never yielded. It was as though plastic surgeons rushed to the scene of every catastrophe and pulled the urban epidermis tight, so that all you saw were traffic lights and on-ramps, gardeners and valets. It was then that I realized how tough an authoritarian burg like LA could be, as tough as any company town with big money at stake. The difference was that no Pinkertons were required to keep the peace: order arrived with the voluntary return of the citizens to their chains. Los Angeles, that crafty enforcer with a smile and a suntan, controlled you because you had internalized its ways. Move along, buddy. Beep beep.

Those early days were excruciating, minutely. And yet. Once I got out of the farting used Nissan I'd bought and into a home of my own, I found it impossible to repress my heart's response. Five weeks into our sojourn, my wife and I discovered a neighborhood east of Fairfax Avenue, full of big apartments with low rents, and the place we took provoked fresh expressions of amazement into our third month in residence. It was a Mediterranean Revival duplex—a stairway, indoors!—with archways and chandeliers and terracotta tiling, two capacious bedrooms, a dining room *and* an eat-in kitchen, fourteen French windows, and—most incredibly, for two people who for decades had duked it out with wily, surly neighbors over the quarter-eating clunkers in the basements of mondo Manhattan—its own laundry room. And all, all for half what I'd been paying for the West Village mouse cave. Beholding this people's palace was like finding true love after a lifetime of settling: you didn't realize how empty was your vessel, and how you suffered from that emptiness, until it was brimming. Our place was comprised of three structures, in a U formation around a central court, and though we had no outdoor space of our own, nothing prevented me from dragging out a lawn chair, sitting beneath the avocado tree, and reading the day's *Variety* in a condition of utter luxury. The twin torments of LA life, fleas and leaf-blowers, notwithstanding, it was Eden.

Having fulfilled one's most optimistic fantasy of love, however, the place revealed itself to be one's worst nightmare of betrayal. There was a reason, I realized, why these places rented so cheaply. Lying fifteen feet from our common wall in my own bed, I was able to hear, one Sunday morning, the camerawoman next door give her boyfriend a blowjob, I could hear, clearly, the sucking and slurping, followed by his hoarse orgasmic groans, followed—clearly—by the expectoration of the wad into a tissue (*two* tissues, actually, I heard them pulled from the box, *pfft, pfft*), and in response to his sighed perturbation her hostile little joke about it ("Would you rather I spit it in your face?"). I was in shock. My love, my refuge, that which was supposed to have been my solace, my stability, proved as porous and flexible as sponge cake.

If the construction's flimsiness belied the bourgeois gentility of the surroundings, so too did the habits of my showbiz-wannabe neighbors. They piled up Styrofoam furniture outside their kitchen doors, pieces that swelled with moisture and filled your nose with a skunky reek. They dragged futons out onto our patches of communal lawn and lounged on them hourly, hanging on their phones and flicking endless smoked-down butts into the street. They dumped cat litter in the gutter, left their doors open and stereos booming, they decorated their terraces with elegantly crafted teak furniture, then pissed off of them into the flowers and trees. One began believing life would be charmed, and ended amidst squalor and entropy.

As with all such tales of seduction and betrayal, this one finished with a small but unmistakable loss of self, as though my essence had wandered a little away from me. Yet it enabled me finally to understand that contemptuous vibe to which we'd first been subjected: why it was that, in the most neutral situations, I would feel so singled out, so judged. The longer I observed my neighbors, the more I believed there was a single controlling idea at work in the city, and that everything was governed by it. The idea was status. Status shaped the grid—that which, like the right-angled Manhattan streets, established the form of one's life and set the pace. I saw it on those occasions when one of the wannabes would break through, with a script sale, a part in a picture, a recurring role in series TV. Promptly the winner, so recently your best bud, would move—not to another crackerbox a block away, but to the canyons or, more typically, the west side, where the rents were high, the temperatures lower, the air clean and sweet. And: you were not going with him. He had exchanged one life for another, completely.

More than once did I watch, as the winner drove away, the newly anointed Little People shoot each other nervous slantendiculars across the courtyard. Then each would suck it up, and do the one, the only thing possible to quash the queasy uncertainty. Each would look at the others, and determine what his or her status was in relation to the other drones in the Dream Factory: who was above and, more usefully, who was beneath.

That was what everyone in Los Angeles was thinking when they checked me out and found me wanting: *This guy isn't better than me.* There was, in that status-gridded town, only one question: What are you? And, to the question, two answers: Somebody, or Nothing.

XXXX

"We're not staying," said my wife.

For all the difficulties posed by the assaultive world, this proved to be my biggest problem: Like the child who hoists the flag of independence by saying no, my wife defined herself in Los Angeles by refusing to in any way accept her situation. She had agreed, on that sad, gray morning in New York, to move; but what I discovered was that she was interpreting the word strictly as a physical relocation, devoid of any behavior that could possibly be construed as settling in.

I, like the parent whose child acts out in this way, assumed it was a phase. Yet dealing with it leaned heavily on my days. Nothing was too trivial to go to war over, to be used as reinforcement for my wife's endlessly restated, conditional vision of our residency.

"I *hate* placemats," she wailed typically, "what's the *point?*"

"Well," reasonably, "let's see. If we want to have people for—"

"I don't *want*. To have *pee*-pull. For *din*-ner," eyes hot, veins bulging, "I don't want to enter*tain*, don't you under*stand*? I don't want to *do* this." Walking away, bare feet *potch, potching* on the wooden floor, downthrusting violently with both fists. "I don't want to do this, so just, just don't—just *don't*."

Worse was how she dealt with our friends. Various couples I knew had preceded us in the westward migration, and I was anxious to mix in their lives. But my wife held them firmly at arm's length. "It's *only* for two years. Then we're going to Paris," she'd proclaim, like Marie Antoinette facing a long, bad patch at Versailles.

So often did my wife repeat this refrain, and in so many houses, that it became the leitmotif of our relationships. "Liking it better?" a friend would ask of an evening.

My wife would reply with a pantomime of a scream, then shrug. "Hey: It's pretty, okay? The foliage? What can I say. But"—and here I would flinch in anticipation—"it's not what I *value*." Her shoulders would go up to her ears, she'd give her head a tiny, incredulous shake. "Liposuction? Big fake titties? I don't *theenk* so." Like her assaults on homemaking, this routine supported our temporary-visa status: rather than threading our way into the community, we remained alien short-timers, crouching behind a wall of suspicion.

As the months passed, and this went on, I became aware that, though the clock on my two LA years was ticking, my actual life there did not feel as though it had begun. Existence delivered events but not experiences: I occupied an apartment, but didn't inhabit it; I saw friends, but from a wife-imposed distance. Increasingly, it became difficult to feel anything at all, except for this strange dissociation from myself. It was as though my intimate life had defected to the outside world, joined up with all the urban and professional adversaries contriving to take away my identity and replace it with their own agendas.

It seemed a kind of mental illness, but the truth was much simpler. It was my marriage. Like the home that had seduced me with its promise of protection, then betrayed me by storming across my underdefended boundaries and shattering my well-being, my wife had promised to stand by me in this challenging stage of life and was instead interfering violently with its prosecution. I needed, just then, to give the fullest expression to the self I'd created. But by forcing her agenda of non-involvement on every aspect of our life, my wife was making that impossible.

I understood this with my nervous system, my primitive brain. Because it was primal, what was happening to me. But, for some equally primitive reason that I didn't understand, I could not convert these feelings into a clear articulation that I might communicate. Instead, I would feel spasms of panic, in anticipation of a dreadful inevitability. And I would explode.

"Can't you be nice?" I shouted one day as I passed my wife on the stairs. "Don't you see what's happening here?"

"Don't tell me how to feel," she replied in a stricken murmur, eyes down.

This was my other, nearly equal problem: even as I snapped and lunged like a cornered weasel, sympathy for my wife poured out of me, as though from a wound I could not staunch. She had no life. There were a few cronies from her dance days, but they lived far away, in the baking smog pits of the northern San Fernando Valley, and the shoestring stage productions that had formed the mainstay of her auditioning career did not appear to exist.

The knuckle of my wife's difficulties, however—in Los Angeles, city of cars—remained her unwillingness to drive. She knew how, but hadn't done so in years, and the thought of wading into the shark tank of LA traffic consumed her with dread. So profound was my wife's terror that she attempted to use public transportation, a nearly unheard-of activity among Anglo Angelenos. My wife found a number in the White Pages, and three days later a packet of bus schedules dropped through the mail slot; "books, books," she said, pressing them to her cheeks as though they were kittens. But when she used them to go downtown, to a late-morning audition she'd managed to secure, I did not hear the pissed-off slam of the front door until dark. She punctuated the tale with furious cursing, bitter tears: the bus was late, she was late for the audition, when she finally got seen the guy cut her off, the return bus never showed, finally she just walked home.

"Sweetie..."

"I *know*, I *know*...Just give me a little more time."

It was the one matter on which I did not feel I could press her. As I had from the first day, I continued to drive her everywhere she wanted to go.

After the bus fiasco, my wife dropped into a consuming misery from which there was no jollying her. Some days I would come downstairs and find her lying on the sofa as though it were a sickbed, staring up through the French windows at the blank blue sky with the lifeless eyes of an invalid. I would stroke her limp curls and promise that things would get better, but I could imagine how she felt— she, whose whole life had been a battle against an onrushing sense of uselessness. I did not dare ask, but suspected that, lying in the quasi-suburban stillness, with only the occasional drone of a leaf-blower for stimulation, my wife was thinking of her mother, the polio victim: in her iron lung, devoid of a past and future, caught in an endless present of imprisonment.

Still, it did not pay to sympathize with my wife too extremely: I had to defend myself, not just against her attitude, but her presence. "I can't paint under surveillance," said the artist Mark Rothko. From my first morning at my desk, I understood him all too well. My wife had remained beneath the covers with an issue of *The New Yorker* while I went to work in the second bedroom, my new office. Rolling my first scene out of the typewriter, I began, as always, to read it aloud. Instantly, I heard my wife— whose head, I realized, was resting on our common, sponge-cake wall—shift, then stiffen. Of course: In New York, I'd gone to her place every day, she had no idea this was the way I worked. I could feel her alertness as she eavesdropped.

The inhibiting effects of being thus on display cannot be overstated. Immediately my performance (which was not meant to be a performance at all) became stilted, my voice low and constrained as I focused, not on my creative problems, but my hyperawareness of the situation; the softer I spoke, the more avid the silence surrounding me seemed, as though not just my wife, but every show-biz aspirant behind every half-open door on the street sat listening to me.

When at last I took a break, I peered into the room next door. Propped up in bed, open magazine held stagily in two hands, my wife was staring at me.

"Hello," she said quickly in a small, high voice, her amusement barely suppressed. Then, booming and stentorian: "*Ac*-ting!"

Given the circumstances—feeling excruciatingly controlled, and forced equally to control myself—I began, as I had not in New York, to feel the burden of my sobriety. The liquor-fueled nights that were like reveries had supplied me, not just with the connections that formed the basis of my work, but the space in which to refine my identity. On the wagon back east, I'd been able to fill the void with long walks that were themselves like narcotic states. My new life was like a drug too—but one that, with its assaults on my identity and independence, seemed to block the aqueducts in my brain that replenished the reservoir of my ego. Since my wife, in my view, was being so difficult—since she was the in-house embodiment of all that was thwarting me—I began, with increasing recklessness, to take out my frustration on her.

Principally, I became hypercritical. In the past, when I had control over more important aspects of my days, I had shrugged off my wife's pathological messiness. Now I called every disruption of my precious order to her attention. "Come in here," I would demand.

"Now what?"

"Just come in. I want to show you something."

My wife would heave a profound sigh and trudge

miserably in to find me fuming over a forgotten dish or dropped sock. Or else I would seize upon a remark and make it a pretext for a harangue. "I don't get it," my wife would say, frowning over some movie star's multi-picture deal. "I mean, she can *cry*. So? I mean, you know? Why her?"

"She does her work," I would reply none too subtly, and there would follow half an hour of abuse that would poison things between us for a day and a night.

Finally, when the hours in which I would whisper reassurances began to be outnumbered by those when we'd pass each other silently, eyes averted and taking care not to touch, something broke in my wife's resistance. Like the survivor that she was, she did what for so long I'd been hoping she'd do: ventured out. Various local attractions lay within our district's radius, and despite the unpleasantness of it, my wife began walking to them. It is not too much to say that this effort moved me. Looking out the window, I would see her striding off, her high forehead and determined look reminding me of a child on an outing, and feel obscurely protective, vaguely proud.

My wife's peregrinations led her to pillars of classical Los Angeles, the standout being the Farmers Market, a ramshackle agglomeration of retro food stalls; here one could get a heaping tray of rib-sticking something and experience what the city must have been like when the Red Cars going from Boyle Heights to Long Beach passed through orange groves, when the long spine of the Santa Monicas was not yet wrapped in a putrefying organ of smog. Here my wife met characters of the most sublime vintage: the homosexual cowboy actor, with his great white pompadour, who in a courtly basso regaled her with tales of the glory days of Gower Gulch; the bitter French bag lady, actually named Fifi, who would have been the next Danielle Darrieux except that she would not, as she put it, "poot out"; the round table of old television writers, guys with Ripley's-Believe-It-Or-Not-sized credits, fifty episodes of *Have Gun Will Travel*, ninety hours of *The Fugitive*, shoved out by an industry that worshipped youth and forced to squander their fortunes on heart-attack food, to spritz and bitch and nense and needle before heading home in a dairy-induced daze to cook up a series idea for Jim Garner or Howard Duff or some other guy who still knew from good.

I had the career and the connections, but my wife was seeing a side of the city that I was not; returning from these adventures with a glimmer of her old eagerness, she could actually make me jealous with her tales. My pleasure in them, my pride in knowing that only my wife could have come up with this stuff, began to restore things between us. At long last, I allowed myself to think, life was beginning.

XXXX

If I believed, however, that I would not receive a bill for improving my wife's demeanor via the magic of my shittiness, I was mistaken. I was banging away at the typewriter one day, in a fugue of inspiration, when there was a knock on my office door. I spun around in my chair, clinging to my cloud, as my wife came in.

"Can I talk to you for a minute?"

I stared at her blankly.

"I'm going to start going to Al-Anon."

Al-Anon: the program, derived from the principals of Alcoholics Anonymous, that helps the families of drunks cope with the difficulties of living with them.

I looked at her. Usually the Manhattan winters left my wife haggard, but she'd been gentled by this soft California March; her expression, moreover, revealed a neutrality of the finest balance, devoid of both antagonism and placation.

I said: "How did this happen?"

She took a step into the room. At the Farmers Market, my wife had bumped into an actress she'd known in New York. Though hardly a friend, this woman had just arrived in LA and, fragile and alone, glommed onto my wife—who in the course of a long coffee had confided her difficulties, with Los Angeles, and with me.

"I thought we were doing better," I interrupted, cranky at having the mood in my mind shattered for this. "I thought things were good around here for a change."

"Absolutely, they are," smoothing the air with her palms. "But, you know." She shrugged. "We still have *is*sues."

I seemed to hear "*is*sues" with my lower back. "Go on."

Learning of my sobriety, the actress "shared" that her father and brothers were degenerate alcoholics, and that she'd benefited from "the program" in terms of separating from her scorching history, and avoiding destructive patterns in her current relationships.

"There were things, you know, really horrible feelings she thought she'd spend her whole life struggling with," said my wife, her silent-film expressiveness fully activated. "And it's taken a long time, but God damn..." She looked to one side, humbled and awed. "I just think it would be helpful."

"What did you tell this woman? That I was a drunk, and you were having trouble living with me?"

My wife took a deep breath, and deflated. She had, in response to the resentment I could not suppress, put on a round-eyed stare that seemed to say *I knew it.*

"I told her you'd stopped drinking," she said carefully, "and, you know, it's difficult. I mean, it *is* difficult, here. We're both under a lot of pressure."

The resistance with which this bone was thrown made it impossible to chew. My emotional well-being, only recently constructed, crashed down like a stack of plates.

"Really," I drawled. "What pressures are you under?"

"Look, you know...Let's talk about this when you can—"

"*No* no no no no," feeling the rush of my rancor like a drug. "*You're* the one who chose to interrupt me. Tell me, I want to hear. *Am* I so hard to live with? Because it seems to me," I brayed, reaching way back to telegraph this punch, "I go *out of my way* to make things easy for you."

"You know how I feel," her sidelong glare fixed on my bookshelves. "You *haven't* dealt with your drinking."

"I—"

"You *haven't* found a way to replace it—"

"How can I, when you get in the way of—"

"You're pissed off at me all the time and it's not my fault, you *blame* me all the time," banging the wall with her hand, "and it's *not my fault.*"

She was angry now, my wife, hugging herself, body trembling with the beating of her heart. But I was angry, too, I knew what this was about. I had not, when I first stopped drinking, characterized my choice as a response to alcoholism, because I did not consider myself an alcoholic. My wife, not surprisingly, dismissed this as denial, arguing that to quit without acknowledging the truth—*her* truth— was akin to not quitting at all. Now—in a new, more diabolical way—my wife was revisiting this disagreement, by using it to try to control, as she had in New York, the proprietary rights to my reality. Al-Anon was her instrument: If I would not declare my alcoholism, she would do it for me.

I was twitching with anger, about to hit back, when my wife threw up her hands.

"You know—..." I'd set our spare dining chair, a ladderback with a rush seat, in one of the room's corners. My wife perched on the edge of it; leaning forward, she spoke in a voice of quiet clarity. "It's not about your drinking," she said, "or, or AA, or any of that. I was so afraid to bring this up. I mean, I *knew* it would go this way, because..."

"Because why? You picked a scab?"

"Because you get into being angry. It's like, it's your new habit. You get into it, and you don't *listen* to me."

"I don't, huh?"

"You listen for your *cue*, you know? And you go off. And it's, you know, it's, it's..." Her shoulders levitated to her ears, and she paused. "I mean, *I* buy into it," sitting back, looking at me. "And we have these—I mean, look at this stupid conversation we're having that's about nothing. Except defending our positions. And it's safe, and familiar. You know, and, and nothing gets...*addressed.*" Finding her subject, my wife had brought a stillness to the room as the words flowed out of her. "It's so *pain*ful."

I hesitated, then nodded. It was true.

The tension lessened, my wife seemed to sink into her lap, as though burdened by the weight of her nature. "I want to work on *my* issues," she went on, "always needing to control everything, being pissed *off* all the time. *Lying* to myself. About who I am, what's really going on in my life."

My wife's eyes burned and cooled, like the heating element in a toaster, charting the flux of her pain. The light, coming through the corner window with its view of the Hollywood hills, seemed to cradle her head.

"I feel so *stuck*," she said quietly, "I don't *do* anything. Which was...*ignorable* as long as I had a certain kind of day. But I don't have that now." Abruptly, she shifted gears. "I need to *connect*."

"You could connect with my friends."

"Maybe this would help," jumping up impatiently, "I mean, *we* could be closer. We could have more *in*timacy." She put her clenched fists to her shoulders and made a comically contorted face, as though she'd been buried to the neck, and was trying to struggle out of the ground. "I need *in*timacy," squeezing out the word, breaking it into syllables, "*in*-ti-ma-cy."

She approached and, as my body language held her off, bent over me with exaggeratedly wide eyes, to see if this performance was having an effect.

"Why are you telling me?" I said, still churlish. "Why don't you just go?"

"Because I'd like your support," said my wife, moving to the door. "I mean, I don't expect you to go to AA. It's like they say in the program: You're not my responsibility. *I* am." She faced me, once again in her balanced pose. "But I thought at least the struggle part was something we could share. Even if we do it differently."

Somewhere, a leaf-blower spluttered noisily to life. I got up and closed the window, then leaned back against it. My wife stood by the door, waiting.

In truth, I appreciated how brave her admissions had been. I also knew enough about Al-Anon to understand that at its core lay the concept of codependency, the sober partner's meddling in the drunk's life. If Al-Anon did indeed teach my wife that she was only responsible for herself, I would receive an enormous dividend.

I extended my arms, and my wife moved into them. She put her arms around my neck and her forehead on my shoulder.

"I'm sure it'll be great," I said. "Knock yourself out."

The hardest part was the logistics. Until she felt at ease, my wife wanted to go to meetings with the actress, whose group met twice a week in Hollywood, at half past noon; as it fell to me to drive her, this threw off *my* schedule, as I typically took a break to go to the gym at eleven. But, in the spirit of the moment, we compromised: I stopped a little later, dropped her off a little early, and picked her up when my workout was done.

I also extracted a promise: that my wife would take driving lessons, then buy herself a car. Though this inflamed her disputatiousness, she too rallied in response to the moment's promise. Soon, I was certain, we would lead independent lives in earnest.

Thus it was that, thanks not to the eons of therapy, but a fellowship of strangers who met in technical-school classrooms and church basements, my wife began to become unstuck. The "qualifiers," those who spoke at meetings, explored their lives with insight and candor; their histories, though more ghastly than my wife's, dealt with the same struggle, and listening to them proved to be immensely helpful. This being Hollywood, my wife also met other actresses enduring professional travails, who tipped her off to the best places to have head shots printed, theatre companies that did readings, acting teachers who knew their stuff—all the tiles that enabled her to fill in the mosaic of life.

This unsticking expanded into other areas. One of her buddies told her that the Fairfax High School track, a few blocks from our home, was open to the public in the early morning; and my wife began to enjoy, along with daily seven-mile runs, acquaintanceships with racist Soviet émigrés, retired athletes playing the infomercial circuit, and other Raymond Chandler-esque figures. Following these marathons, she would take a long breakfast in our sunlit kitchen, do the *Times* crossword puzzle, and still have sufficient leisure to shower and dress before knocking on my door at Al-Anon time.

My wife even bit the hardest of all bullets and took driving lessons: I cheered her on one morning as, her sobs audible over the gargle of the catalytic converter, she jerked spastically off toward Melrose in a K-car, an alarmed-looking instructor in the passenger's seat. It was, in every sense, a shaky start, but within weeks she was leaning on her horn, changing lanes without signaling, cutting people off, and screaming cunt and motherfucker out the driver's-side window like a proper Angelena. As my wife had kept this part of the bargain, I assumed she'd begin a used-car hunt as soon as her confidence increased.

I was gratified by my wife's happiness—and yet Al-Anon unbalanced us somewhat. The contrarian who had bedeviled my first months disappeared. But her replacement was someone other than the warm, insightful companion who'd interrupted my work that afternoon, someone considerably more self-centered and cold.

What I discovered was that "You're not my responsibility," that clarion of a nag-free existence, had morphed into a reduced respect for my needs. When my wife began attending meetings, I asked that she honor my anonymity and not mention it to my friends. But Al-Anon assumed such importance that, my wife argued, it would be dishonest not to speak of it—especially, she added, with a challenging uptilt of her chin, if I expected her to "bond" with these people.

I relented (a better option that being defied) and my "alcoholism"—to which I had not even agreed—immediately joined "only two years" as a favored topic of conversation. When I told her to stop flogging it, my wife replied that what she did was no reflection on me, she was—again with an uptilt of the chin—*not my responsibility*, any more than I was hers. Besides, she added with semantic craftiness, she never referred to me directly, only in regard to how the program affected her responses to my behavior.

Rather than elevating our status as a couple, moreover, my wife's sudden ascent made me look less substantial. For this, she could not entirely be blamed: her entrance into the program coincided with the onset of difficulties with my producer. When not writing, I was often on the phone, prodding him to put a director on my script, the need to get started having been given sudden urgency by the revelation of *another* screenplay, very similar to my own, that had attracted the interest of one of the biggest actor-directors in Hollywood.

My producer, however, had a higher-priority project, with a start date and a raft of concerns that consumed his energies; having professed delight with my first draft, he now began suggesting changes, some substantive, for which he would not pay, and with which I did not agree. I had to take him seriously, and so I was trying to finesse this, doing enough tinkering to seem like a team player, the while noting that it was counterproductive to assay anything significant until a director was on board. The result was that while my wife—who, thanks to her running regimen, had begun to glow with health—entertained everyone with tales of celebrity-filled program lunches in Trancas and Beverly Hills, I became the dry dipso with nothing on his tongue but his stalled project.

More perplexing was that I had begun to complain about my work. This was entirely out of character. One of the hallmarks of my discipline was an unwillingness to judge the process, my conviction that a day spent writing was by definition a success. This view had buttressed me with a tremendous sense of power; and now I seemed to be giving that power away, ranting on and on, to my ever more powerful wife, about how poorly things were going, how *hard* it all seemed.

My wife was sympathetic. She did, she said, understand. But wouldn't it help to put the writing aside at day's end, to enjoy one's life and vary one's experience?

Her nostrums only inflamed me. How could I relax, I had so much *work* to do—didn't she see what I was *going* through? No, I decided. She *didn't* understand.

These difficulties mooted, finally, my anxieties about my friends as—being at my desk all the time—our connections began to wither. Instead, my recreational life increasingly grew out of my wife's, in what came to be the single ongoing social ritual of my life: the Al-Anon party. These gatherings seemed to loose all of my complicated feelings—not just about Al-Anon, but what seemed to be happening within me.

My wife had a sponsor, the individual who, as one's primary contact within the program, helps one get the most from its teachings, and the Christmas party she threw revealed what it was that I admired about Al-Anon. Betty, or Bets, was a woman in late middle age, with a hennaed pageboy that, though not a wig, seemed askew, and a nose that, in the thirty-odd years since it had been bobbed, had acquired a kind of crazing, like porcelain. She was married to Vern, a stunt-man-turned-general-contractor, a white-haired, gravelly-voiced cuss who, despite throat cancer, chain-smoked Larks, and whose gut, despite chemo, hung over his T.J. Hooker belt buckle. They lived in a bungalow in the San Fernando Valley, at the end of a cul-de-sac beneath the fumy, roaring Ventura Freeway; Vern had been a hunter—"back when I's drinkin'," as though blowing away small fauna was something only a lush could enjoy—and their home, all 900 square feet of it, was filled with the stuffed varmints he'd potted, their Jujube eyes staring out with game, feeble ferocity.

Bets stood too close and talked too much, the kind of woman who haunted laundromats and cafeterias, tormenting the kind and the tolerant. Yet she'd managed to carve out quite a power position for herself, as the sponsor for about twenty-five B-minus celebrities: actresses mostly, still girlish-sexy in their fifties, who'd slipped from nighttime soaps to daytime talk shows, plus a smattering of male standups trying to break into sitcoms, and a few TV tabloid hosts. It was, I thought, a kind of parallel-universe version of being an agent—better, in that her clients never left her.

On our first Christmas in LA, Bets held "open house," and though my wife and I took pains to be an hour late, we were the first guests to arrive, and two of only five to show up at all. The environment, which at its best must have owned all the cheer of a beer hall on Sunday morning, had been tarted up with tinsel; there was white bread and mayo, Oscar Mayer bologna and Pringles New-Fangled Potato Chips. Fortunately, these were among my favorite foods, and Bets was pleased that I had a second sandwich as, since the onset of Vern's illness, the pair had lived on little, it had been a hardship for them to put on this spread, and they didn't want to see it go to waste.

The small turnout surprised me—until I realized, looking around at the unfamiliar faces, that the only sponsees to show were the ones who, like my wife, weren't famous. Then I understood: In the mind-bending calibrations of status that ruled The Business, it was de rigueur to have someone like Bets as a sponsor—it indicated humility—but out of the question to go to her house. The famous attended her "wedding," when she decided to reaffirm her vows to Vern on their twenty-fifth anniversary, but the church was in "good" Brentwood, west of the 405, they could knock back a cranberry juice and slip away without being accused of snobbery. But no way was a woman who appeared bi-monthly on the cover of the *National Enquirer* going to eat a bologna on white beside a dead raccoon, no matter how important or needed it would have made this lonely couple feel.

Certainly, Bets must have known that she would be humiliated like this. But it was imperative that she offer her chickadees a refuge on this most difficult of days; that she set out enough for all, lest she be seen to be acknowledging the truth of her situation. What impressed me was the dignity—the acceptance—with which she endured the experience, the cheer in her voice as she fielded my wife's nervous questions: "Is Jackie coming?" "Aw, nah, she couldn't make it. Obligations. Yeah, I'll see her at the Tuesday." It was simple: Bets wanted to be in show business, this was the only way she could do it, and in Al-Anon she had learned to take responsibility for her choice and live with the results, one day at a time.

It was, I thought, excellent training for a life in the movies, in which frustration rode on the airborne particulate that one breathed. But what I most appreciated was that Al-Anon had separated both sponsor and clients from their reticence. Bets used her stable of big names to lure in others, she played favorites and bored and tortured people beyond all seemliness. Equally might her charges ring her up after midnight and sob about this or that trauma, then decline to return her calls until they needed her again. But neither side held it against the other, and both could have cared less how it made them look: however much guilt, fear, shame, or embarrassment these individuals might once have felt, the program had helped them cut it loose. They were ruthless, I considered, inhaling the odor of old taxidermy; and though I had grown wary of this quality in my wife, I respected it.

With that, a part of me granted that I might do well to try it my wife's way: shed my pride, make the necessary admissions, and join the rest of the Writers Guild member-ship in AA. These thoughts made me anxious, an anxiety magnified a billionfold by the Al-Anon baby showers I attended. If Betty's Christmas party demonstrated that committing to change could transform me into a guilt-free arriviste, the showers set in high relief the perils of avoiding that choice. Here, in the backyards of tiny houses in Rancho Park, Culver City and other starter neighborhoods for upwardly mobile left-of-centrists, one saw men—husbands—who, having declined to act on their dissatisfactions, had become the absolute servants of their self-centered wives.

I found it hard, at first, to source the husbands'

cowardice. Their partners didn't *look* tough. They displayed more hair under their arms than on their prematurely gray, close-cropped heads, their faces remained undecorated by anything other than a few discreet moles. They had chosen, these women, to view "a few extra pounds" as a proud badge of motherhood, they wore Birkenstock sandals that drew one's eye to their fungoid toenails and girded their midriffs with fanny packs that were like colorful nylon colostomy bags.

It was only when one unwrapped these frumpish packages that one found the trouble: a galling smugness that was absolutely unassailable. These women had it all figured out, nothing could shake their certainties. If you did take issue with them, they'd compose their faces into elaborate masks of solicitude and say, "You know, you should really look at why you feel that way," and if you then lost your temper and accused them of arrogance, they'd smile, faintly—pleased at having gotten to you—and say, "*Whoah.* Come down off that testosterone kahuna, big guy."

This self-satisfaction extended to their children, whom they regarded as "choices," and in whom they otherwise seemed to take very little interest. Child-rearing was man's work, and it was clear, watching these husbands—all of whom were sober—that they did not want the degree of responsibility they'd been handed. Rather than fighting back, however (or, given the futility of argument, walking out), they had chosen to dramatize their resentments. A more repellent show one would have been hard pressed to find.

These men, I observed, as I slouched in an Adirondack chair with my club soda, turned every parental action into a display of selflessness, so that one could see just how abused they were, how overworked and underappreciated. They could not simply be with their children. Instead, they bent over elaborately at the waist when addressing them, peering into their little faces with exaggerated attentiveness; took them on their laps and read their little books to them, exclaimed over the illustrations, pointed with long fingers at the sentences and laughed with delight when the kids recognized a word; refused them television, snatched away magazines with gun pictures, reminded them, these three- and four-year-olds, to say "African-American," not "black," "Asian-American," not "Japanese"; and managed to keep this up without forgetting, every few minutes, to refuse all food and drink, even if none was offered.

Painful as this was to witness, it was preferable to engaging the fathers directly. "Bruce Knoll, camp counselor," one guy invariably greeted me, to remind me that he had no life, and having no life was what he was about. Another would wait until you'd spooned tabouli onto your paper plate, then snatch it from your hand, saying—in a tone at once accusing and defensive—"It's for *Max*," as though hiding behind his son's needs let him be the prick he'd always wanted to be. The apotheosis of this passive aggression was a guy I nicknamed Johnny Appleseed, who had been the sperm donor for no fewer than five Lesbians, and who loved it when the issue of his wanks, Noah, Joshua, Jonah, Zoe, and Zoe, jumped on his back and tore his clothes, as though encouraging the notion that he was only carrion for their mothers, Rachel, Mindy, Ellen, Pippa, and Diane.

The dynamic of these relationships would so depress me that I would fall asleep, often in mid-conversation, the buzz of traffic on nearby Pico Boulevard soothing in my ears. After attending half a dozen showers, however, I recognized that it was not my negative feelings about the participants that was knocking me cold. What I didn't understand— what filled me with an anxiety so engulfing that my mind would switch off to escape it—was *why* these men would not stand up for themselves. Was this cravenness the counterpoint to the empowering narcissism Al-Anon bestowed upon their wives? Were these marriages a portent of what was to become of mine?

XXXX

As I pondered the uneasy notion that life's options came down to sociopathic self-interest, or the conversion of need into allegory, in the hope that another might decode and fulfill it, I was unexpectedly saved: Out of the blue, my producer put a director on my script. He'd given it, he explained, to his own agent, and this man, after examining his high-octane client list, had come up with an inspired choice—a creative partner, I believed, who might restore me to myself again.

As it happened, I had met the director almost twenty years before, when her first feature, an autobiographical docudrama called *Ovarian Cyst*, screened at my university. It was the early 1970s, a romantic time to be an aspiring filmmaker, a rough moment to be a man: with sex roles and their assumptions under challenge, the future of male/female relations heavily in play, even the most enlightened among the XY-chromosomed could be flung unexpectedly into the doghouse. A week before the screening, in fact, I had been called "pig" and ejected from a seder, for remarking that the pooled wine drops signifying the Ten Plagues looked a bit like menstrual blood.

Centering on a young woman's cancer scare and its consequent redefinition of her femininity, *Ovarian Cyst* owed its sensibility to the second-wave feminist Zeitgeist. But it was a story, not a manifesto, and the film's personal take on its politics, while compromising nothing, deftly drew together the sexual sides of the audience. *Cyst* showed that a movie about politics and culture could still be one from the heart; and in those first New York years, distilling my own theme, I took it as an influence.

Appearing for the post-screening Q-and-A, the director did not disappoint. A tiny peaches-and-cream redhead in her early twenties (I was nineteen), possessed of a soldier's posture and a snorting laugh, she was smart and spunky, girlish and vulnerable. Answering our questions, the director synthesized a reverence for cinema, a commitment to doing her own work her own way, and a strength of vision devoid of stridence and certainty and leavened by sensuality, humility, and wit. By evening's end, she was every male's muse, precisely the sort of woman whose approval (and affection) we hoped, in our hearts, to earn.

Now here she was, in an office smelling of new carpet, in the crook of the elbow of Sunset Strip. I had missed the half-dozen Hollywood pictures she'd made, excepting the most recent: a superbly judged period piece about a girl's sexual coming of age, one that had reverently served its script. The film was a surprise hit, the director was for the first time in demand, and she had selected *my screenplay* to be her follow-up film.

Shaking hands, I was nervous. The waist-length tresses had been shorn away, revealing a middle-aged mother with a mainstream career. The director's large head and breasts, all proportionate, presented a power triangle that was formidable in every sense. I wasn't sure how to play it.

Gambling, I decided to tell her about my long-ago crush: show her that, unlike most industry birdbrains, I respected what she was about. "A *crush?*" the director boomed in her Connecticut Yankee voice. "*Gad.* Where were you when I needed you?" Then she threw back her head and laughed—a knee-slapping guffaw that had replaced her horsy snort—and immediately we were off. Ferociously, we yakked about *voice*, the struggle to preserve that individuality in everything we did; the director was only too happy to reaffirm her original identity, point out how the signature themes in *Cyst* had ramified in *Hot Date, Oh Dog!* and the rest of her subsequent oeuvre. And she was smart enough to question me, closely, about my progress and my life (I got points for dating a woman who'd made a short about menstruation). Leaning forward in her Mies cantilever chair, she planted a fist on her thigh and nodded like a banker. "I like what you've made yourself into," she declared.

Taking up the matter at hand, the director was all business. Crisply, she encapsulated my script's motifs, then ticked off the points at which they seemed under-realized. She offered no concrete solutions, but the session was bracing: Hollywood people didn't usually talk about the quality of the work, only the reasons why it was uncommercial. This was not complaint, but good criticism.

The rewrite was due in a month. It would take a solid week, we decided, to vet the material; I'd write as we progressed, so as not to fall behind. Hurrying home, recounting the joy of it to my wife, I was certain we'd create an interesting film, the synergy of our voices would produce, not Hollywood boilerplate, but something recognizably *special.*

"Can I take the car?" said my wife.

I laughed: my wife, the driver. No problem: I'd work out at dawn, she could drop me at the director's office and pick me up at night. In fact, it was ideal: my wife could use my car to search for one of her own.

I was not so naïve as to expect a smooth ride. But I was surprised by the form the bump took: every morning, the director was late. For fifteen, twenty-five, forty minutes would I sit, getting wired on coffee and irritation until, as I was putting on my coat, she would hustle in, huddle with her assistant, then claim her son, Foster, as an excuse. Foster was having separation anxiety. They weren't paying attention to Foster at school. Foster's turtle had escaped, Foster wouldn't eat. These reports, moreover, were delivered grudgingly, as though the director knew she had to explain, but resented it.

After a week of this, our deadline ratcheting my anxiety to the moon, her assistant let slip that the director was dependably early for studio appointments. When she walked in, I stood up.

"We have to negotiate," I began.

"I have a child," she snapped. "Doesn't that mean anything to you?"

"Sure, but I—"

"*Look.*" The director breathed heavily through her nose, like a boxer. "I've been in this business a long time, and I've seen this...*abuse.* Do you know," rattling her words off with escalating pique, "that I once had a meeting with a studio executive, and the moment I stepped into his office, he stuck his tongue in my mouth?"

My eyebrows took off like boomerangs. "I don't see what—"

"*Ob*viously you have no concept of what it is to be the primary caregiver," widening her eyes imperiously. "So don't—don't *crucify* me on a *cross of gold.*"

Thrown as I was by this reference to William Jennings Bryan's century-old speech regarding the monetary system, I understood. The director felt that I was punishing her for being a woman. She was also damaging our project, then flattening my protests with her feminism, which she knew I respected. I chose to take the charitable view—that prospering in a high-testosterone profession had made her hyper-sensitive—and proposed a compromise: I would write in the morning, and she could call before leaving her house. This obliged her completely. She assented.

But she was more Hollywood than I realized. The director didn't have to respect me, and so she wouldn't: she did indeed call, but arrived later than ever, as I had to be taught a lesson. Catching on, I'd wait an hour after hanging up before leaving my apartment, and arrive, invariably, minutes before she did. Thus did we solve our first problem.

This was schoolyard silliness. More alarming was that, when we did sit down to work, nothing got done—after two hours, the director would claim "pressing business" and return me to my desk. At first, I laid it to poor concentration—what business could be more pressing?—but as the days evaporated, I saw that, for some reason, she simply wasn't engaged.

Baffled by what was happening, I rented videocassettes of the director's movies that I hadn't seen, and spent a night reviewing them. They were grimly mediocre—visually flat, dramatically ham-fisted, emotionally predictable. Her only good pictures were her first, a pitch-perfect autobiography, and the most recent, which had an idiot-proof script, a dream cast, and a first-rate director of photography.

I was heartsick, but not surprised. The director had been

shrewd enough, in our first meeting, to talk a good game. But whenever we came to a piece of problematical structure, an ambiguous character choice, a house-bound scene, she fell back on the worst clichés: "There's no drama without conflict," she'd declare, or "The character has no arc," or even "I'll reset the scene at a circus." The director, I knew perfectly well by now, was winging it.

What was fascinating, however, was that in an entirely unexpected way, she was indeed being creative. When she wasn't obsessing about her favorite subject, her bad back (a drama more consuming than the one on the page), the director digressed, and each of these side trips touched on a perceived wrong: she'd been misunderstood, unappreciated, underpaid, her creative, sexual or intellectual currency debased. The director, I realized, had sustained her success by mythologizing herself—as much for her own benefit as the world's—and our meetings were vehicles for its burnishing: performance pieces, one-woman shows. Small wonder that we were getting nothing done. We were working on different projects.

This recognition—that the movie would only be good if I solved the script's problems—lashed me to ever more feverish extremes of effort. My wife counseled me to talk to the producer, but I resisted this, for fear of jeopardizing the production. Instead, I went into overdrive, combing each of the director's utterances for a clue to her intentions, working late into the hot, chopper-riven LA nights. And yet, though my enclosure in the bullet train of the project seemed perfect, I started to hear, intermittently, another motif, unsettling flashes that came, not from the nuisance world outside, but from within.

Watching the director on the phone, lecturing her publicist, dropping names, I began to consider that, in The Business, one was some*thing*, not some*body*. The American cinema had little to do with having a personal vision. It was about the excruciatingly difficult task of getting a picture made, and that meant following, not leading. The work might lack originality, but one sustained a career and, no less valuably, a reputation.

Considering my director in this context, I realized how completely I'd misjudged her. I had assumed, when she said she was a feminist, and committed to a vision, that she meant it. What I failed to perceive was that she had been these things when they were the things to be—and when "the things to be" changed, she changed with them. I thought the director wanted to "say something," because that's what she told me. What she really wanted was to be a Hollywood success, which her actions demonstrated all too clearly. I had somehow completely missed this, and what tore at me, as these bursts of dissonance grew sharper, was that so massive was my blindness that it could only have been deliberate.

One's pleasure, I considered as I printed out draft after draft—as I *worked*—did not come, in The Business, from work. The reward was success, on the town's terms. And since it was *so hard* to get a picture made, that success was well deserved, since it had been earned, generally, through the most naked, bare-knuckled aggression.

This wasn't what I, or my work, were supposed to be about. But perhaps, it occurred to me as I wrote like a fiend, if my director wasn't what she said she was, neither was I. Perhaps I had not seen the truth about the director because we were not all that different. Like her, I had created, and played, the character of myself. Like her, I had cultivated an ambition that gave me cachet. The critical difference was that, if a producer said to me, "Your work is very 'smart'" —which, in Hollywood, is the kiss of death—I took it as a compliment. The director, conversely, *stopped* being smart, she objectified her talent the way starlets objectified their bodies, butchered and restitched it into something that suited the marketplace.

This, arrantly, was beneath me—but, if that's how I felt, why had I chosen this path? Why had I not become a playwright, or a poet? Out of a love of cinema? Or because there was something at work in me of which I remained unaware? Worse yet, though I would do anything to improve the writing, the writing then had to take over, it had to be enough. I had run with predators in New York, but—I realized now with a jolt—I was not one of them, I was a *watcher*. I'd gotten used to thinking of myself as tough. But I was not prepared for the kind of combat with which everything, even a parking space, was won in Hollywood.

Writing, writing, the script getting better and better, I became overwhelmed with the sense that there was something terribly wrong with what I was doing. Wanting to have a strong personal vision as a Hollywood screenwriter was like aspiring to perform circumcisions on a trampoline. All it took was one glance at the situation to know it wouldn't fly. So, I wondered at 4 AM, as I printed out the final draft of what, I was certain, was the best thing I'd ever written—just in time for my four-week deadline—*what was I doing here?*

All of this was swimming in my head as I staggered into the director's office six hours later, right on schedule to receive the shock of my professional life. Giving me a thumbs-up as I tossed the script onto the coffee table and collapsed on the sofa, the director continued her in-progress telephone conversation; unavoidably listening, I realized—gradually at first, then all at once—that she was talking to a different producer from mine, about a film adaptation of a Pulitzer Prize-winning play—one that, according to what I'd been reading in *Variety*, had been fast-tracked by the studio putting it into production.

I gathered myself into a posture of hypervigilance. The instant she hung up, the question popped out of my mouth: "How can you direct *that* if you're doing *my* script?"

"Ha!" the director ejaculated, in her best by-gum, gee-whillickers mode. "Irving knows this isn't my next picture."

My head jerked forward between my shoulders, I goggled like a chicken. "Irving" was my producer. "This" was the script that lay between us on the coffee table.

"What?" I yelled. "What are you talking about? Nobody said anything to *me* about this."

"Well it hardly matters. Yours is still going to be one of

my next projects." The director picked up my rewrite, put on a pair of half-glasses, and made a show of reading it.

Bullshit. I could add. If she really had committed to the other project, she'd be completely unavailable for, at the least, six months. The director knew perfectly well that we weren't going to wait that long for her. My heart started to pound, I set down my coffee cup with a loud, unmistakably angry *bang*. I had, I realized, been trying to make something work for someone who'd never had any intention of doing it in the first place.

Instantly, the director read my mind and, in the best show-business tradition, faked sincerity. "Are you questioning my integrity?" she snapped. "Because if you're questioning my integrity, this conversation is over." The director got to her feet, offering a back-pain wince worthy of Quasimodo. "I have to go. I'm taking Foster to Disneyland."

I went to a pay phone, called my producer, and demanded an explanation. The producer, an enormously wealthy, cheerfully amoral man whose face habitually wore the most untroubled expression one could possibly imagine on a member of the human race, blew it off: the director's other movie wasn't a sure bet, even if she did leave my project the studio's greater investment would make it more likely to go forward. Revealing my miserable working experience, I changed my demand to one for a meeting: if the director *was* doing this job, she had better start doing it, and stop jerking me around.

The meeting, the next day—for which, as it was at the producer's office, the director arrived early—played like a bad movie: overly plotted, with too many new characters introduced, as multiple deus ex machinas, late in the third act. After screwing the tops off their water bottles, the two major players began discussing, not my script, nor the one the director proposed to do in its stead, but a third, entirely different project. The producer, it transpired, owned the rights to a "literary" novel that the director wanted to film, and the two were trying to determine, as I sat there, whom they could get to write the adaptation. I put my elbows on my knees and stared at the floor. Not only had the director never intended to make my movie: she had only signed on to my project to get her hands on *another* project.

What I did not understand was how it served the director, if she wanted to get into my producer's good graces, to do a bad job with my script. As I looked up at the stack of screenplays on the faux-Chinese coffee table, the answer was, literally, in front of my face. Angry, humiliated and bored, I opened, idly, the script on the stack's top to its title page. It was none other than the competing project, allegedly so similar to the one I'd written—a script I had assumed I'd beat into production because *my* script had a director attached.

I noted the name "Bob" penciled on the title page. Bob was the famous actor/director who had been flirting with directing this competing script. I had not been unduly concerned, because Bob was famous as well for taking forever to pull the trigger. Now, I thought unhappily, my competitor had an improved chance of beating me to the starting gate.

I closed the script and looked at the agency logo emblazoned on the cover. If only *I* were represented by a big agency like this, I thought, like my director was, and my producer...and the writer of the competing project...and Bob. I frowned as I remembered: not only were they all at the same agency, they all had the same agent.

The sudden silence, after so much amiable chatter, caused me to glance up. The director and producer were looking at me, the latter with an embarrassed grin.

"How do you like that?" he said, with his customary relaxed affability. "Bob finally said yes."

I looked back at him, utterly expressionless. Bob had committed. My script was now, officially, dead.

Dead.

"When?" I finally said.

"Just yesterday."

I cleared my throat. "I guess the fear that *my* script would get made lit a fire under Bob's ass. Forced him into a decision."

The producer shrugged. "Who knows what goes on in these people's heads?"

I looked at the director, who had put on her half-glasses, and was making a show of going over her notes. All at once, I realized what the fuck was going on. By agreeing to seem just busy enough with my script to make Bob nervous—while waiting for her other project to start—my director did a favor for her agent, and was rewarded with a crack at the novel my producer owned. But what, I could not possibly fathom, was in it for my producer? How did it serve him to have my script lose out to the other one?

Once again, the director read my mind. She looked up abruptly, as though remembering something, and smiled at my producer.

"Congratulations," she said.

Immediately, I said, "For what?"

"I'm directing my first picture," the producer replied with shy pride. He named the other, higher-priority project he had been working on.

Now it all made sense. By agreeing to let my script be used as bait, my producer also did a favor for his agent, who in turn went to bat for him with the studio. As a result, after thirty years of having to settle for the money while the other guys got the glory, the producer could play the auteur.

The producer picked up the script closest to him on the blood-colored coffee table and tossed it in front of me.

"What's this?" I asked.

"Your next job."

I took a look at my next job. It was an original piece by an Oscar-winning screenwriter that needed, I knew, a substantial rewrite. So I was to receive a reward, too: I would do back-to-back gigs for a major producer, my price would rise substantially, and if the rewrite got made, I could end up sharing credit with one of the industry's classiest brand names—all of which meant that I had now, officially, made it.

I put the script down and stood up. "I'm going out for a cigarette," I said.

I didn't smoke, but I had to get out of there—not out of anger at the participants, but at myself. I had misjudged the director even more completely than I thought, she had proven to be, not just a self-mythologizing narcissist, but a strategist of the first water. After wandering for years in a wilderness of flops, the director had stumbled onto a winning formula with her most recent picture, a boutique project written by a major playwright. It had made her interesting again, in a way that she had not been since *Ovarian Cyst*, and she was determined to sustain this, by moving on to another boutique project written by another major playwright. The director knew what she wanted and what served that desire, she had pursued it with a driven, ruthless, single-minded intensity. And she had won.

The director appeared now, putting on her sunglasses, checking her watch. She extended her hand and I shook it.

"I am truly sorry," she said.

"Tell the truth," I said, in as jocular a voice as I could manage. "You were never going to do my script. Were you?"

"I'm sorry you feel that way," the director replied, without a trace of hostility. "In fact, it grieves me to hear you say it, because *I* felt, at any rate, that you'd done exemplary work under my guidance. Why is that funny?" she asked when I laughed.

"Because you didn't do any work at all."

"If what you're saying were true," the director said, still without hostility, "there was always the chance that everything could have fallen through, and I'd've had *nothing to do* but your movie. And I'd never put myself in the position of making a film I didn't believe in. I think you know that's not what I'm about."

She was her old self again, the woman I'd met that first day in her office.

"I understand," the director said. "You got whipsawed and you're hunting for someone to blame." She shifted her shoulder bag, then looked at me from behind her sunglasses with something like real human interest. "Let it go," she said. "Learn your lesson and move on." With that, the director walked off toward Wilshire Boulevard, heels clacking on the sidewalk.

I had very badly wanted to ask her if it was all as Machiavellian as I suspected. But I might have gotten my face slapped. I had no problem asking this of the producer, however, when he strolled out the door a moment later.

Utterly relaxed, he grinned, hands in his pockets as he considered me. "What, you think this was all some grand scheme to ruin your life? Don't flatter yourself."

"Isn't it all just a little too close for comfort?"

The producer shrugged, looking up and down the street. "We assumed, or hoped for, the best. But the best didn't happen. At least not from your standpoint." He grinned again, enjoying this needle. "But you came out ahead."

"I didn't *want* to come out ahead. I wanted my picture to get made."

This had been said with some heat, and my producer stopped smiling. He was as nice as anyone with $100 million can be, but he was very particular about having his ass kissed and didn't like to be challenged.

"Listen," he said, regarding the rewrite job, "I'm offering you something of value. You can take it or not, it doesn't matter to me. You're a talented kid and you can do very well, if you don't get in your own way."

"How am I getting in my own way?"

"By arguing with me. I don't need you. I'll get somebody else." The producer was looking at me frankly. I understood him, of course. He put his grin back on and clapped me on the arm. "Look, it was a bad break. But the ratio to scripts written to scripts made is a million to one. I don't have to tell you that."

"No. You don't."

"You want the job or not?"

"I'll take it."

"Good. Now go buy yourself a big breakfast and a Bloody Mary. You're going to be rich." He patted my cheek, got into his Maserati Quattroporte and drove away.

And that, after almost a year of work, eight months of anxiety and a major relocation, was the end of that.

I walked toward the Beverly Wilshire Hotel, a few blocks away, to get a taxi. I was still angry at myself, but not because I'd been gobbled up by these two piranhas. I'd read the script I would be rewriting, it was perfectly decent and I had ideas for how to improve it, but I had no connection to the material whatsoever. I'd accepted the producer's offer because it would have been foolish not to accept it. This was my career.

But, I reflected, watching black-clad agents streaming antlike out of the William Morris building, I had not wanted to *be* a "Hollywood screenwriter." I'd wanted to find and refine my voice, and had spent ten years learning to put that voice into a screenplay. But because I had not considered what it was that I *genuinely* wanted—because I did not, somehow, understand myself—what I'd achieved was tantamount to building, in the last years of the twentieth century, the world's most perfect dirigible. I was, I realized, in a business I disliked, in a situation I did not want. And this strange miscalculation—revealed in the moment of my "success"—had cost me the thing that mattered the most, as it contained the essence of who I was: my work.

XXXX

"I'm not buying a car," said my wife.

A divertissement:

In 1995, O.J. Simpson, the football great, actor and product pitchman, was acquitted of the murder of his ex-wife and an extremely unlucky waiter. Though the crime and the trial, which took place in Los Angeles during my years there, were the objects of torrential analysis, it would be useful to revisit *l'affaire Simpson* for a moment. So doing might be helpful in explaining what happened to me next.

Contributing my own bit to the moment's babble, I suggested that O.J. should plead not guilty, by reason of the insanity of celebrity. He should explain to the court that decades of being deferred to, having his ass kissed, of having each of the evils he committed excused or explained away as "not really you"—that year upon year of the serial separation of his actual and public selves, and the ever-increasing certainty that it was the image that was real—had finally severed the connection between O.J.'s assessment of his own humanity and the nature and consequences of his actions and left him capable of anything. The defendant might have added that, quite apart from the many-splendored manner in which fame discouraged personal responsibility, they carved up people in Hollywood every day and nobody said a word. Deliberate cruelty was essential to the calculus of status: not being nice, the number of people you didn't have to be nice *to*, established your position in the industry with the surety of a sextant. How big a jump was it, really, to slaughtering the mother of your children like a barnyard animal, then leaving her in a sea of blood while you ran to catch a limo?

I mention this because, following the debacle of my script, when I was profoundly uncertain about my vocation and my identity, this selfsame psychopathology took full possession of my wife. Certain Al-Anon fundamentals, in particular those counseling separation from the alcoholic's daily drama, helped her to shape the equivalent of a celebrity personality—one supported by her fans in the program, a world at least as rarefied as show business—that stood apart from the realities of life. This personality, moreover, gravitated naturally to the casual cruelty that was the currency of all Hollywood transactions. To my misfortune, "You're not my responsibility," that glaze daubed upon my wife in the program, baked into armor in the Hollywood kiln of delusion and sadism, and became, in effect, "You don't exist." Before my eyes, my wife turned into O.J. And she behaved in character.

It all coalesced around the issue of the second car, which my wife had promised to buy and did not. We fought a battle over it that owns, in memory, the quality of myth. It was a signal incident in my life and our relationship—for both, the turning point.

The fight took place in my office, the day after my meeting with the director and producer. The rewrite job sat before me on the desk, but—unusually—I couldn't force myself to work on it. To compensate, I was trying to put on my John Huston persona, to view what had happened dispassionately, as I imagined that coolest of all customers might. This had, in the past, been an effective psychological gambit: If my own feelings about something proved unworkable, I'd don the aspect of a personality that, in my estimation, would be better able to bull through the moment's miseries.

But the trick wasn't working, a failure I understood all too well: it grew out of my suspicion that the prototype of this technique—playing the character of myself—was the true cause of my difficulties. I could not keep from mourning my dead screenplay, with which I'd lived for so long and loved so much; and mixed with this was guilt, as though the script were a child I'd fathered but had not been able to care for.

My wife knocked, and came in. I was surprised, then remembered: she was here to drive me to the gym, it was Al-Anon time. Encased in the aspic of my script, I'd forgotten how intrusive these disruptions could be.

I didn't turn around. Moments before, I had sensed stirrings of recognition, a subterranean but certain coalescence. By giving her my back, I hoped, I could hold off the interruption until my thoughts solidified. But the damage had been done: that which had been knitting itself together unraveled in a rush.

"Are you ready?" said my wife.

Her voice crackled like cellophane, with a clarity that rendered unmistakable even the subtlest intention. It was that kind of day, theatrical: dark and muted, the colors outside my windows heavy and saturated. Rain rumbled like a low, ominous tympani.

I turned in my chair and studied her. Fit, she looked, with a focus so deliberate that it felt almost threatening. My wife's face, youthful yet eternal, had taken on the hauteur I had always associated with Garbo.

My wife smiled blandly and tapped her watch. Being nice, but waiting.

"Am I ready," I said, recasting the question as a consideration. "Uhm..."

And then, on the brink of getting up, I froze. The rumble of the rain notched up, a herald: understanding was upon me with the onrushing urgency of a bullet. The connection I had been struggling to make, between the disaster of my circumstances and the glitch in my nature, was there, right there. All that prevented me from completing it was the situation.

My wife made her bland look more emphatic. Was there something else?

"Listen," I said—and again I hesitated. Her presence made it impossible to think the connection through. But I could *talk* it through, perhaps, with her. Of course—was not conversation the bedrock of our relationship? And yet I was aware that until recently my wife had been part of the problem, one of the outside forces conspiring to separate me from my instincts. There was no telling how she might react to—there was no other way to put it—my need for her.

"I'm sitting here," I began, "and I'm wondering: how did I get into this? And, uh…" My wife's impatience, her evident lack of interest, was distracting me. "I wonder," I said quickly, "if you could help me examine my choice."

"Choice of what? Can we talk in the car?"

"Look, just give me a minute, okay? I...I need you to listen to me."

My wife folded her hands in front of her.

"I'm afraid that I'm missing the point about myself. That I made the wrong choice, that...that I became *this person* for the wrong reason."

"What wrong reason?"

"I don't know. To *hide*," I said vaguely, thinking aloud. Turning my head, I saw, on my desk, the new script. "I mean, this job...I don't know if this is what I *want*."

"Does that matter?"

I looked at her. My wife's expression was one of incredulity, tinged with distaste.

"Doesn't it?" I replied.

My wife shrugged twice, eyes upturned, the picture of bewilderment. "You're going to get paid more than you've ever been paid in your life," she said, "to do what *you want to do*. Even if it *isn't* what you want, whatever that means, can you really afford to say no to it?"

"Afford," I echoed tonelessly. "Right."

My expression, I knew, was that of a man who has tasted something that has curdled. The rain sound was soothing now, reinforcing the moment's familiarity.

"Look, how long will this take you?" My wife had softened her tone, though I could hear the cellophane crackle of resentment underneath. "Three months?"

"I don't know. Yeah. About."

"Well won't that buy you a lot of time? That three months' work?"

"Yeah."

"Do you want me to tell you it's okay?" she said, terse and dismissive. "Fine, don't do the work. I just wonder how much you'll get if you turn things down."

"Do you hear yourself?"

"What do you want me to say?"

"I *told* you," I barked, "I want you to *help* me examine my *choice*." My wife remained silent. I took this as encouragement. "It buys time. But it burns energy, too, it burns..." I struggled to find my feelings. "Doing the wrong thing, for the wrong reason, kills your talent, it kills *you*. I mean, I've just, after what? A year of work? And turning my life upside down—"

"I know, *my* life, too, remember?"

"Oh. Oh, *I'm* sorry. This is about *you*."

"Well, you know—what did I come *out* here for?" said my wife a little wildly. "I mean, I went through this whole...*thing* of readjustment, and, and you're actually making money—"

"Money. Ah—"

"Well?! I just think you're being very self-destructive. This could be the last job you get for a *long time.*"

I sighed, heavily. I'd switched off the desk lamp, and the room, already dark, had grown gloomy. My wife's face, with its exaggerated, emphatic expressions, seemed to glow, as though my office were haunted by an imploring ghost.

"Look," turning away from her gaze in my swivel chair, "I wasn't asking for a...a *judgment* on what I'm going through. I need you not to tell me that what I *want* for myself is *wrong*"—I could hear the plaintive note in my voice, and it sounded weak, as though I were an Al-Anon husband pleading with a recalcitrant child—"but, you know, to be on my side while I'm trying to sort out some really difficult—"

"Look, we need to talk in the car, okay? If I'm going to drop you and be on time, I need to go now."

"Weren't you going to *buy* a car?"

Abruptly I saw it: the stone in the road of our life.

"What?" said my wife.

"'What?'" I mimicked. "I mean, I know you have contempt for my needs and belong to the world of commitment and responsibility. But wasn't there a commitment *here?*"

The question caught my wife off-guard. She folded her arms and looked murderously to one side, her manner exasperated but covering, I could see, a wariness.

"Well?" I said, cocking my head. "I would have been perfectly content to continue pondering my problem in peace, and we could have discussed it at our leisure. Instead, you've interrupted me. *Won't* talk. And are interpreting my unwillingness to hop to and attend to your needs as a function of my irresponsibility. Don't you see what's happening here?"

"No."

"You were suppo, you *promised* to resolve this stupid little problem, and because you haven't, life is getting worse."

My wife was still hugging herself, but an impatient calculation had replaced the wariness, and the moment I stopped talking, she was off:

"Oh, so, you've been *ignoring* me for a month—"

"*Working*—"

"But you weren't available, right? And I *stayed* out of your way, and I was *really* respectful of that. You know, and on the *first* morning you're back, I'm the bad guy, I mean, what's *that* about?"

"Taking some responsibility!" I yelled. "What don't you understand? The fact that I have to stop what I'm doing every day and drive you, or *be driven*, is *ruining* my *life*."

As if on cue, my wife exploded. "Don't *blame* me because *you* haven't made a *life*," whacking her chest for emphasis, "that's *not my fault*. I mean you *dragged* me out here, I had *no* friends, *no* job—look how much more you have than I do! And I said, Okay, I'm *here*, I'll make the *most* of it, and you don't give me *any credit*, you just blame me for all your problems and it's not my fault."

"I don't blame you for—"

"Yes you do, you blame me for everything." She was marching back and forth, working a furrow into the flea-infested carpet. "Let me tell you something," stopping before me, "something I've learned. Nobody's twisting my arm and making me react to you. I mean it was wrong of me to blame your drinking, your rages, your, uhm, your distance and, and absence and abusiveness for my unhappiness," jabbing a finger into her palm, "because I don't have to buy into the *whole bad dynamic* of that."

"Yeah, but—"

"All I can control is my own behavior, that's all anyone can control—"

"*Hey!*" She stopped, miffed. I stared at her. "What *I* need now is something from *you*. You're right, we can only control ourselves, but right now the control I need is over my own life, and to get that, I *need* something from you."

"Well I disagree."

"It's not a *matter* of agreement. I need something and you have to do it."

"Well I think I'm doing pretty well, okay? I mean I'm

staying out of your way, and I'm doing pretty damn well."

I exhaled, frazzled. The heels of my hands were on my forehead, my elbows on my knees. "The things you're doing," I said, looking up at my wife, "are for your*self*. Not *me*. I need you to do something for *me*."

Rather than address this, my wife frowned at her watch and threw up her hands. She did not, however, leave, and this was telling. My wife, with this outburst that managed to put forth a self-serving philosophy, highlight her sacrifices and achievements, and enumerate my flaws—all without speaking to my complaint—had opened a new door in the relationship. Important as Al-Anon was, something far more significant was going on between us; and though she wasn't quite sure what it was, I could see that she was chasing it, and would not now leave until it was caught.

It was my move, but I wasn't sure how to make it. Listening to the rain, I reflected that there was an after-the-fact quality to the conversation. My wife and I had always been on different wavelengths. Even after getting married, we had maintained separate lives, and this had suited both of us. In New York, it had been easy: our days were spent apart, we returned to each other's company every evening from entirely different worlds.

In Los Angeles, however, we were compelled by circumstances to behave like what we, nominally, were: a couple, with a mutual responsibility we had, by the act of marriage, chosen. The problem was that, while I was asking for something and believing in it, in the reality of my need for it and the legitimacy of my insistence upon it, expecting my wife to be there for me, in this new, more demanding way, violated the basis on which the relationship was constructed. Given this fact, was my request not, at heart, unfair?

It was a grotesque bind, and the most difficult question—a version of which had been nagging me professionally—was: *Why was I in it?* Just as I'd been struggling with why I had chosen the film business if my desire was to cultivate an original voice, I had now to ask why I'd chosen to get married to someone who was unwilling to meet my needs. This question brought me to another, yet more unpleasant one: What, in personal terms, would be the equivalent of my dead screenplay? What price would I have to pay for this?

There was a muted branch-break of thunder, the distant seesaw of a car alarm. Alive to the urgency of these sounds, I struggled to steady myself, to locate the discussion in what I knew to be reality. "There's a difference," I said calmly, "between blaming you for my problems, and having legitimate desires. Our deal was: while I was working, you were going to use my car to buy your car. Right?"

"I don't know."

"Excuse me, what don't you know?"

"I don't remember that that was our deal. I don't remember that we *had* a deal."

"You *don't?*" My voice had risen, and I heard, rather than belligerence, woe. My wife heard it, too; I could feel her quicken. "Our deal was," forcing my voice down, "you're buying a car. You haven't looked, picked up the paper, nothing. Right?"

My wife folded her arms and scowled uncertainly.

"Did you hear what I said?"

"We don't need another car."

"*Whaaat?!*" I spluttered.

"Yeah," arrogantly, opening the door wider. "*I* don't have a problem taking you to the gym. You take a break now anyway—"

"*Look,*" practically strangling on the word. "All this is about, as you perfectly well know, is that you don't want to spend the money, and you don't want to spend the time."

"Well why should I?" said my wife, seeming to gain strength from the throwing off of pretense. "This *wasn't* my idea, I *loved* my life in New York, I *hate* Los Angeles and everything it stands for, so *why*—when I'm *all too happy* to drive you to the gym, and I *only* go to Al-Anon four times a week—why, why, *why* should I have to buy a *car?*"

"Are you going to use that to opt out of everything you

don't want to do?" My voice was quavering, I struggled to bring it under control. "'This wasn't my idea'? You run, you go to Al-Anon, you're having a great time, fun, fun, fun, but when I ask you to participate, it's, Oh, this wasn't my idea?"

"Well it wasn't."

"*Stop saying that!*"

She looked at me cooly. "Don't abuse me, please."

"Don't abuse *you?*" The quavering in my voice had worsened. "Do you really expect me to arrange my *entire working life* around your *Al*-Anon meetings? This is my job, I can't not..."

I trailed off, with a sharply exhaled sigh. I was on my feet now, hands out in supplication, but my wife wasn't listening, I could see her struggling—as I had been before she knocked on my door—toward something elemental. Understanding was coalescing like a cloud formation in her eyes.

"Look," I said pleadingly, the thunder breaking closer, setting off more car alarms, "don't do this. I mean, don't you see how *unfair* this is? I *paid* for everything, I *moved* us, bought the first car—"

"And I really appreciated it—"

"Well then—I mean, what am I asking you to do? Two weeks with the classifieds and three thousand bucks. What am I asking you to do?"

"Why should I?"

"For *me*. Okay? I don't have time to go out and buy another car, I'm *working*—"

"I thought you didn't want the job."

"Now you *don't* want me to take the job? You want me to turn down an *$80,000 job* so I can buy a *car* for you?"

My wife's eyes were looking inward. I got in her face. "What's the *matter* with you?" I yelled, trying to get through. "You're supposed to be on *my side*, you're supposed to be *helping* me. Don't you see how insane this is? This isn't some stupid argument about housekeeping, it's...It's about my *freedom*."

As I said it, I recognized it, that which had been

struggling to come out: my understanding of what was at stake. It was met, by my wife, with silence.

"I need you to do this. *Do* it for me."

"You're not my responsibility."

There it was: that which my wife had been struggling to release. Also a variant of freedom, but, whereas mine was personal, her quest was, in effect, artistic: my wife needed to release all vestiges of guilt about focusing upon herself. Now, bravely, she had done so.

In keeping with the moment's significance, my wife seemed to rise above me, a parade float filling with the helium of power, her chin uplifting, as if to accentuate the lack of apology. Above, the tympani exploded: rain attacked the windows with snapping teeth, pounded the roof deliriously. Pagan gods had been freed.

I had been in similar positions with my wife before—asking and not receiving—but this was different. It was, of course, a bad time for me, but it was more than that, it was the *kind* of bad time I'd been having: the way in which everything I encountered, in the city, in my living situation, in my work, threatened my boundaries, attacked how I saw and what I wanted for myself; the way these assaults, and their outcomes, had replaced my jauntily optimistic certainty with the most private forms of doubt. By insisting upon driving me wherever I wanted to go, my wife was proposing to take control of the last remnant of my freedom, to make me completely dependent upon her in a situation in which I had almost nothing left of my own except this small bit of independence.

As clear as the moment's meaning was my course: I could not, must not, let this happen.

"Look," articulating as forcefully, as clearly as I could. "I can't be dependent on you. It's not just how disruptive this is, your coming *in* here and saying, Your work is done now. I mean, that's bad enough. But more than that, I have to have..."—I saw it lucidly—"the *illusion of power* to write. I have to get up every day with a kind of unreasonable faith in myself, to give my life to creating things that are essentially unnecessary."

"That's got nothing to do with me."

"Yes it does, if you're taking away—"

"I'm not *taking away* anything," said my wife pitilessly. "What you're calling your needs are, are just, you know. *Bourgeois dilettantism.*"

I was stung by this, but shouldn't have been. My wife had reached for the blunt instrument that had enabled her to survive her childhood: faced with a challenge, she counterattacked, she denied the humanity of her enemy and thus the validity of any claim he might make.

"You *can't. Share.* A *car,*" she sneered. "People share cars all the time."

"They have to. I don't."

"Why? Because your life's so much more important than someone else's?"

Perhaps I was mistaken. Perhaps she held a new weapon, or else, in my attenuated state, I was feeling its edge more sharply. But it was as though, having worked through her process to its unsparing finish, my wife had found a new, more awesome power.

"Do you *hear* yourself?" I said.

"You said that already," she drawled pleasurably, then leaned in. "You're a *perpetually dissatisfied person.* Your dissatisfaction is just taking this form *today.* You're saying, *today,* that because, for *one hour,* we're driving each other, I'm ruining your life, and that's bullshit, I'm not buying it, uh-uh, no way."

"I'm saying—"

"Because, you know what? I can buy a car *today,* and *tomorrow,* you'll find something else to hate me over, because you won't take responsibility for yourself, for your"—she leaned in further and spoke harshly, face contorted by a preening snarl—"*al*-co-hol-ism."

"Fuck you," I said, slapping the desk with the flat of my hand.

"Fuck you, too," the pleasure streaming out of her like sweat. "Fuck, fuck, you, you. *Deal* with yourself, and believe me, your 'needs' will go away."

With that, my wife turned on her heel and left the office—a good morning's work completed.

I hurried after her down the stairs, which she took swiftly, her aqua socks a blur on the brown tiles. "Oh, yeah? My need for what?" I demanded. "For freedom?"

"Leave me alone." She ground her feet into her shoes and snatched up her keys.

"How can I make you understand," I said, "that I can't let you take over my life this way? Drive me around, like, like a child, like you were my *mother*—"

"Your *mother*." She grabbed her jacket from a chair.

"Yes! I have to know that my life and my time are my own, I mean you, of all people, know what it's like here when you don't have wheels. My dignity demands that I not be isolated and imprisoned, that my need for freedom not be belittled as, as. A neurotic expression of dissatisfaction."

"That's what it is."

My wife plunged toward the door, her finger on the release button of her umbrella. I put myself in front of her.

"I can't survive," I pleaded, "if I can't keep my distance."

"Get out of my way." She was looking, it seemed, at my sleeve.

"Baby," I said, embarrassed now by the jargon I was spouting, the fact that I was, nakedly, begging, "I can't ask you for, for *permission* to gratify my most basic need."

"Are you coming?"

"*Listen* to—"

She stepped around me and reached for the doorknob. I grabbed her arm. My wife tore loose and turned on me, seeming to draw back like a snake; then she swung her umbrella, pivoting and putting her weight into it, cracking me on the temple with the handle.

I touched my eye, which had been lashed by the tip of one of the umbrella's ribs. Bent over at the waist, I looked up at her, blinking.

"To buy a car would be to accept blame," said my wife, "and I'm not going to be blamed for your life. It's *bullshit*.

Bullshit, bullshit, bullshit. Are you coming?" When I didn't reply, she took the skin of my arm between two fingers and twisted. "*Are you coming?*"

Minutes later, I found myself in the passenger seat of my car, clutching my gym bag protectively with both hands. Driving, my wife cursed the Sunset Boulevard traffic with an outsized savagery, spewing out such a vile condemnation of the local motorists' inability to handle a little precip that I leaned away, as though her words were a sewage with which I might be sprayed. My wife's demeanor was frightening, her rage at being made late to Al-Anon unprecedented. Before we'd come to a full stop in front of the Hollywood Y, she reached across me and flung open the door; before I'd closed it, the car was accelerating away.

Throughout the drive, I'd sat stunned, as though the blow I had taken moved me a step away from myself. I felt numb but, walking up the Y's front steps in the rain, I realized that I'd not been able yet to process my feelings about what had happened. My rational brain, of course, ground on, and led me to the unhappy understanding that, in the moment of my wife's refusal, I had known exactly what I'd needed to do: take her car keys, take her keys or send her away. I had done neither, and now the moment had passed, it was receding as palpably as an object seen in a rearview mirror. My emotions had yet to pull into the station of my heart. But this much I knew: the conflict with my wife had been a test of character, and I'd failed it. I had turned a corner, irretrievably.

The deeper feelings—the anguish—hit me on the treadmill. Muttering, mulling over how else I might have played it, I caught myself delivering a fantasy monologue to my wife, ranting under my breath about how difficult was my work, how miserably went the struggle with it—and realized that I had become that most detestable of all creatures, the Al-Anon husband. Looking at my streaming face in the mirror in front of me, I read in its contortions the pain of recognition: that for a long time, I'd been begging, begging my wife to accept my needs and fulfill them. Of course she had not, and today had demonstrated that she would not, but what pierced my heart with woe was how incapable I was of *doing* something about this. An hour ago, my wife had effectively plunged a knife into my talent, and though I'd dodged and protested, I had let her do. Even O.J.'s wife, I thought, arms pumping as I ran and ran, put up a fight. I had let it happen.

I flattened my thumb against the treadmill's speed-advance button and began running insanely, trying to escape the inescapable: What my wife wanted for me mattered more than what I wanted for myself. And because of something in me—in *me*—there was nothing I could do about it, *I could not act to save myself*.

There began a screaming in my head, a sound, I imagined, akin to the engulfing scrape of tectonic plates, as my world began to unmake itself. At first I seemed to go crazy with rage and hatred—rage at my wife for doing this, hatred of myself for accepting it. Then I felt electrified with terror, like an animal that finds itself trapped in a cage, except that it was a cage of my own making. This nudged me over the precipice. Cutting the treadmill's power so abruptly that I almost hurtled into the mirror, I ran full-out down a hallway with high yellowish walls, one made institutional by the sallow glare of flourescents, and into the boxing room behind the basketball court. There I found a heavy bag, and laid into it bareknuckled, first with jabs, hooks off the jabs, straight rights, then whirling, imprecise body shots into which I threw all my weight, punches that deformed my skeleton and caused the bag to swing as lightly as a Japanese lantern in a hurricane. But it was useless: I could not fight my way out of the prison of my nature. Throwing a final overhand right, I shouted hoarsely, turned to walk away and, for the first and only time in my life, passed out cold.

XXXX

If I retained any optimism regarding my choice of profession, the rewrite job put it to bed. Determined to throw off despair, I attacked the work with the same adrenalized savagery with which I'd pummeled the bag, and completed a gorged, misshapen draft, a pig-out of clashing savories. This was by request: the producer asked that I release all my ideas quickly, so that we might polish them together. Fair enough; but what I discovered when we sat down to work was that I'd met this man, considered to be the finest producer of his era, at precisely the moment that he'd decided to become a director, a task for which he proved entirely unsuitable. Developing his own screenplay, this two-time Academy Award winner mistook violence for reality, ponderousness for gravity, schmaltz for lyricism, quirk for character. "Theme" was the music that sugared the credits: throughout the process, he remained incapable of expressing a clear view of what the movie was about. I shouldn't have been surprised. His motivation for directing was my old friend status: he wished to tell his friends, over cigars and wine, "I'm a director." When after four months the producer read the revision and pronounced it crap, it seemed a fitting end. He thanked me, paid me, and caught a plane.

It was of course unfair to blame him, given my own disengagement: For the length of the job I remained at precisely the pitch of rage I'd reached in the moments before my collapse. If I spoke at all, it was to shout, in a voice so contorted that it was hard to decipher the words. The message, however, was unmistakable: *Buy a car.* I had become obsessed with making my wife obey, it was my failure to do so that had ruined things, and I was certain that, if I could reverse this loss, everything would be right again. This was equal to assuming that, if one could find a missing limb, one would once again be whole.

Like many obsessives, there came to be little distance between my inner and outer states: So loud, clear and constant was the shouting in my head that I was often surprised to discover that it was issuing from my throat. This proved especially true when my wife and I had to deal with the car itself. The scuffed little Nissan had assumed such outsized significance that it practically glowed; flashes of light, bursts of static, would rip through my brain when I saw it.

"Do you want to drive?" my wife would ask, with a martyr's indulgence.

"Want to drive? Want to *drive*?" I would snarl typically, going white, my hands trembling. "Is that supposed to give me the illusion that I'm *the man*? Is that some *sop* you're throwing me, to make me feel like it's still *my car*?" Eyes would appear behind windows as my rant echoed off the stucco façades.

"No," my wife would reply, mixing resignation with a faint, unmistakable pleasure. "I just know you hate my driving."

Off again my head would go, barking about inequity and manipulation, a harangue so consuming that it would cover the complex of feelings within me as thoroughly as an explosion erases a whisper. And the more I raged and sulked and fumed, the firmer and more intractable my wife's position became.

My emotions were indeed complex, but I remained trapped in this condition precisely because I couldn't bear to look at them. What I could not confront was *why*: Why was I, a mature man, incapable of fighting for my life? Why would I not act to save myself? Whenever my mind would drift too near to these speculations, the rage would kick in, it would course through my nerves with a pounding violence. It was easier, after all, to be angry at my wife. Wasn't it her fault? Wasn't it a rotten, destructive thing she'd done to me? No, there was no *why*, I didn't know what it was about and didn't want to know. I knew enough. Buy a car. Bullying, haranguing, kicking over chairs. *Buy a car.* "Stop blaming me for your unhappiness," my wife had said. I hadn't before, but I was now.

Hiding behind my anger licensed behavior that, had I observed it in another, I would have judged shameful. The buy-the-car jihad, I decided, would restore my self-respect. But the hostility with which I pursued it served an unadmitted purpose: it let me punish my wife, pay her back by making her life as miserable as my own. "Intimacy," she'd cried out for in happier days, "*in*-ti-ma-cy!" The worst thing you could do to my wife was withhold yourself, it was equal to withholding water from a flower. But she had given *me* an intimate wound, it was inevitable that I would withdraw; inevitable, too, the pleasure I took in it. Had I examined my feelings, I might have dealt with her more humanely. Instead, all the tenderness went out of the relationship.

A little tenderness would have been welcome just then: in a pastel-tinted office on Beverly Boulevard, we learned that my wife's childbearing years were over. "You have no eggs," said Dr. Leslie, Gynecologist to the Stars, a tall, cool, hatchet-faced neo-Bess Myerson whose bedside manner owed much to Josef Mengele. Glancing at her watch, calling out to have the car brought round, it was time for her *Today* show taping, this woman casually informed my wife that her most cherished dream was, like Humpty Dumpty, irreparably broken, no matter the number of horses and men. "Have you considered surrogacy?" with a joyless showing of bleached teeth, a disdain for our un-modern wasting of her precious time. In a lifetime of rage, I have never felt closer to killing someone.

Yet this was more hypocrisy, for though I fulminated against the doctor's insensitivity, I offered nothing to put in its place. Traumatized by the outrage my wife had committed against me, I found myself incapable of the kindness I would have shown, under similar circumstances, to a stranger. Even in my condition, this struck me as ridiculous, as I had practically a genetic inability to *not* sympathize with my wife when it came to my own needs: in every dispute within the marriage, I took her side against myself. Now, flipping this principle to reveal its moronic obverse, I chose to redress the emotional imbalance by giving my wife nothing: perhaps I cannot be kind to myself, went the message, but I can be cruel to you.

This infantile punishment held a certain poignant irony. During those months, we were both in mourning: my wife for the child that was not to be, I for the loved one I'd spent my adult life nurturing: my identity. The character of myself, the hard-drinking, erotically venturesome writer-dreamer, met its own Humpty Dumpty end on the morning my wife refused to buy a car: that identity became, on the spot, insupportable. Though this perception was as dim as all the others, a component of the white wall of pain in my head, that tectonic screaming, was my anguish at the murder of the imperfect but necessary child that I had raised, the "I" that contained me, a murder in which—shockingly, shamefully—I was complicit.

It was this above all that I couldn't face. And in my rage at my wife, my need to rush away from responsibility and blame her for everything, I could offer no tenderness in her own period of mourning.

As for my wife's behavior during this time: Lashed by the pain of loss, she slipped the tethers of interpersonal rectitude entirely and pursued the liberation she'd discovered with a blind, savage mania. It set the difference between us in high relief. I had learned to survive by playing a part. The strategy's flaw was that it taught me how to hide but not to fight. My wife had survived by denying any reality but her own, and if this had previously been in the service of staying alive, she sensed that pushing her guiltlessness to extremes—especially when this involved the joy of hurting an intimate who criticized her—held the key to unblocking her talent. That meant—as she could not otherwise do her work—that the marriage became my wife's Theatre of Cruelty. Needless to say, she played Sade.

She would hammer away, my wife, at any aspect of my life that she did not yet fully control. I wouldn't smoke cigars, she railed, if I'd go to AA and face up to my need to have self-destructive habits, suck at one or another tit, in place of fulfilling activities. A vegetarian, she attacked my meat-eating as an example of my profligacy: throwing away money on *meat*—and she would spit out the word bitterly, as though I were squandering my savings on ermine underwear or diamond-studded teeth—was just another addiction, no different, or less contemptible, than compulsive shopping.

Always, always, my wife worked to equate desire with dysfunction, my unwillingness to go to AA and admit that, yes, everything in my life of which she didn't approve surely *was* bullshit and *should* be stamped out, a ceaseless, insidious linking of need or aspiration to personal failing, to weakness. Thus did my wife, cleverly, turn me inside out: she made me feel weak, not because I couldn't beat *her*, but because I couldn't beat my own lust for life. It was infuriating, incredible, and finally a little impressive: My wife wormed her way into every clean impulse I had and gnawed away relentlessly until it collapsed and decayed. Rust never sleeps? Compared to my wife, rust was Rip van Winkle.

Toward the end of the months it took to complete the rewrite, I managed, finally, to badger and bully my wife into allowing that she would "think about" buying a car. By then, however, I was utterly depleted. So I had wrested this vague concession from her. At what price? The wrongness of a relationship that proceeds on these terms ultimately militates against the very idea of winning. More to the point, though I'd made inroads against my wife, she'd made far more substantial ones against me. Weakened by her relentless hammering, I'd crossed the line between not being able to take my freedom to beginning to accept its absence as a given. Combined with my awareness of our battle's existential nature, this extra measure of despair left me incapable of consolidating my victory.

Once again, deus ex machina, in the meddlesome figure of Bets, my wife's sponsor, intervened. She called to tell us of a new gym, right nearby—only *forty minutes* on foot. It was hardly a solution. But four months of non-stop anger had left me near to ruin. Changing gyms would end the daily battle, we could sort out the particulars, my wife and I, "later." We agreed to see a couples therapist, who would teach us to "negotiate." And I began to walk.

And to suffer. Oh, yes. I became the anti-Piaf: *Moi, je regret tout.* "If only" became my favorite words. I had *known* that nothing in the marriage proceeded except via ultimatum, *if only* I had given my wife one immediately. Our windows of opportunity are few and far between, the gaps between them swamps for the will and soul, and I had choked, I had blown it. If only. *If only.*

That was the smallest part of it. If regret was my Everest, my rage was scaled to the whole of the Himalayas. I had thought it would abate, but it got worse, my rage, it picked up force as it rolled like a shock wave across my interior landscape. This was nowhere more apparent than in the course of my daily death march to and from the gym. Erewhon: Nowhere, approximately, spelled backwards. The name of a food market on the ground floor of the Broadcast Center Apartments, on Beverly at Stanley, two blocks south of my home. Every day, I would sprint across the former thoroughfare, pass Erewhon, and enter Nowhere, in the form of a limited-access road that ran between Pan-Pacific Park and the car lot that serviced Television City, the nearby CBS broadcast studio. On the CBS side ran a row of eucalyptus trees; on the road's other edge, the gently downsloping bowl of the park. Not an unattractive stroll—except that what it was, in my rage, was both a park and a parking lot giving me their backs: an alleyway. Lined with cars: this being LA, despite the benches five feet away, people chose to kill their lunch hours in their vehicles, eating Cheetos, smoking fags. I would stalk down this alley, between idling cars and the park's public toilets, and rage, aloud, grinding my way through one fantasy argument with my wife after another, in a fury so physically annihilating and spiritually desolating that I felt my heart would burst.

Reaching Third Street—the end of the road—I would once again sprint as cars bore down on me, then cut through Park La Brea, a postwar housing development in which I would invariably get lost, until I'd arrive at Wilshire Boulevard, where the clean new gym awaited. I would work out, and reverse course. Two forty-minute walks; raging both ways. Returning home one afternoon, I passed the Villa Stanley, a group home for deinstitutionalized mental patients; muttering, snarling, spitting out my hate, I looked up and saw a bunch of them, nodding gravely, recognizing my state. Yes, the brethren at the booby hatch awaited, and no surprise: I was suffering the pangs of the knowledge that I had made this bed, a knowledge that was driving me insane.

XXXX

As Humbert Humbert might have put it, it is now my duty to report a shocking decline in my wife's morals. Or, to paraphrase the protagonist O'Shaugnessy of Mr. Mailer's *The Deer Park*: Just when things seem as bad as they can be, they get worse. Approaching the end of our second year, things began to go bad in a way that seemed out of control, as though I were inhabiting a dreamscape suffused with catastrophic inevitability. This was, to be sure, my doing. My rigidity, to which my conscious mind clung as proof of my indomitability, was in reality just the opposite: it was my will, holding out stubbornly against the prospect of a new, perhaps better life that is not, alas, the old life, not the feral emotional knowledge embedded in the bones. The spirit can endure far more punishment than one can imagine, when the alternative is to do something else. Of course, as I had learned from repeated temblors, that which cannot bend, breaks. In the land of the earthquake.

"You *what?*" I shrieked, voice cracking on the second word.

"I joined a writing group," said my wife. "I'm going to be a writer."

"*Oh* no. *Nooo*-no-no-no-no-no-no-no-no. No way."

"A meditation writing group, actually." She struck her signature pose, to which she invariably resorted when dealing with me: arms folded tightly beneath her breasts, weight on one hip, the leg opposite turned out and extended, head lowered and angled. A pose bespeaking defense (against the flume of abuse that met her smallest effort to live her life) and disgust (with my serial unwillingness to deal with myself).

"What the *fuck*," I said. "Is a *meditation writing group*?"

My wife sighed, eyes wide with resignation: she could explain, but I would just judge it, piss on it, hate her for it. "Junie gives us a word," she began anyway, and despite herself with a trace of pleasure, "and, you know, we meditate on it, like it was..."

"A mantra."

"Right, except it's a *creative* mantra, the idea is, you know, you just let it...*take* you where it's going to take you. To whatever associations."

"And? What do you do with these associations?"

"This is just what I've been told. But then she passes around a basket with strips of paper in it, and we each take one, and it has a *sentence*. And it's your point of departure for writing your shortie."

"Your *shortie*."

She shrugged, twice, head shaking with the speed of a hummingbird's wings. The next beat in her choreography, designed to express bewilderment at so contemptuous a reaction to something so inoffensive. "A short piece. Okay? It's what she calls it, I mean, the word unlocks our imaginations, and the sentence gives us a push, why are you so hostile to this? I mean, I thought you'd, you know. Be happy I *found* something."

"Thrilled. Who's Junie?"

A pause. "Someone from the program."

I groaned. My wife went into the kitchen. I heard the refrigerator door open and close; the release of gas as the top of a bottle of sparkling water was unscrewed. I remained in the living room, looking at the staircase, which I had enjoyed descending grandly in our first weeks of residence, a time so remote that I could scarcely conjure its pleasure and possibility.

"When does it meet?" I said.

Pouring of water; open and close of refrigerator door. I went into the kitchen. My wife was at the sink, her back to me. I walked to where I could see her in profile, her blank eyes staring at nothing, fingers loose around the water glass on the countertop. A spasm of empathy went through me, for her unhappiness, for the pain—which I knew so well, because she had inflicted it on me—of optimism undermined, enthusiasm spoiled.

"When does it meet?"

"Two nights a week."

"How will you get there?"

Silence. I dropped into a red metal folding chair and laughed softly and shook my head and sighed. It was a still, clammy late morning, on the sort of day that feels stale before it even begins. The exhaustion in the room, the longing for an end, was palpable.

"Ah, God," I said.

"I just don't know what to say, you know? I mean...I made a life—"

"Don't start..."

"I keep trying to make a life. And..."

"And now you'll have the car five days *and* two nights a week."

It never, as the saying goes, ceased to amaze. We could be half-gone with the boredom and depression and stink of it, slumped in our corners of the marital ring and consumed with a lassitude next to death. And yet, at the clang of the bell, my wife and I would tumble off of our stools and flail— a jab of martyrdom here, a hook of manipulation there. Until, on points but nevertheless, she won another round.

What could I say? I couldn't tell her not to do something. Indeed, I thought, as I slogged up the stairs and packed my gym bag, it was the logical next step. The marriage as medium of expression was reaching its limits, and having acted, painted and danced, my wife's options were few. Writing, moreover, offered continuity: even as she moved in new creative directions, she might continue to replenish the well of my misery by doing what I did.

Does that sound paranoid? Could my wife really have been innocent of the effect her decision would have on me?

She must have sensed, with her impeccable killer instinct, how upset I'd be with this latest choice of endeavor. At the least, I had zero interest in living with another writer—living with myself was bad enough. *What next?* I wondered. *Where will it all end?* I had visions of my wife publishing slender volumes of heavily autobiographical white womanist short fiction that got made into movies (for which she wrote the first drafts, guaranteeing her screen credit), her gripping lineage profiled in *The New York Times Magazine,* her ability to go on after the suicide of her alcoholic husband a testament to her Al-Anon-derived inner strength.

Quite apart from this phantasmagoria, the very notion of the writing group pushed my buttons. "Writing group"— the ultimate oxymoron. *I* was a writer, I penned myself like a rat and went at it alone, and I was certain my wife knew how extra-infuriating I found the prospect of her taking off in *my car* so that she and her fellow circle-jerkers could indulge their artistic velleities.

Having studied mate manipulation at the bunioned feet of the maestra, however, I did not come out with this. I played, instead, on the historic intractability of my wife's acting career, based as it was on the need for a text, space, lights, sets. Why, I asked guilefully, hoping this would pulverize the whole idea, had she taken a craft that could be practiced solo, and chained it to a roomful of strangers?

"But I *love* groups," my wife exclaimed, with a bit of the old brightness in her eyes, and I became cognizant of a truth that, despite the years, I had been missing. Another route to intimacy was to *belong*, in a positive way, via creativity: to make, in short, a family, one that worked for a change. She began writing, my wife, and the link between the private act of imagination and her affinity for group endeavor proved magical: within weeks she was filling spiral-bound pages from edge to edge with determined, impressive density. It had nothing to do with me. I *was* being paranoid.

My recognition of the value of the writing group caused me—inevitably, it seemed, as I found myself now on an honesty kick as compulsive as my drinking had been—to reconsider my objections to it. Apart from snobbery, my feelings were based on the concept of protecting the work. A central group activity was reading aloud; and I would not have exposed a script in progress to the spitballing it would receive from a bunch of insensitive amateurs.

Yet considering the facts of my life, it was hard to take this seriously. I had failed to protect my writing from Hollywood, and failed to protect it from my wife. Given the trashing my creativity had taken as a result, wasn't a fear of writing groups a bit like worrying about birdshit on the roof after leaving one's bungalow unbattened during a tornado?

I didn't buy it. And I began—compulsively, pulling harder at the threads in the fast-unraveling tapestry of my nature—to dig for what it was about writing groups that really bothered me. Listening to my wife's reports of her own spitballing sessions, in which group members would point out each other's mannerisms and miscues while also praising and encouraging their strengths, the answer revealed itself: these people really mixed it up, they were not afraid to take a few hard knocks if they thought it would make them better.

This was not something I could or would have done. I fought it out in meetings, but only after the script in question was as good as I could make it: my writing did not leave its room until it was perfectly groomed, clean and neat. In a way that went beyond self-protection, I did not show what I did not want seen. It was as though my writing was not my work but my emissary—the "me" I did not feel that I could be. This was a more truthful explanation of my mistrust of writing groups. The people with whom my wife met had personalities that stood behind their writing. My writing was a personality behind which stood nothing. How could I have offered it up for criticism?

In the aftermath of my most recent failure—which, as I'd rewritten a major writer for a major producer, everyone else considered a walloping success—an old script I'd had optioned suddenly Lazarused, and I was hired, for more money than ever, to rewrite it. The studio demanded speed,

I juiced myself up and got down to it, and yet I found my attention drifting, my mind wading into existential reveries. If my personality (I reasoned typically) existed to enable me to function, and the writing went forth as the face of that personality, then, yes, logically, the writing's true purpose was to give the personality expression. Pondering this, I reflected that it was the real reason I could get none of my vast oeuvre into production. Perhaps my Hollywood readers were not as clueless as they seemed. "You're very smart," said the town, then took a pass; and whereas I had assumed, bitterly, that the town couldn't handle smart, perhaps it saw, as I had not, that I was not really writing movies. "You're very smart," meaning—nudgingly, kindly—that I was trying to make myself *look* smart—in which case, how smart could I really be?

Here, I considered, was the true problem: not only did I have no audience, I didn't want one. I was not doing the work to write scripts that got made into movies, but to give safe expression to a dishonest self-fantasy. A fantasy that— by virtue of the fact that I could not even stand up to my wife—I knew to be unworkable.

Emerging from my office one day, after a session so unproductive it had left me terror-stricken, I found my wife, on the big bed in the pretty bedroom, writing madly. "Can I read you something?" she asked, and promptly commenced. My response to this—a blow to a brain unready to receive— was recognition: I could not have cut it in a writing group because my focus would have been on protecting myself from *invasion*. Here at last was a bit of my life's design: I could not be invaded. Invasion, I repeated to myself, struggling to keep hold of the word. *Invasion*.

Unfortunately, the more I understood this fear, the less able I was to defend against it. This became apparent in a situation that arose from my wife's writing. As the densely printed spiral notebooks began to pile up, my wife realized that, if she ever hoped to edit any of this output, she had better get it typed. Technology utterly defeated my wife: sound systems, kitchen appliances, anything with a mechanism more complex than an ON/OFF switch, reduced her to narcotized bafflement. Yet, rather than using her mother's old Smith-Corona, my wife became fixated on mastering the intricacies of my Macintosh—which meant that I had to teach them to her. The hours of explanation dissolved into afternoons, which melted into days; and my wife, at first tentatively, then with her trademark entitlement, became a presence beside me in my office.

The office. It had, in this marriage in which nothing was sacrosanct, remained the one part of my existence that even my wife acknowledged was my own. It was not merely that I worked there. It was also that I *worked* there: objectively, I had never been more productive or more successful. I was going from one job to the next, my price continued to rise, and my writing, though no one was making it and I myself questioned its value ceaselessly, continued to be well-received. In my isolation—which, given that my wife, literally, held the keys, had come to resemble a glorified home detention—my work remained my sole connection to reality. It was, startlingly, all I had.

Thus the sensory peculiarity I experienced when my wife invaded, the weird distancing that felt like the beginning of the end, the separation from the last of the self that I was used to thinking of as me. Having nailed the basics of word processing, my wife asked if she could use the computer while I was working out, and there was no reason to deny her. But I would feel, as the moment approached, like I had been up for too many hours, or taken a drug that made my hands seem far away, as though viewed through the wrong end of a telescope. Before going to the gym, I would take a last backward glance at my wife as she sat down, in *my* chair, at *my* writing machine, and began to put her words into it; this image would perplex me—vaguely, uneasily—the whole time that I would be getting nowhere fast on the Stairmaster; and it would deepen when, upon my return, I would find her still in place and have to go somewhere in the big, still apartment and wait—five minutes, sometimes ten—while the upstairs echoed with the click of the keys. When confronted, she responded with that now-familiar look of wounded contempt; and I saw, with grim certainty, that she had taken title to the last vestige of my old identity. Shortly thereafter, I bought another computer, "loaned" her mine, and put it in the bedroom, on the other side of the wall. My wife never used my office again. But it was never entirely mine again, and the slightly nauseated feeling of dissociation never completely went away. Too late did the end of the two years finally come into view: there was not enough left of the man who'd begun the race to reach the finish line.

And yet that line remained the dominating image in my life, the single, hard hope I'd continued to hold in my heart. Though she was leading a golden existence, my wife had continued to rail against LA and cudgel me with Paris, my promise. She needn't have worried—I was more than ready. I even developed a version of nostalgia for the entire LA experience, ultra-nihilistic in that it was for what had never been. My plans, I sighed, ah, my plans! Ah, well. Fuck it. I was still punching, still on my feet. The rueful pride this produced enabled me to throw off my lassitude and, not just sprint through the rewrite, but polish off outlines for two new scripts, provocative ideas awaiting only the writing. Twenty-three months after our arrival, I finished up in a blaze of glory, heart roaring, muscles burning, my chest breaking the tape. I'd written three screenplays, saved enough money to last as many years, established a high price and a sterling reputation. Mission accomplished. I was home free.

<h2 style="text-align:center">XXXX</h2>

"I'm not leaving," said my wife.

Even as I was hearing it, I didn't believe it. I had insisted that, if we went to Paris, she do all the planning, and she'd agreed—that, surely, was the problem. What she didn't realize was that I hadn't the slightest intention of holding her to this. What would have been the point? *My wife* was never going to plan a *three-month trip to Paris.* So we'd knock around a bit until we found a place. Don't worry, I assured her, it's a no-brainer. We even had my wife's studio apartment waiting at the end of our Parisian sojourn, a cozy place to camp while we searched for something permanent. Let's go, I said, ragged and distracted but, for the first time in years, in sight of a sense of ease.

She said it again. With emphasis this time: "I'm. Not. *Leav*ing."

"All right," I said. "*I'll* pack. I'll"—the familiar refrain—"pay for everything."

But she was serious. Yes, said my wife, she hadn't wanted to come. But she had tried very hard to adjust, and had finally made a life for herself—more than *I* had, tilting up her chin. It wasn't *her* fault that I hadn't accepted responsibility for my happiness, it wasn't *fair* to drag her away after the effort she'd made. I'd complained about New York, I'd hated LA, now I would hate Paris and then New York again, I was a malcontent, perpetually dissatisfied, I always blamed people or places and never looked within. Why should *she* have to pay for that? Especially now, on the brink of winter? Why should *she* suffer through a damp, gray Parisian fall, then stagger around the pee-drenched streets of New York, in the bitter cold, competing with richer, wilier people for the one or two small, dark ratholes that would both suit us (barely) and be affordable? Why *now*, she howled, when we had a big, beautiful place, the sun always shone and it was 78 degrees?

And (she, my wife, added with emphasis) the *business* was in LA. *I hadn't gotten a picture made*—did I really think anyone would remember me two minutes after I left town? Was I that de*lud*ed? LA was *full* of screenwriters, none of them ungrateful or whining or ambivalent like I was, any *one* of whom would have *killed* to have an opportunity like mine— how could I leave it? Was it really worth it to trash one of the most fragile, tenuous careers in the history of motion pictures, just as it was *finally, maybe* going to get off the ground, to punish her for my dissatisfaction? Was I insane?

Was I *ever* going to *deal* with myself? No way, my wife said. No *way* was she leaving. It was bullshit. She wasn't playing along.

To use the cinematic model: this is the moment in the picture when, after a series of ever closer close-ups of myself and my wife, climaxing with an extreme tight shot of her chattering mouth, followed by an equally claustrophobic angle of my bulging, twitching eyes, I grab a heavy object—call it a candlestick—and bash in her brains.

Movies, however, are movies, and life is life. "If we stay," I said, "will you buy a car?"

"How long are we staying?"

"I don't know. I don't *want* to stay at all."

"Then why should I buy a car?"

"Because you want to stay!"

"*Are* we staying?"

"Will you leave?"

"Eventually."

My lips tightened in resignation. "In the spring?"

"Maybe."

"Then buy a car."

"By the time I find one, it'll be January"—this was said in October—"and we'll be leaving in March. I'm not going through all that for two months. It's bullshit." She looked at her watch. "I have to go, I'm late for my meeting. I know *you* don't respect it, but people depend on me."

"I depend on you, too."

My wife folded her arms tightly beneath her breasts: first position. And: "Do you want a ride to the gym?"

Minutes later, I found myself—once again—following a traumatic failure of character, taking the passive position in my Nissan. Yet this time, things were different. There was no violence, no fainting; I felt, instead, a preternatural calm. The truth was that the dynamic of my marriage had become routine—no longer a source of desperate conflict so much as the way things were. The distancing from myself that accompanied the invasion of my office had returned—overlain, this time, with an element of fantasy. Everything's going to be fine, I told myself, just fine. Surely, we would leave in the spring.

This sense of peace evaporated later that day when, getting up from my desk, I went into the bathroom and caught sight of myself in the mirror. What I beheld stopped me cold. I had repaid my wife for what she'd done to me by denying her the intimacy on which she thrived. It had somehow not occurred to me, in my state of rage, that if she was being denied intimacy, so was I. This realization—which, once I came to it, seemed almost absurdly obvious – led me to realize as well, and with an abrupt spasm of anguish, that I had not taken hold of my wife—or, for that matter, anyone—with unfettered affection for well over a year. There in the mirror, the legacy of my strategy was staring me in the face: the frown, the hot, angry eyes, the pinched mouth of a perpetual lemon-sucker. I am not an attractive man, and whatever appeal my looks may own derives from an animating pleasure, a sly but genuine joy in life that, when apparent in my face, can be infectious. All of that, I could see, had long ago left the premises. What remained was a rictus—one that, having been so long abandoned, had begun to decay.

I went back to my desk, picked up my pencil...and set it down. Whatever I was doing—whether it was punishing my wife, protecting myself, or both—I was dying. Once, I'd enjoyed a wide range of interests, I'd filled notebooks with one idea after another, I'd written—my God—*comedy*. Now, all I thought about was my unhappiness. There was no pleasure to be found for me in anything, and I stuck to my misery stubbornly, against all attempts by my friends, associates, and even my wife to jolly me out of it. It had become my identity, as being a writer once had been.

Faced with this realization, I could think of one question only: *How did it serve me?* The answer seemed beyond imagining—unless it was that I'd never realized I *needed* intimacy. I had always been a loner, fanatic about preserving my independence; intimacy was something I equated with a loss, in every sense, of control. This explained a lot, I thought, it explained my marriage, which had begun with rigid separations and proven to be no marriage at all, it explained—I paused to put together the thought—it explained why my first solution to every threat was to cut myself off. It stood, in my life, as a leitmotif—the first weapon I reached for, seemingly the only one I had.

Examining this from the mirror's other side, I wondered: What did my wife and I give each other? I had, I told myself, married a woman I loved, but was not absolutely in love with (to cite that tired chestnut), in exchange for getting a life companion with whom I was simpatico. This perspective, however, struck me as violently inaccurate: my wife and I were on the same creative and intellectual wavelengths and enjoyed each other's company, but otherwise occupied completely different planets. And yet the bargain might have worked, I felt, if I had only known how susceptible I would be to her will. This, more than anything, had spoiled our potential: I had not known that, when backed into a corner, I would not fight to save myself. I had not known my flaw.

Glancing at my bookshelves, I saw the long row of red-spined Chinese notebooks I favored as journals. I crossed the room, found the appropriate volume, and flipped to the entries surrounding my wedding. On the night before, I had written (in a scrawl suggestive of inebriation): *If it doesn't work out, I can always drink.*

I went to the window and opened it, letting in the LA sounds of car alarms, helicopters, leaf-blowers. Of course. At the time, my notion was that I'd still be able to enjoy my usual roistering. Now, sober for over two years and in an intractable crisis that was tearing me apart, I recognized, in this unguarded notation, the truth: my drinking was a barrier, the most dependable means I had of cutting myself off—a defense against a world against which I was otherwise incapable of defending myself.

I paged through my journal, thinking as I did so that I'd misunderstood my interest in my wife. Yes, I had been drawn to her because we clicked. And yet another part of me had been attracted to her destructive potential, my recognition that—I found the sentence in my notes—"she would out of her own anxieties convert my love of life into a disease, and characterize every part of my life that she feared as an aspect of that disease."

"Out of her own anxieties" struck me as the critical phrase. My marital compromise was not that I didn't love my wife, or wasn't *in* love with her—indeed, it was not so much compromise as fact: I had married a woman with whom I had a lot going, but who would always convert fear into manipulation, who *out of fear* would try to limit our life together.

It might have worked, too, the marriage, if I had only perceived my susceptibility to that manipulation. But I had not, and this was because—I saw it now lucidly, and for the first time—*I was an alcoholic.* Rather than fishing my flaw out of the murk of my unconscious, I had instead put up a wall, with an over-the-counter drug that ensured that I could sustain a space within me that no one could penetrate. The upshot was that I had a problem—ticking away inside me like a bomb—that I didn't know was there.

And why, I reflected, sitting down again, would I have known I had it, *as long as I was drinking?* I assumed that I was free because I *felt* free. And look how far I'd gone—quite a ways, from writing car brochures and public service announcements to within an inch of the pinnacle of my profession. Alas, having not been sober enough to understand my situation, just at the moment when I was ready to claim my prize—when I had rolled the rock of my writing to the lip of the industry mountaintop—my flaw came and tapped me on the shoulder; my bomb went off. I stopped drinking, and thereby removed the wall I had erected to keep out the world, the barrier that protected my carefully designed self-fantasy. And the world, in the figure of my wife, came rushing in and overwhelmed me, the rock teetered and rolled back down the mountain, my confidence, creative energy, self-respect, and my identity were all, bit by bit—beat by beat, as they say in the movies—stripped away, and everything I had wanted for my entire adult life was utterly, irrevocably lost.

I sat motionless—the word is inadequate: I seemed, rather, to turn to stone—as the implications of this understanding seeped through me. My first thought was that she, my wife, had been right: I should have gone to AA and "dealt with" myself. Had I done so, I might have anticipated what the withdrawal of drink and the change of venue would do to me. Part of the reason I did not, of course, was that I'd never believed in my alcoholism, and thus could not progress to an understanding of alcohol's function. What I found interesting—again, the word is inadequate: *stupefying* is more like it—was that swearing off drink had done nothing to change my personality. Not understanding the problem's true nature meant that I'd simply found another way to cut myself off: I was now as addicted to unhappiness as I had been to liquor, and it performed precisely the same function. It was with no small shock that I realized that, for my two sober years, I might as well have been drinking.

I could feel the toxic stain of my understanding making its way to the extremities of my consciousness. *Destroyed.* Was I really destroyed, I asked myself almost plaintively. I could not, I felt, even begin to repair the damage. To reclaim everything that had been lost would require finding out why it was that I could not act to save myself, and this was not a journey I felt able to undertake. No, I considered grimly, it was hopeless. Like a fighter who lays off for months, then tries to train for a title bout in a day, the outcome was preordained.

I stared at the avocado tree in the courtyard, scarcely breathing, as the implications of what I had done saturated me completely. Augie March's observation, on page one of Saul Bellow's great novel, came back to me: when you hold down one thing, you hold down the adjoining. I had suppressed, rather than corrected, a conundrum of character, and though it hadn't happened right away, that central suppression eventually came to hold down every other aspect of my life. I had lost my success—I, and no one else, had destroyed my talent.

What this meant, in practical terms, was that it might be impossible for me ever to write again, as this self-knowledge exposed—more irrefutably than the difficulties with my wife—the insupportability of my character. By "character" I mean both the man I was and the man I played. For twenty years, these states of being had preserved a balanced relationship, and it was this that enabled me to get through the writing day. If I was in many ways obtuse, it was also true that one cannot be a professional for as long as I had been without developing a sense of one's strengths and limitations; and I'd long had to do battle with a shallowness which came directly, I understood, from anxiety. Even at its best, my voice as a writer owned a frantic quality, as though I were a nervous person meeting a group of strangers, and wanted only to get through the occasion as wittily as possible and leave a good impression; and this anxiety could prevent me, I'd found, from elevating a scene or screenplay above cleverness to well and properly done.

Nonetheless, I judged that the problem could, with application, be fixed. And while I worked at it, I clung with energetic jauntiness to that contrivance, my adopted character, the way a man might cling to a runaway train: knowing it was out of control, but certain that, if I could manage not to get flung off, I would arrive, eventually, at my destination.

I looked at my desires and said: Act as if. But I had assumed that I knew myself. What I discovered now was that one cannot build a useful fiction on top of a destructive lie. I based that fiction on a belief in myself as a fearless seeker of the truth. But my self-fantasy, formed as it was behind a wall of alcohol, was not based on an equally fearless self-appraisal. I had, at the beginning of my career, thought of myself as an interesting writer, but sought reinforcing opinions from those with the lowest possible standards: trade-magazine editors, milky men who'd long ago scuttled their own big dreams, or else swinging-dick bond traders, too clogged with Kobe steak, Stoli and cocaine to read anything more complex than the laundering instructions on a designer label. I had believed my work to be cutting-edge, but didn't seek the edge in any of the arts, about which I knew little more than what I read in the papers. I had considered myself an adventurous pursuer of the outer limits of eros, but didn't challenge my bedroom skills with anything more formidable than a long string of silly, needy girls. I had created a character to help build my character, but that character proved to be a character, too.

Realizing all this, the raft on which my discipline, imagination and optimism had enjoyed a decades-long float disappeared beneath the surface without a trace. From this central death, others seemed to radiate like spokes from the hub of a wheel. Most notably, I suffered an abrupt cessation of paying work. I had picked up that most unenviable of profiles: the promising nobody who gets a couple of breaks, then fails to crack the big time. A screenwriter in the middle is a bad investment, one of hundreds of overpaid known quantities, good but not good enough. And so, having failed to become the next big thing, my blip dropped off the radar screen and I was gone, history. A silence settled over my professional life as perfect as that of the tomb.

On a personal level, I bore helpless witness as this inner death began to exhibit outward manifestations. It was as though I had undergone chemotherapy and emerged fragile and wasted, attenuation drawing down steadily over me like a veil. It was, of course, a disease from which I suffered, if not a physical one, though depression does have its metabolic components; if anything remained of my former clarity, it was the ability to perceive how, under the right circumstances, a cheerful spirit could become so undermined that discouragement could seem biological. The calm I'd felt when my wife declared that she wasn't leaving, I understood, had been the first symptom of this condition.

I raged, I rebelled and made demands, but these flashes of spirit became ever more distant; my wife's natural sweetness reasserted itself, and we passed tolerable days. We showed up for Al-Anon parties, took walks on the beach; I drove my wife to Trader Joe's, pushing the cart as I followed behind her, and out to Costco in the Valley, to help her stock up on cheap bulk toilet paper. Life went its way.

I was only reminded of my reality—the horror and fury would only flash in me—when, once a week or every ten days, we had sex. The sense of violation I experienced as I approached these transactions—the certainty that, having been denied every form of recognition and respect, I was now to have my body used, my genitals touched and my orifices probed—frightened and disgusted me. It made me sick and furious that I had to drag out every pleasant memory and fantasy, had to search and search the tissue of my sexual hagiography until it became threadbare for every touchstone of pleasure that still bore enough novelty or power to arouse; and it embittered me beyond measure when these methods failed, and I was impotent and had to "talk about it." Most times I could tolerate the relationship, however odd that may seem; I could force myself to see my wife's good sides, and though the incessant tympani of resentment and self-loathing permeated every aspect of our life, I endured the connection. Except when we had sex: when she reached through the curtain of her beastly cruelty and touched me. Then, truly, I hated her.

A year went by, then another; I spent nearly $80,000 supporting us, a grubstake I'd expected to carry me through three or four screenplays as I reestablished my life in New York. My discipline wilted like a newspaper left too long on a stoop; I reported to my desk, but mostly just watched the fat squirrel outside my window eat avocados all day. I was, finally, trapped: too paralyzed with regret and grief to write, to think, to contemplate the possibility that there might be a better day.

Thus it was that I found myself, after four years, at the point at which this confession begins: caressing the pulp of my inner wrist with the point of a blade.

Yes, I was dead; and in my state of self-mourning, I came around at last to blaming everything on the playing of a character. If only I had been strong enough to be myself, I might have perceived the true nature of the problem before it was too late. But the equation of the creation of the character of myself with the evasion of living behind a wall of drink was a significant mistake. I had indeed been dishonest about my alcoholism. But in condemning my character for its dishonesty as well, I was forgetting that, to create, one must make things up, that one's first, most important work of fiction is oneself. I blamed my alcoholic denial for everything except that for which it deserved the blame: it deprived me of the maturity required to understand that one's initial character cannot be a fixed thing, it must evolve in response to experience, die to be reborn. I blamed myself for my "bad character," failing to see that the phrase had a double meaning. I was dead, in the sense that my character had gone bad. But the story was far from over. For all my self-analysis and self-flagellation, the endless raking and re-raking of my motives, my mistakes, I had yet to make the essential discovery: that I would not have allowed my life to be demolished if I had not wanted it to be.

I did not cut my wrists. Instead, toward the end of that fourth year, when I had become so paralyzed by depression that, many days, I could not get out of bed, I took the first of my healing steps: I began drinking again, secretly. Every evening, at the end of the "work day," as the sun set and the sky turned that mixture of cobalt and gold that is so indelibly LA, I would get in the car, drive six blocks to a liquor store on Third Street, and buy a miniature bottle of Jack Daniel's, of the size served on airplanes. I would drink it in two or three eye-watering gulps as I drove home, listening to National Public Radio and watching for the police; then, with my last spark of insouciance, toss the bottle out the window onto one of the darkening suburban streets. The entire transaction took no more than ten minutes, my wife was never the wiser and, even though I'd grow sleepy and forgetful from the suddenness of the jolt, to tell the truth, I didn't care. Finally, I had some peace. Without it, this tiny bit of release, I would not have been able to begin again.

Not that I understood what I was doing. All I knew was that I was getting a little rest and doing my wife a little dirt. As for the indignity of it—of being a middle-aged, unemployed hack, tossing airline bottles of bourbon out the window of a used car: no big deal.

Besides, if she, my wife, got wise, she might leave me. And then where would I be?

TWO

Within half a year, I had been consumed by a $5000-a-month addiction to prostitutes and cocaine.

If this seems like a poor definition of "beginning again," consider that I was, however imperfectly, taking care of myself. At the point at which I returned to drink, I did believe that I was, on some profound level, dead; I'd taken to creative visualization, to seeing, upon the white desk, my head, lapped by a red pond fed by the wellspring of my wrists. Had the ice of my misery not cracked, that vision would have prefigured my final peace.

My longing for death's release was, I now see, the passive man's desire to be rid of the nag of freedom. But the urge to be a free man—to live—dies hard. The impulse was operating within the catacombs of my consciousness with the heroism of a partisan, and though I harried it to the limits of its ingenuity, it found the light. The key onto which the agent of my resurrection locked was permission. Each step gave its blessing to the next until, finally, things did change for me. Step one—and whether it was dumb luck, or the first shot fired by the partisan, I cannot say—was drink.

As noted, I consumed very little, no more than a single mini-whiskey a day. But it did not take long to reactivate in me the drunk's signature mental condition, that of pornographic seediness. This is not because we feel we deserve nothing better. Rather, we are addicted to the goosing of our primitive brain, and degraded sexual fantasizing effects this almost as well as liquor.

In New York, my booze smuttiness had found a home in the Times Square peep shows, in the pre-video era when they still reeked (among other things) of good American furtiveness. There were, however, no peeps in LA that I could, or cared to, uncover. What I found instead, on nearly every corner, were newspaper machines, which for a quarter dispensed editions of "L.A.X…Press," a weekly publication featuring "Photo Ads" for "Models – Massage – Escorts – Dancers – T.S." and, mysteriously, "Horoscope – Jobs." Though I lacked the mind to think it through, I was lonely: I needed the tenderness of sympathetic female contact. And so I turned, in my seediness, to the ads—the hundreds to be found in each issue—and began to craft detailed fantasies out of their brief but vivid come-ons. It was only a matter of days before I picked up the phone.

In search of a kind word, and assuming that "Escorts"—prostitutes—would be less talkative, I began with the page labeled "Massage." Stepping across the threshold, leaving my barren existence behind, I found a tantalizing world of seductive femininity, perched on my shoulder, purring in my ear. It was not long before I developed a miniature craving for these calls, for the nuanced blend of tact and avidity needed to tease out a nugget of truth.

"Hel-*lo*," the girl would answer typically, in a voice that seemed to put quotes around the word. "Who's this?"

"Mike." (Not my real name.)

"Hi, Mike."

"Hel-*lo*."

There would be a nanosecond's pause, in which the girl decided whether she was being kidded, playfully, or mocked. If one hit the note correctly, the conversation warmed up: you had demonstrated, with your smooth savoir-faire, that you were not a nervous cretin.

"Where do you live, hon?"

"The Beverly-Fairfax district."

"Oh."

I heard that vague syllable often enough to improve my neighborhood to West Hollywood—realizing that, if one resided in the low-rent flatlands east of Canter's Delicatessen, one would be lying when one answered the next question, which was:

"And are you an upscale gentleman?"

This one, I confess, always deflated me. Though I could appreciate the desire of the businesswoman to determine how much the customer might be good for, "upscale" seemed such a dispiriting word, so product-and-lifestyle oriented.

Still, there was only one answer if one hoped to continue. "Uh-huh," I'd reply, with a slightly knowing emphasis on the second syllable. As in: You don't know *how* upscale, *hon*.

Then I would use the usual innocuous questions to nudge us toward the personal. "Are you in a private apartment?" I would ask—neutrally, so as not to suggest that I'd be showing up with a hatchet in hand. This would not appear to be an intimate line of inquiry. Yet I was probing for something human and—as was frequently the case in "real life"—asking a girl about her space often resulted in expressions of pride.

"Oh, you'll like it, all the guys do. There's white shag carpet, and it's nice and quiet because there's central air."

What upscale gentleman could refuse? I would imagine myself visiting one of those motel-style complexes above Hollywood Boulevard, the swirls of its stucco grimed with smog, the contralto trill of the birds animating the lush vegetation; a studio apartment with a cottage-cheese ceiling, maybe a push-button fireplace, plastic sinks.

"So the guys really like it, do they?"

"Yeah. Especially at night."

"Well"—sensing my moment—"I'm sure they're not coming for the carpet."

The girl would laugh. "No, but, you know. People can be particular."

"Have you ever lost a customer because he didn't like the way the place looked?"

"Well…no. But, you know…" And here the girl would hesitate, as if deciding whether or not to let "the enemy" in on a secret. Then, if I'd done my work well: "Some *detail*. A lot of guys have this whole thing going on. They can leave 'cause they don't like your *feet*."

Quickly, jocular: "What's wrong with your feet?"

"*Nuh*-thing!" Now we would both be laughing. "C'mon,

you know what I mean."

"Yes. I do." A pause, in which we silently appreciated each other, for transcending the particulars, for being—even here—real.

"So. You want to come over, give it a try?"

"I'll…"—drawing out the word—"think it over."

And that would be that. I'd get the urge to make a call with my morning coffee, but would mentally harrumph at it, this pathetic hankering that was, self-evidently, beneath me. It wasn't until the evening, when I'd be in my one-drink fog, that I'd reach for the phone and begin. These women, our transits, were real, yet more than real, being launched, then manipulated, by my drives and imagination; even in my depleted state, I understood the double gift I was receiving, the two things upon which I thrived, and had been too long deprived of: the joy of life, and the pleasure of creation. I would come downstairs to my waiting wife then with even a little gratitude: for the world of the normal, her smiling face and good cheer.

It wasn't until I got into coke that I made and kept a date.

What can I say—what is there *left* to say—about cocaine? As with my observations regarding Los Angeles, all I have to add is the personal. If there is anything unique to my experience, it is perhaps the complete lack of precedent with which the mania for the drug consumed me. For the truth is that I had only a passing acquaintance with coke: I hadn't done any, or even given it much thought, for almost ten years.

Like others of my generation, in a certain place and time—New York, the nineteen-eighties—I had partaken of what were then still regarded as the drug's harmless satisfactions. My experiences were entirely joyful. Think of a December night: when the crisp, clear air rings each streetlight with an aureole, the vodka pours thick and frigid and arrives in a crystal glass, when a woman's smile is bright, her laugh musical, and every scrape and snap has a satisfying bite: cocaine at its best is all that, a great winter's eve in a small cylindrical bottle, and no honest individual who has ever spent (a short) time on (a moderate amount of) cocaine (when he or she is still new to it) could deny its charms.

Then the flip side of paradise kicked in, coke's glamour crashed meanly to earth, and the drug and I went our separate ways. Until suddenly, in the course of my daily internal debates about how far to push my masseuse obsession, like a disease that has been in remission, and then, in the manner of a horror-movie incubus, RETURNS!, the urge for cocaine rose up in me with a terrible ferocity. I had no clue as to why; I only knew that I wanted it. Within a month, I was completely, helplessly hooked.

When the urge hit, I assumed—surveying my friends, all of whom had cultivated an impenetrable amnesia regarding the excesses of youth—that scoring would be difficult. Cocaine, however, turned out to be the Sheridan Whiteside of narcotics, the Drug That Came to Sit at the IKEA Glass-Topped Table and never went away. I mentioned my interest to an acquaintance, a personal-injury attorney with whom I had a weekly boxing-class-and-Chinese-food date, and he assured me that it would be "no problem, bro." We departed Genghis Cohen's (our restaurant of choice), returned to his West Hollywood pad and, after wrestling with his conscience ("I'm not startin' nothin' hinky, am I?"), he made a call.

In the ensuing hour, as his dealer took her sweet time to arrive, I wondered if the motivation underlying my desire would reveal itself. I received my answer within the four minutes it took my first two, collar-stay-sized lines to hit. My craving, I discovered, as an excruciating pleasure flooded through me, was for a substance that utterly erased the part of my brain that cared what others thought of me. This was entirely different from what I'd experienced previously, a pleasure beyond pleasure: two lines of coke killed the conundrum of my character—of my *life*—with the simple, brute finality of a mousetrap.

Dumping nearly a gram onto my slightly shocked buddy's coffee table, I cut it into six fat furrows, and began packing my head with the stuff, as though my skull were an ice cream container to be filled with frosty, palate-aching vanilla. I did not want this incomparable feeling to go away—and it did, I discovered, within minutes of my initial rush. Here was something I'd not previously experienced: the "crash," a nerve-jangling nose dive that plunged me into depression. The solution, of course, was to do more, and *more*, in slow, slurp-sounding snorts, until I'd packed my ice-cream carton cranium with enough to transform me into a silent, bug-eyed maniac—twitching like a stretched-out Slinky that had been plugged into a socket—but at last, and indisputably, at peace.

No, this was not the coke I remembered. But I had been a different person the first time, sailing through my days on a bottomless reserve of hope. What I did not realize, sitting down to cocaine again, was that depression had altered my brain chemistry. The drug, entering my head, encountered a changed environment: its job now was not to underscore the fun, but to reverse devastation.

What I find remarkable is that some part of me knew cocaine would do this; there remained, in my memory, enough of the drug's essence to whistle its way through my mental vacuum tubes and whisper in the ear of my spirit. It felt like the return of a beast, and I suppose, in a way, it was: not a horror-movie monster, but my impulse toward freedom—the partisan at his most ingenious.

Make no mistake: I was about to fall much lower than I'd imagined possible. Sometimes I find myself in mourning, for lost brain cells, certain delicacies of feeling, most of all for time, squandered and irretrievable. But it is pointless to judge experience. That first night, the drug unlocked the most difficult door in my psyche and gave me a glimpse of Nirvana. There would be questions and hesitations, reconsiderations but no regret. The Nirvana I saw was myself, and I was determined to reach it.

I began doing coke on a regular basis. Twice a month,

but in quantity: three and a half grams—an eighth of an ounce—per session (largely unstepped-on, and entirely unshared: I'd buy the boxing ambulance-chaser his own eightball, and keep our piles strictly separate). My routine never varied: I would sit in my buddy's living room, and an upscale place it was, with its beamed cathedral ceiling and mirrored wet bar, completely motionless, utterly silent, listening to vintage Giorgio Moroder soundtracks, locked into an electrified state of perfect, impenetrable uncaring.

Uncaring. How can I describe the pleasure of it? Maybe only by invoking its opposite, the lesson of the battle with my wife: that the desires of others mattered more than what I wanted for myself. Caring had ruled my life, I had *died* of caring. High on cocaine, the walls of this prison vaporized completely. So impervious was I to obligation and guilt, those nightmare constrictors that had broadcast their weight upon my heart, that *I didn't even notice they were gone.* I was free, free to focus on what *I* wanted, which proved to be—and in this I was abetted by my buddy's porno collection—pussy.

In particular, hooker pussy. This desire was ten times more potent than my yen for coke, and every bit as inexplicable. I'd never had sex with a prostitute and did not see the urge as the outgrowth of my obsessive phone-calling. Yes, I had battled the impulse to get a "massage," but this was different, this was, to quote *The Wizard of Oz*, a horse of a different color. Two lines of coke, a few bars of "Theme from *Midnight Express*," and the words would begin to pound in my mind with the violence of a pile driver: *hooker pussy hooker pussy hooker pussy.* I understood that drugs can clamp the mind in a bear trap of obsession, I knew about how coke was supposed to be a sex drug, but this was beyond sex, it was beyond even obsession. It was *monstrous.* BOOM BOOM! HOOKER PUSSY! BOOM! Why, I wondered, had all these things been stirred together? I started to try to figure it out…and then I had a novel thought. I would not *figure* it out. I would *find* out. By *doing.*

The reality of "doing," however, threw me off my game. Making the short, critical transit from the "Massage" to the

"Escorts" page, the factuality of what I found there alienated me. This was what I'd sought to avoid with my telephone muses, whose invisibility had enabled my imagination. Now, confronting photos by the score, seemingly identical in their smeary inscrutability, I faltered. Drugs had pushed me past my first success to this more urgent shore. But it was not yet apparent what I was looking for.

There loomed also the more difficult question of my wife. There are men and women for whom sex with third parties, secret or otherwise, does not open up any more of a gulf within the primary relationship than would a particularly good lunch date with the proper stranger. As the moment of my first betrayal approached, however, I understood that I was not one of these gifted individuals. Going forward demanded an accommodation with my nature. It was the initial phase of my cocaine use that enabled me to make it.

At its center lay the fact that, despite my habit's conspicuousness, I was able to conceal it. The particulars of this deception—the emotions it released—revealed aspects of myself, my wife, and our relationship that sprang the lock protecting me from the labyrinth of greater betrayals. I am not saying that, as my wife was too dense to notice what was happening, she "deserved" it. What I discovered, rather, is that living inside a dishonesty leads one to examine its construction, to ponder the means by which a dishonesty is lived. The longer I did this, the further it drew me from my inclination toward fidelity.

My discoveries were many. None was more surprising than the first: betraying my wife with drugs, I faced the extent to which guilt and anger infused, not only the bad, but even my *positive* feelings for her. On those days when the urge for coke became irresistible, I would become, with my wife, uncharacteristically affectionate. Guilt over my imminent misbehavior would form a caduceus with my anger at her for making the misbehavior necessary; and since I felt unready to wrestle either of these snakes, I would hide from them by sentimentalizing my wife, reassuring myself with excesses of improvident emotionalism.

These warm fuzzies would float away in the aftermath, when, after I'd run out and crawled home, my coke-fueled contemplations would dissolve into the miseries of withdrawal. Then I would use the obverse of this sentimentality to try and shame myself into quitting. *The poor, sweet, decent woman*, I would moan inwardly, *if you don't care about yourself, at least think of how you're humiliating her.* It had been thus, of course, in the pre-Los Angeles days of my drinking. The difference was that, now, my wife remained entirely unaware of what I was doing. I was not greeted by anger, tears, ultimata when I returned from a late-night rout; yet I experienced the identical complex of remorse and self-disgust that had oppressed me previously. During the years in LA, I had come to believe that I'd mistaken tumult for love, that little of our relationship came down to affection or regard, but it was worse than that: the violence of my feelings did not even depend upon her participation. It was impossible for this knowledge not to lead me away from her.

The subterfuges required by my addiction taught other lessons. To mislead my wife, I hit upon a means of deception as unconscionable as it was foolproof: I exploited the part of the marriage that still endured as true feeling. My willingness to do so shamed me. It also showed me—the writer who had been doing his own work his own way for twenty years—how much more ruthless I needed to be if I expected to accomplish anything.

To cover my tracks, I fell back on a pre-existing condition: periodic sinus headaches, upon occasion so severe that I would be temporarily incapacitated. In the past, these had elicited concern and sympathy from my wife, and we would engage in one of the small, satisfying waltzes that collectively comprise the choreography of happy marital relations.

"How's my sweetie?" she would ask as I lay in bed.

"Oy," I would reply (thankful for the Yiddish monosyllable, often all I could manage).

"My poor sweetie. Maybe a few head kisses would soothe the brains."

And she, my wife, would lovingly, indeed soothingly, kiss and caress my skull until her tenderness set off some sort of endorphin-laced response, and my agony would recede.

This routine stood as a touchstone of our affection. Yet when I began to indulge seriously—to return home from my buddy's pad in a condition that required, make no mistake, *an explanation*—I trashed it without hesitation. After easing the car into our garage, I would gather the spilled peas of my brain functions for two efforts: the first, to compose a smile; the other, to gasp out the sentence, "Can you soothe the brains?" Immediately my wife's suspicions would ease, and she'd embrace the pleasure of having her affections returned without irony, cruelty, or any other gambit I might use to hold her at arm's length.

I got away with it; I fooled her. Still, even through the anesthesia, I felt twinges of remorse, twinges that evolved into throbs as my addiction worsened and I began to get high at home. Yes: despite my best efforts, I was not always able to root my way through an eightball before the hour grew dangerously late, and no amount of lying would get me off the hook. Thus I had, on those inconvenient nights, to run on parallel tracks: to get up every quarter-hour from my sweat-soaked side of the bed and sneak into the bathroom for a toot.

Fortunately, I had a second infirmity to exploit, a weak stomach—an excuse made more plausible by the fact that, so far as my wife knew, I had been overdoing it in a Chinese restaurant. And so I learned to say a second sentence: "Your sweetie's guts are killing him."

This would elicit a sad-clown-faced display similar to the one inspired by my headaches, with the addition of gently administered suggestions for moderation.

"Sweetie," my wife would say, "maybe you shouldn't next time have the sweet-and-sour pork *and* the fried fillet of yak Peking-style." Then she would smite herself: "Oh, Christ, haven't you learned *anything* in Al-Anon? Mind your *bus*-iness, shut *u*-up…"

My wife's assumption of blame for this minor act of codependency further served me, by opening the way for—incredibly—expressions of *forgiveness* on my part.

"S'okay," I would gasp, taking her hand limply, "I unnersta'."

"My sweetie."

"Oy."

And as I would feel her lips caress my amphetamine-constricted guts, through the thickly paved road of my uncaring, blades of pain would sprout. I was deceiving my wife intimately, as only I could, and even stoned, this struck me as the essence of junkie behavior: the use of human things to destroy human things, in the service of a drug.

Yet in the middle of all this lay something new, a thing hard, lucid and cold. In retrospect, I recognize it as Graham Greene's famous sliver of ice in the heart, the writer's ability, amidst the worst sort of chaos, to stand back and observe. What I saw was that the drug was teaching me to do something at which my wife had already proven her mastery: to live with the reality that, in the service of one's desires, others get hurt. I was learning to balance how I felt about betraying someone against what I received in return; to negotiate, day by day, with a troubled conscience.

Neither did I beat myself up exclusively. My wife, it was plain, owned a felt need to let sleeping dogs lie, lest they bark her out of LA; I was not such a genius of deception that anyone wishing to see the truth could not have done so. Ironically, what I perceived as my wife's looking the other way wounded me more than her manipulations. I found it hard not to wonder: How intimate could we *ever* have been? What did our connection really mean to her? Not much, I decided bitterly. Perhaps it might all turn around. But for the moment, my bitterness made it easier to go, as did she, my own way.

In my third month on drugs, that way led me, for the first time, to whores.

I had been looking for a sign and, poring over my bible

one evening, the pilot fish of my unconscious found it on the "Escorts" page. The ad featured a snapshot of a girl, in a perfect side view, with long legs and narrow hips, on a rumpled bed, in a string bikini; on her elbows and knees, her feet in high heels upraised, ankles crossed, soft belly encircled by a thin gold chain; her coarse-seeming blond hair cascading over her face (for anonymity's sake) as she looked down at her forward-pointing, steepled fingers. Beneath this photo, so neutral as to strip its object not merely of identity but of sexuality, were the words: "Carleen & Friends. $200/hr. Sunset/LaBrea. Anytime." Certainly there were prettier, sexier women on the page. But something about the flatness of the presentation, and the matter-of-fact recitation of the salients, intrigued me—indeed, it seemed a goad. It was as though the ad were saying, "You're not doing what you're doing, and you don't even know *that*, because you don't *know* what you're doing—and we promise not to tell you." It was a communication aimed, to borrow a phrase from Ralph Ellison, at the lower frequencies, and those things operating beyond my conscious knowledge clamped onto its implications with the precision of a heat-seeking missile. I called, I got the information from a voice of similar neutrality—not informed neutrality, it was more the tone of someone hard-used but guileless and wanting only to get the facts straight—a voice perfect in the tact of its appeal to me. I called my coke connection immediately, and took off.

Riding my instincts, I did two things that first time I'd never done before. First, I told my wife, as I came hurriedly down the stairs, that I had decided to take a long ride up the coast and might not be back until morning. When she looked at me, eyes burrowing into my soul, I explained that I felt a headache coming on and thought a drive beside the ocean might fend it off; if my gambit failed and I got sick anyway, I could pull into a beachside parking lot and snooze in the car. Whatever my wife thought, there was something about the improvisatory nature of my decision—and it was an improvisation, I thought of it as I descended the stairs—

that reassured her. She pressed a bottle of Tylenol into my hand, kissed me with reassuring concern, and sent me on my way.

My second smart choice was to stop at a pay phone, call my buddy, and double my personal order to a quarter of an ounce. Eight grams of coke is a lot for an individual to consume in a night. But my instinct was that, once I arrived at my final destination, I would not be indulging alone.

With these two decisions, everything I needed for the next stage of my life was in place. Over the ensuing months, I would pursue many such nights; collectively, they comprised the blueprint for my resurrection. As they were so similar—and their lessons so specific—I will not describe one or another but conflate them all. So that you may see how I came to be.

XXXX

I learned to savor the going as much as the arriving. At the start of each evening, as I grinned with crooked world-weariness at my coke-tooting partner in crime, I'd marshall my powers of speech, lay my hands on my thighs, and say, gaspingly, "Better head home."

My buddy'd nod—it would be, roughly, eleven, time for him to swallow a handful of Valium and a tumbler of gin and pray for sleep—and escort me to the door.

"Okay for drivin'? You don't want to get nailed by the LAPD with beaucoup product, bro. In a motor vehicle."

"I'm cool."

"Goin' straight home?"

I'd smile, to indicate that this was a foolish question.

"Okay. See ya."

Bye-bye…But in my mind, I would already be on my way. Fully armored with my five remaining grams, pockets bulging with ATM cash, my pleasure was exquisite, keen. Straight home? Please. Shame, guilt, remorse, had been excised completely, I was going to have sex with prostitutes and nothing could stop me. I had slipped now into a monomaniacal mental groove, wreathed in the gratification of being comfortable with desire. I was about to become myself, and, in my becoming, not merely unrepentant, but free.

Essential to the act of becoming, I learned, was the drive. If the coke represented the overture, then the drive was my first movement, a blues allegretto that enabled me to work my way through strata of mood to the condition from which I might do business. Sunset Boulevard was integral to this: its transformations along my route—an arc that began with hope and crashed into desperation—mirrored my own Los Angeles experience, they reconnected me to that which had brought me to the moment. I liked that, it felt right to me—so much so that it was the repetition of this fifteen-minute transit from my buddy's place to the whorehouse, the burning into my brain of a skein of recognitions, that taught me to appreciate my adopted city: to give real due to the dream in which we all oscillated unendingly between longing and dread.

I would, on these nights, ascend to Sunset via La Cienega, a steep grade, with a long light, that left me hanging below the boulevard's lip for long, nervous minutes. Then the signal would change, I'd take a hard, swiveling right and, beneath a rain of billboards, head eastbound on the part of Sunset known as the Strip. *Sunset Strip*: Not even coke can fix a mood more indelibly than a cruise down its velvet macadam—indeed, what earthling can think those words without feeling a frisson of iconic cool? Yes, the Strip was cool, all right, but more than that, it was fast, a paean to the stylish motoristic hum of the American Mechanical. It imparted a suave dynamism, the way it banked and curved like a racecourse, until you were no longer yourself but Steve McQueen, the cab of your Cobra combed by passing headlights with the steady deliberation of prison searchbeams.

Over the years, I had visited most of the places I passed, and my mind as I drove would go in and out of them, long shot to close up and back again, the memories weaving themselves into a textured thicket that flooded me with the pleasures of the past. This was appropriate as, more than New York, which looked and felt old and rotten but was entirely of the moment, Los Angeles was at its best when you felt its history, when a real-time experience was burnished by a sense of legend.

I gave myself up to this pleasure within an instant of hitting the Strip. First I pondered the corrugated-tin bulk of the House of Blues, a Tara-sized chicken shack, blisteringly hip, occupying real estate that had once, I knew, belonged to the Garden of Allah, favored hotel of the Algonquin Round Table set, and the scene of much tweedy debauchery in the Roaring Twenties. Looming up past it, as I nudged the accelerator and one-handed my Nissan-turned-Cobra into a snug curve, was the Argyle, a sleek Art Deco high-rise, now a Brit-friendly hotel, once, once upon a time, the Sunset Towers, swank apartment digs where Bugsy Siegel had been busted, over the objections of his pal George Raft, for making illegal bets.

My mind ping-ponged across the Strip to Thunder Road, a motorcycle shop owned by a cartel of actors, the name which bestowed its hot-rod wallop plucked from a Bob Mitchum movie, the one about moonshine runners made in the late of the great fifties, decade of dispiritment the off-cuts of which still rule the globe's pop culture. And here comes Carney's, next up to the left of my whining tires, a burger joint in a Union Pacific dining car, and how I loved this funsome relic of the drive-in age, last big when psychedelics were the rage, selling "probably the best hamburgers & hotdogs chicken & tacos...in the world!" And then, *boom*, abeam the Marlboro Man billboard, the cowboy beefeater guarding the Strip's eastern portal: the Chateau Marmont, legend of legends, where everything had happened—Nick Ray had popped Natalie Wood's cherry in one bungalow, John Belushi had choked his life out in another—and where everything happened still, in the form of book parties, product launches, food tastings, fashion shoots, and myriad other unmissable eventoids involving the making and spending of cash.

Among these glittering jewels, side stones winked, the interestingly crappy little "theme" buildings, Hawaiian this, Chinese that, Tyrolean the other, all of them morphing ceaselessly from production office to nail parlor to Polynesian Poo-Poo Palace, any one of which could have been 77—the best, the only address to have on Sunset Strip. That, *enfin*, was always the time and temperature on that stretch of blacktop for me. I was always drag-racing, in my mind, cream-colored ragtops, gleaming pompadours bobbing within their vinyl cabins, the boys wolf-whistling chicks with fishnet stockings and go-go boots and chalky lipstick that made them look like they'd been drinking Milk of Magnesia, giggling away as they clustered on the sidewalk and palpated with utmost caution the hairdos that were glued to their heads.

That fifties-into-sixties thing supplied the iconography that burnished the Strip for me. But as I hurtled along the banked track toward my nefarious destination, the adrenaline of my euphoria would kick up my coke high into beatitude, and I'd welcome one and all—not just Kookie Burns, but every ghost I imagined on the Strip: Gable, in a tux, pulling Carole Lombard from Ciro's to the Mocambo in 1935, brushing past Roger McGuinn and David Crosby as they hustled to a gig at the Whiskey (as always, eight miles high) in 1967, the both of them ignoring young Jack Nicholson, recently arrived from Neptune, New Jersey, goggle-eyed, dreaming his dreams, circa 1959. I even spotted, one night, old William S. Hart in 1943, climbing up from his rancho beside the Garden of Allah; I watched as he stood between Mabel Normand and James Dean, and considered what had become of the paradise he'd helped to make. I welcomed them all. In the first upward flume of the drive's arc, I had the perfect LA experience: I felt, for the 180 seconds it took to run the Strip, what every nobody in Tinseltown longs to feel, and so seldom does: like I belonged.

These feelings would then vanish, within two blocks of passing the Chateau, at Crescent Heights Boulevard, where

I confronted the Sunset Plaza Mall. Considering its two-story arched windows and portholes set into a curved exterior wall, its colonnade through which one passed to reach a circular piazza, it was hard to imagine what had been meant—until, watching the cars roar up Crescent Heights and screech, practically on two wheels, around the curve that flowed into the eastbound lanes of Sunset, as though they were chariots in a demolition-derby version of *Ben-Hur*, one took a few connective steps (architecture, chariots, Rome) and realized that one was in fact gazing at a crackerbox rethink of the Coliseum, a contemporary arena in which we Christian slaves of culture might be thrown to the lions of commerce.

This was entirely appropriate: leaving behind the Strip, one abandoned all hopes regarding one's private legend, and faced up to how much life here was about greed and exploitation. This would become increasingly irrefutable the longer I sat at the stoplight, as I'd recall that the mall sat upon the bones of the final location of Schwab's Drugstore. Schwab's had been one of the great Hollywood destinations, and I'd often stopped by in the seventies to grab a bacon-and-egg on a roll and soak up the vibes. There was a lunch counter, and a cigar case, and patrons would linger over coffee and smokes in a spirit of camaraderie that still owned a whiff of what Hollywood must have been like when it was an easy-going company town full of world-famous, surprisingly folksy wage slaves. I had, in a small way, experienced this the night I hurried in to make a call, and turned to discover, on the next pay phone, Taryn Power, daughter of Tyrone, then beginning her own film career, and so heart-stoppingly beautiful that my head snapped back in astonishment—which elicited, from her, a becoming blush and the sweetest, most unaffected smile.

That was Then, I'd reflect, as the light would change and I'd proceed—carefully, for now I was, not Steve McQueen, but an exceptionally stoned motorist at an extremely treacherous intersection. In the Now, my memory-induced sorrow reminded me that my sense of belonging was illusory—a trap, set by powerful interests to draw me in and exploit my resources. I would feel, as I rolled past the Laugh Factory and the Gaucho Grill, that we had no control at all, we multitudes, we were victims—whereas once there had been Taryn Power, shyly acknowledging one's awe, now, signing soundtrack CDs in the mall's Virgin Megastore, there was this or that leather-suited superstar, eyes invisible behind shades, unsmiling, bored. This sickening recognition—that one's dreams and tender feelings would *never* be more than fodder for the town's rapacious hierarchies—always increased as I passed, on my right, the Directors Guild building, a cluster of mirrored volumes I dubbed the Reichstag: here, the architecture seemed to state, resides a power you will neither possess nor comprehend. I would roll to a stop at Fairfax Avenue, realizing that I had passed the apogee of my arc, I had peaked. Now would commence the next phase of the Hollywood hopeful: the spiral down.

The intersection of Sunset and Fairfax was the perfect place to begin it. Once, the area had been desirable: a block to my left, on Selma, a married silent film director had built a mansion for his mistress; to the east, in the foothills above Hollywood Boulevard, stood a house recognizable to TV-watchers (of a certain age) as Ozzie and Harriet Nelson's. The homes on the blocks to the immediate north and south could be nearly as nice—not mansions but substantial—and young film folk stepping up in the world often settled here. Yet this also signified the start of Seamy Hollywood, and of a commercial district that could smack, after hours, of the unsavory. Here began the blowjob blocks, and one never knew, returning from a parent-teacher conference, if one would discover, beside one's shrink-wrapped LA Times, a used condom on the front lawn.

This worked for me: I too was transitioning, from the safe and the known, into my personal parallel reality, that of addiction, the vice that coexists with the mundane; and since coke led me to perceptions, locked me into them and laced them with significance, this unity of inner and outer landscape thrilled me, I traversed these blocks feeling a bombardment of understanding that was almost sexual in its sublimity.

I would proceed with caution, maintaining a steady speed, until I reached Genessee, where there resided a diner called The All-American Burger. This establishment emitted the embryonic whiff of what would come to be, a mile or so to the east, total desperation. I was approaching a stretch of Sunset that evinced, not the suavity of the Strip, but the staleness of a long-sealed storage closet crammed with the detritus of Hollywood failure, businesses that had lingered though the parade had indisputably passed by. All-American Burger heralded this condition, and I would try to stop momentarily to savor the subtleties of its message. In accordance with its name, All-American Burger was red, white and blue, and announced itself with a grimy plastic sign that reeked of patriotic cheer, a sentiment, one suspected, that had been grievously mistimed. The diner, I guessed, had opened in the sixties, just as being All-American was on the wane; I could imagine Nixon supporters sitting in the windowside booths, watching as the easy-riding freak brigade flowed past in VW buses. It had lasted, All-American Burger, barely—I seldom saw a customer—but its originator had bet on the wrong horse, reality had mocked him, a truth apparent in the irony of the neon sign out front, red letters that promised, in this low-grade sexual combat zone, DAILY FRESH MEAT.

Once again, I understood: I, too, had made mistakes, seemingly innocuous choices that were in fact ruinous misreadings of reality. Accelerating, I braced for the consequences, implicit in the transit's next phase. I continued to the intersection of Sunset and Stanley, where there began the part of the boulevard to which I referred, in my overheated brain, as the Dead Zone.

Here, in a quarter-mile-long no-man's land, one knew the tension of feeling truly exposed. The little structures with poky charms abruptly gave way to a string of squat, enormous monoliths with almost entirely blank façades. On the north side of Sunset they followed one upon another: the twin Butterfield & Butterfield auction houses, resembling a pair of gigantic sugar cubes; an Indian and a British restaurant, just as white, just as blank; the Guitar Center, daddy of them all, a block-sized volume against which the streetwalkers stood out as indelibly as bloodstains on a sheet. The Dead Zone, I would feel as I drove it, was about buildings that turned a blind eye on what transpired beneath their noses—declining to judge, but offering no succor. You got the message as you passed (and how it summoned up my own life then, when not even friends would return my calls): *You're on your own.*

That was the north side of Sunset. Across the street, one found the situations in which the monoliths declined to get involved: little businesses, most of them either provisional, like the emporia selling perfume and clothes, their wares touted by signs in Cyrillic, or dodgy, head shops and tattoo parlors, operations that seemed like fronts for all the desperadoes trolling the concrete in front of them. Contemplating the silhouettes of these hard people, the pimps and the whores, bodies backlit by fizzing neon or the sallow flourescents of shop windows, I thought of the line from *Heartbreak House*: "Money is not made in the light."

But it was risky to get too lost in contemplation, as all the illicit action ensured the presence of the police. I would monitor my speed, stop at yellow lights, try not to seem like I was checking out the whores—try not to become hysterical at finding myself suddenly, irretrievably off-base. It was with relief that one finally struggled to shore, passing the Tuxedo Center (Established 1952), remnant of an era when black tie was de rigueur, which reasserted slightly that legendary quality, and enabled one to catch one's breath.

Except that—as I had never quite returned to normality after that rain-soaked morning with my wife—you never really recovered; in a way that could only be quantified via a cataloguing of small details, abandonment and anxiety had changed you. At Poinsettia, I passed a temple-like Ralph's supermarket that seemed to announce the return of the everyday as though it were the Second Coming. But this was excessive protestation. The daily grind did reassert itself, but the company had become dotty, the respectability frayed. Here the citizens existed in the real world but did not entirely inhabit it. Of course, in LA, no one did, but there was a difference—a hair's-breadth but critical—between living in a present touched by fantasy, and doing the opposite. Here, east of the Dead Zone, past the Temple of Ralph, one observed the latter—a normality of delusion, disillusion, and degradation.

In the motel-style apartment structures above and below Sunset, forgotten people entertained fantasies of making it in a place, indeed a time, that had long since ceased to exist. Mostly they were older, men and women who'd come west in the CinemaScope era, in the hope of being signed as contract players. I would spot them as I drove, they were night owls, the gals especially: in soiled clam-diggers, angora sweaters layered against a nonexistent chill, badly applied lipstick as red as a gash as they wobbled, in their mules, through intermittent amoebae of streetlight.

But they were not all old, these people. Passing, on my right, a copy shop, I would recall the time I'd rushed in to xerox a script, and noticed a small plastic sign, suspended far above street level: beside the painted silhouette of a ballerina, the words BALLET DANCE ART and, beside them, the name J. Erglis Smaltzoff. I'd sighed with pleasure at discovering this fossil (for surely the studio was long gone), my mind resurrecting a room full of would-be Audrey Hepburns (a few aspiring Troy Donahues among them), bending sideways from a barre, one-*two*, one-*two*, as an old babushka with a Bull Durham in her mouth banged out Chopin on a piano and Smaltzoff, stiff and unsmiling but handsome as Charles Boyer, kept time with a baton. I was halfway to my car, my errand finished, when—as though I'd imagined too feverishly—I caught the harmonics of a piano. Following a driveway to a structure in the rear, I peeked through the diamond-shaped window panes of a parlor, and there it all was: the rattling baby grand, a Balanchine manqué with a soaring pompadour, a dozen maniacally grinning, desperately clumsy "gypsies," drenched in sweat and hope for the resurrection of musical comedy—all of it as quaint, as removed from the reality of fin de siecle Hollywood (or even the reality of ballet dance art) as the man in the moon.

Yes, I understood everyday madness, and the long-term toxicity of casual illusion. Now, as well, I was coming to understand criminality, which had also been normalized on these downmarket blocks. A few streets to the north, I knew, lived many of the masseuses I once had called; in their apartments, the off side of the Hollywood Dream also persisted, as bent as it was at Smaltzoff's, but toward what Louis Calhern, in *The Asphalt Jungle*, called "a left-handed form of human endeavor." Here the dark doings of the Dead Zone became less exposed but more routine, they were baked into the crust of the neighborhood; here one saw the minor-key players who made their livings off the day-to-day grind of vice.

The presence of all this corruption—specifically the matter-of-factness, the sense of being surrounded by people who had, whether by necessity or choice, crossed a line—would improve my fluctuating mood, and I'd proceed a few hundred yards to the place that nudged it into its final shape: the Seventh Veil, a famous strip club, its façade adorned with Roman columns and statues in blue-tinted niches. Like the landmarks of Sunset Strip, the Seventh Veil was burnished by legend. It had been, in the fifties, a notorious mob-run dump in which various strata of LA society furtively intersected: crooked vice cops, pervert pols who knew better but couldn't help themselves (like Tweety Bird, they were gonna get a whippin', except that, often, that's what they wanted), z-grade actresses on the slide. Considering the place and its lurid history, I would think, always, of simultaneity, of how it felt like the 1950s both here and on the Strip, but not the same fifties: from the House of Blues to the Marmont, it was the era of black-&-white television, A Quinn Martin Production, glossily photographed, neatly groomed; while here, on Sunset and Formosa, amidst the gasoline fumes, the brash horns and hacking coughs of engines, the decade belonged to Mike Hammer, the crude avenger hatched by Mickey Spillane, who punched and sapped his way through novelettes with titles like *Kiss Me Deadly* and *My Gun is Long*. This was the mood I had been seeking, the fifties fatalism that so accurately reflected the man I had become; the mood that enabled me to access and appreciate the only pleasure that was left to me—to experience, at long last, the eros of desperation. Passing Formosa, I would cut the radio and soak up the racket of the boulevard, understanding why I was in this town: the noise, like the ad for the whorehouse itself, was anonymous, yet thickly textured with inchoate need and its consequences, an equation that was the story of my life, and the spine of the history of LA.

And there it was, on Sunset and Detroit, one block west of La Brea, just as advertised. It sat, my whorehouse, in the middle of the short leg of a triangle of urban blight that, to my hyper-cool consciousness, quivered semiotically. To its left, a murdered motor lodge called the Hollywood Hills, the plastic letters on the sign—the sort that can be changed, to WELCOME the SHRINERS or the ELKS—announcing NEW M MT, the whole cinder-block ruin trussed up with rusted balustrades and chain link, the effect like that of a corpse that, as a warning, has been tossed into the street. Across the boulevard, at the triangle's peak, a biggish mini-mall, the Sunset Galleria, its vertical sign advertising the usual inedible commercial smorgasbord, yogurt, copying, bagels, beepers, thematically ideal for my purposes, in that it epitomized the impulse buy—as with the streetwalkers of the Dead Zone, you pulled in, did your business, and moved along. To the whorehouse's right, a building of similar vintage but different in style, the usual inedible architectural salad, Spanish tiles, Greek columns, French details, one half covered by plywood boards that ran from earth to roof and advertised, in faded, hand-painted letters, "China diesel generators – marine diesel engines – submatic drip irrigation systems," the house's other half given over to "psychic reader and adviser," and this too suited me thematically, as one could not have imagined a more incompatible couple under the same roof.

As for the whorehouse itself, it wore, I thought, a gothic air. Just beneath the flat roof, the façade bore a delicate relief of flowers and ampersands; below this linear design ran a row of windows, two on each side of a little balcony that extended out over the front door to form an entry and was supported by a quartet of Greek columns. The design of the balcony railing, and its gracefully turned balusters, repeated on the ground floor, enclosing a poured-concrete verandah that ran the full width of the house, the railing divided neatly in the middle to accommodate the cement path that led from the entrance, across fifteen feet of lawn, to the sidewalk. The past gentility of this rooming house— for that, apparently, was what it had been—seemed evident: it was easy to imagine it having once sheltered respectable midwesterners, in the days before Sunset was a paved road, when folks migrated to Hollywood to pick fruit, start ministries, or beat TB. Now, perhaps a century on, the place was a barely standing ruin. Each of the façade's eight windows was of a different vintage, ranging from the most recent, a solid pane of UV glass, to an apparent original, two sets of spider-webbed six-over-sixes in rotting frames, behind a screen that hung as slackly as a stroke victim's cheek. The concrete verandah, like the path, had been broken and split by weeds, the pillars supporting the little balcony were cracked and splintered, and it would not have required a child's strength, let alone a Samson's, to push them down. To complete the effect, a long fissure ran jagged and irregular from the façade's upper right quadrant to its lower left, as though one were looking at a photograph made from a broken glass negative. The impression of utter dereliction, of the end of the line, was finalized by—of all things—a *billboard*, its twenty-foot-high pylon sunk into the front lawn, advertising a miniature submarine that ran underwater tours from the Queen Mary in Long Beach.

Obviously meant as a take-off on the film *The Hunt for Red October*, the copy line proclaimed, in crimson letters: THE HUNT IS OVER.

And so, for me, it was. The first time I saw the place, I thought, This cannot be occupied, I have made a mistake. Then I saw the dim light leaking through the cracked shades, the new maximum-security gate over the front door, and realized, I am home, I am here, I have come to the right place. For as I parked, and walked the few yards up the sidewalk, I saw that here was a remarkable summing up, an anonymous yet provocatively dreary old dump, its dimly lit doorbell glowing like the light at the end of my tunnel, its cracked, columned entry giving it the air of a haunted house in New Orleans: haunted, in this case, by all the brutal LA men, all the leopard-skin pedal-pusher dames, all the foul memories of bindles, and backhanded, knuckle-heavy slaps, glasses knocked askew and the crunch of stomped dentures, of cheap perfume and hysterical laughter and misused luck and shame—a true and genuine, almost comically exaggerated temple of woe. My vision grew narrow and focused and locked-in every time I walked—slowly, unfurtively—up the wretched path, I even dawdled, even swayed, in my pleasurable apprehension of this true classic of the American psychodramatic landscape, this Baby Jane enacted by Blanche DuBois, this *Dragnet* penned by Edgar Allan Poe.

I pushed the bell, turned—showing myself to the video camera, its red light barely visible through the security gate and the smeary glass of the blistered front door—and waited. And in the moments, the very few moments, between the pushing of the bell and the loud buzzer that rattled the gate, the experience, my night, began in earnest. As I waited those brief seconds for approval from whomever lurked within, one eye on the lookout for a prowl car, my sore, slap-happy heart rose. Those who have been truly addicted to something that is dependably the same—cigarettes will do—will have some idea of the extremes of relief and pleasure that would flow through me. For it was then that I knew that, for the coming hours, while the drugs held out, the cash held out, I would be *away*, in the clockless moral-free twilight of the feeding of my very deepest need; I would be, in a word, *satisfied*. This joy, this relief, would arise in me with such power that it would leave me all but swooning; and the pure physical sensation of it, the warm-bath, world-go-away pleasure of it, was so all-consuming, so *good*, that it would take my breath away.

Then the buzzer would rattle the heavy gate, I'd push through into the urine-and-dry-rot-smelling gloom of the vestibule, the gate would crash shut behind me, and I'd climb, slowly (for the sake of my racketing heart), the steep, narrow staircase with its worn-out treads, my hand resting lightly on the uncertain banister, in the yellow light that made me think of a tapioca that had sat out too long, listening to the rapping of high heels as a girl came to the door above me, the report of the deadbolt as she threw it and hesitated, waiting for my face to appear in the peep hole. If I made that walk half a hundred times in the entire transit of my experience, it might have added up in total to less than a few minutes. But with their promise, their assurance that for the coming night I would have permission to be truly myself, they were the most obscenely happy and blissfully unhampered minutes of my life; and I fear, as all addicts know too well, they always will be.

XXXX

With the opening of the door, that preparatory narrative ended, and I began to write a second story, one that evolved out of the first but went in its own direction. Now other people entered the picture, and to achieve my ends required that I mix it up, and with women whose success depended, as did my wife's, upon controlling me. What I had gained on the drive, I needed: in this challenging next passage, it would be money in the bank.

The best first face to see, in the dim, particled lamplight, belonged to Wendy, a pug-faced girl with dirty-blond bangs. We had, over a string of visits, gotten a good thing going, and whenever she opened the door and half-looked at me, murmuring a neutral "Hey, how yuh *do*-in" in a voice like mud, I could relax, I was home free. I would wait as the bolt was thrown, then follow, intoxicated not by her rag-doll body in its pink-and-black teddy but the rapping of her heels, the leitmotif of organized prostitution, as she led me the seven steps to the waiting room. "Siddown," she'd say, "you want a be'?" and off she'd go to procure a flat Bud, leaving me in an exploded club chair, Chaka Khan thudding on the Kenwood, to face, across a glass-and-brass coffee table, the other available girls.

They would look me over, these practiced hands, arms folded, legs tightly crossed, smiles tinged with a satisfaction unmistakably cruel. This I could not begrudge them: I sprang from the species of which there is one born every minute, and it was only a matter of time, the girls understood, before each took a turn at the trough of my drugs and cash. Typically, I'd find my old friends Bonnie and Lupe (a whorehouse is a nest of things, not the least of them pseudonyms), and after we'd exchanged the obligatory "how is it out theres" and "long time no sees," there would be a silence, a hesitation, as they waited for me to choose.

Almost always, if she was on—and she almost always seemed to be—I would begin with Wendy. Alert to my racing heart, I'd follow her into the darkness of one of the two hallways, then wait a blind moment until a door opened and released, onto the carpet, a parallelogram of light. Entering, I'd perch on the edge of the narrow platform bed as Wendy set my beer on the night table, murmuring "Make yourself comfortable, be right back," before closing the door tightly and rapping off down the hall.

A page from the whoremonger's Baedeker: "Make yourself comfortable," alternate usage, "Make yourself *completely* comfortable," means, "Be naked when I get back, or I'll know you're a cop, and that will be the end of me and thee." It was one of several precautions taken in such places to evade the law (cops are not allowed to strip), which included never discussing price (all negotiations were conducted prior to one's arrival) as this might be construed as solicitation, and never accepting payment until the sex act had been completed (cops are not allowed to screw). I learned them all, and forgot how I learned them, having quickly—like a good criminal—made them part of my second nature.

Thus Wendy hadn't needed the coded order to disrobe. But it was part of the odd rigidity of the situation, the system by which hookers attempt to hold johns in place. Though I assumed, upon my entry into the game, that both parties had their reasons for doing what they did, I had not been prepared for the extent to which prostitution was about sex as a means of control—the titanic struggle for domination, the hypervigilance it demanded, bordered on the hallucinatory. The mechanisms through which the participants achieved their objectives were so convoluted and strained, moreover, that anything other than the most qualified trust was inconceivable. Each proceeded on this wisp of faith—which amounted, really, to the promise not to kill or maim—and tried to work out their crabbed and twisted needs, reacting to every gesture with excruciating attention, lest the slightest thing go wrong, and the exchange deflate.

Not much fun, on the face of it. But I wasn't there to have fun. I had, famously, a problem with being controlled, a problem I had not solved but masked, by learning how to hide but not to fight. Here, in a space barely big enough to stand face to face with one's nemesis, naked, hiding was not an option. Nor was the dynamic entirely adversarial: the underpinnings of one's need for control, one's awareness of the identical foundation in the other, contrived to create, however obliquely, an intimacy that was real. Understanding drew hooker and john close, as close as two boxers married by skill, rage and terror. Achieving a certain kind of pleasure was impossible, perhaps. But I could learn to get my way, and to respect my opponent, as we had given ourselves fully, and taken each other's full measure.

I'd do as instructed, tossing my clothes onto the

collapsing Danish Modern chair, reclining on (to borrow a term from Van Morrison) the TB sheets. I have been told that the essentials of equestrianism have remained un-changed for centuries, that an experienced rider can mount any horse, anywhere in the world, and the animal will respond predictably. Whorehouse décor owns a similarly timeless dependability. On those occasions when I was untrue to my school and went elsewhere, I discovered that more or less money bought only a classier or tackier version of the same old thing.

The style was instructive. The room in which I found myself most nights—the "big room," taking this as proof of my favor—had faux walnut paneling, a moss-green carpet so hard and worn that it shone, and a water-stained acoustical-tile ceiling that quivered like a frightened Yorkshire terrier every time a truck rattled past. The platform bed, topped by an ascetic cookie of foam, had been wedged into a corner of the windowless box, and mirroring attached above each of the two sides that hugged the walls; as these mirrors conformed in width to the dimensions of the bed, and rose above the mattress the same number of inches that the mattress rose above the floor, a sense of volume had been created, giving the narrow slab the aspect of a fish tank—so palpably that, once ensconced, one became reluctant to violate the imaginary "tank walls." Beside the bed stood a glass-and-brass night table of identical provenance as its cousin in the waiting room, on the lower shelf of which sat a stack of arcane stroke books (*Back Door Monthly, Close Shave*), on the top of which had been placed a lamp. And that was that.

Suburbanites will know the typology: the den, to which everyone repairs to veg out, the one part of the home requiring neither manners nor dignity. It is for precisely this reason that dens—as did the rooms of my brothel—desexualize their occupants; and the bed's aquarium aspect performed further neutering by turning the would-be satyr, not merely into a Dorito-eating lummox, but a goldfish, floating in a volumetric prison. In the better houses I visited, management gussied up this formula with shag carpeting or gold-veined mirrors. But the objective, I understood, was the same: to blunt the edge of the patron's purpose by slipping him a cultural mickey; to keep, as always, control.

I defeated this tactic variously. The cocaine had the physiological effect of warping my vision, and this infused the ostensibly folksy room with a sinister air. Shadows writhed on the walls, Munch faces formed out of the rumples of the counterpane—a wrench of the brain, and the whores' suburban fantasia morphed into the fabled motel room on the outside of town, locus of dark doings. This drew in the mood of erotic desperation that hung about the house's exterior, filled my room with it like a dirty fog.

An extra mirror helped, too. My tiny box had been dubbed the "big room," not merely for the additional centimeters it had stolen when the house's five upstairs bedrooms had been subdivided into nine cabins, but for a design flourish: an outsized marble mantelpiece, over which hung, amazingly, a gilt-framed Rococo mirror. How I loved that looking glass. Despite my dissolution, I'd remained devoted to my workouts, and coke, the appetite suppressant, had chiseled me further, so that I'd come, in my misery, to resemble an underwear model (below the neck—atop my shoulders still lolled the same portrait of Semitic peevishness). It became an indispensable prelude to my pleasure, when in this room, to lie back, having "gotten comfortable," and admire my reflection, surrounded appropriately by a halo of gold. As an act of shameless narcissism, it compelled me— the man who had come to hate himself—to enjoy the contours of my long-muscled thighs, my broad, flat pectorals like twin slabs of slate, my swollen, serrated, handsomely crafted balls.

Finally, I defeated the room's energy by using it. For if den design is predictable, so too is addiction. I'd come, as centuries of compulsives had come to every manner of narcotic, both chemical and experiential: to arrive at a specific state of being by repeating a highly particular routine. What better place to do so than on a familiar, indeed ubiquitous, stage?

Then, in the few minutes in which I'd been left to myself, I would relax, as secure in my certainties as a child on Christmas Eve. As I lay there, I'd reflect that what had been given back was nothing short of the optimism of early manhood, when all of life's rewards lay ahead, and I owned the confidence that my plans would unfold perfectly. What had been returned was my innocence; and what was better still was that it had made its way back to me from the most fatal kind of knowledge. This time, I had done my work honestly: I'd imagined, not a literary career, but a life the peace of which arose from not caring, a release from everything but arithmetical certainties—the number of girls, the quantity of coke, the sum of cash, and the figures on the clock. I did not consider that I'd run from responsibility— no, I had *embraced* it: recognized my goal, accepted the sacrifices, then shoved myself through successive barriers of resistance until I arrived at my destination. Listening to the onrushing rap of Wendy's heels, shifting my eyes to study her as she slipped in and shut the door, it all felt right. This was mine; this was me.

XXXX

Wendy, then.

When, with a distinctive twist of the doorknob, she would enter my room, I'd sit up with the alacrity of a man who has bet on a horse—who is alive during the thunder of the race, and for whom everything else is waiting. Detoxifying from this life, it was the memory of Wendy that drove me from bed before dawn, onto walks wherein the quiet would settle me down. It was with her that everything—the sex, the *meaning*—came together.

Having said as much, I must answer a question that will have arisen in the minds of certain readers, those familiar with the drug's side effects. Yes: cocaine made me impotent. As my addiction found its shape, even the thought of it was sufficient to suppress tumescence, in the way that thinking of women makes other men erect. The comparison is apt, for if I had not understood the craving for prostitutes that exploded within me, I recognized immediately the feeling I experienced the first time I had sex with Wendy. It was that of revelation: the profound satisfaction of understanding, after trying a thousand keys, why it should have been *this* one that turns in the lock.

As noted, my intractable problem was my wife's ability to manipulate me into acting against my interests, and the seeming impossibility of extracting myself from this dynamic. But I did have a card to play: to salvage a crumb of self-respect, I refused to take any pleasure from the relationship. The flip side, of course, was that I *wanted* to be close to someone, wanted it desperately—I would walk the streets of the Fairfax district, it seemed to me, literally dying from a lack of affection, feeling that I would do anything to give myself unreservedly to a woman. Yet this was precisely what I'd decided I could *not* do.

By the end of my fourth Los Angeles year, this conundrum had pinned me in stasis. But if first coke rid me of caring, it next proposed an alternative to this unappetizing choice between self-denial and self-annihilation. Sex with a woman while on drugs, without the possibility of erection, I found, created a magical construct: it removed the expectation, on that woman's part, that I might take conventional sexual pleasure. This proved to be critical, as an essential component of expectation is judgment—and judgment, approval or disapproval, was my very worst enemy.

I had always assumed that, in sex, good marks depended upon being a good lover. What I realized, having mutually orgasmic but unaffectionate sex with my wife, was that one's talent resided ultimately in one's ability, not just to give pleasure, but to take it: it was precisely a willingness to lose control that created intimacy and satisfaction, whereas withholding oneself, and substituting technique, disappointed both parties.

And there was a larger fact, one I would admit privately in the aftermath of our arid relations: even when things were good between us, my lovemaking did not transcend performance. Lying stiffly beside my wife, pondering the truth of this, I would wonder: if I had chosen to define love as giving myself to a woman unreservedly, why had I persistently remained unwilling to do so? The answer was that, although I wanted the closeness that came from giving myself, I understood, if only instinctively, that I *had* no self, and so was *afraid* to give it—my identity was a manufactured commodity, for public consumption rather than personal gratification. Herein lay the glitch in my approach to my wife. Certainly I was right to withhold myself—but in guarding my freedom this way, I was also clinging to an evasion. I feared surrendering to further humiliation, but I also feared the unknown: "revealing myself unreservedly" while that self remained a mystery.

This was where sex on cocaine, in a condition of irreversible impotence, proved its value. Making the sex act entirely about another's gratification enabled me paradoxically to be intimate in this self-revealing way, by locating my pleasure in someone else's. With no expectation that I lose control in the usual way—and thus no risk of disappointing my partner or losing my autonomy—I was, as if by magic, free.

This amounted, I knew, to a convoluted equation. But it worked, and with each successive whorehouse visit, my hopelessness grew less monolithic. Revealing myself let me coax the frightened beast that was my true nature from the murk, to nudge him into the first steps of his dance. This was why my brain, sensing the outcome, began screaming for a whore within minutes after I did my first two lines: so that I might begin to medicate the disease, and not the symptoms.

The treatment proved, in practice, to be cunnilingus. What I discovered was that, for many girls, receiving oral gratification amounted to a time out, the area they'd cordoned off for self-solace (as opposed to being poked inexpertly by dirty fingers). In this, as in all else, I was abetted by the drug. Apart from being, for women, a sexual stimulant, coke created, for the whores as it did for me, a discrete mental space, a soothing distance. Its introduction not only increased the likelihood that a girl would let me pleasure her; it made the experience in every way more successful.

As for me, cocaine waved the wand of dexterous sympathy over my tongue. This suited me exquisitely. I liked to talk—to me, oral gratification was a monologue. Alas, what was true in sex also applied to conversation: insecurity compelled me to substitute technique, rhetorical pyrotechnics that ultimately left their object feeling empty, even cheated. The intimacy of oral sex, however—the conversion of out-loud language that, contorted by anxiety, seemed to float above the truth like a gas, into a whisper slipped secretly into the private ear of a woman's wet pink lips—healed my shyness about the things I needed to say. The difference, thanks to a drug that made me, not only impotent, but silent and nearly immobile, was that I made myself understood by understanding someone else. For me, cunnilingus on cocaine was like a conversation in which one forged a powerful bond by really listening, creating a safe harbor in which another could bring her own truth into port. Here, at last, was intimacy without penalty, and the joy it inspired, the passion and emotion, would flow from me as freely as the sweat my blast-furnace body emptied into the sour, yellowed sheets.

I was at my best at it with Wendy. With her pushed-in, freckled face, her pug nose, she looked like the kid you see with a Band-Aid on her knee, organizing mischief in the schoolyard. There was nothing about Wendy, however, that was playful. She said she was 24, but her body bespoke thirteen: the small breasts with nipples the size and color of tarnished pennies, the few fine tendrils of pubic hair: it was the immature flesh of the girl with whom you first play doctor, but any excitement at the prospect of a return to innocence was tempered by unease, the inescapable sense that Wendy had arrested, developmentally, in the moment in which she'd first been molested. Her exhausted silences, her mental vacancies and empty face, suggested a void in which unimaginable extremes of abuse still echoed, heard only abstractedly, but there, always there. Once, after a long night, I asked if she saw clients privately. "I sleep during the day," she replied, in a trailer-park croak that conjured visions of someone waking on a cheery midafternoon with agonized slowness, coughing up a mountain of cigarette phlegm, dragging herself narcotically to pee. Here, I knew, was not someone who would last; soon I would see Wendy on the parched stretches of Sunset Boulevard, on the streets.

But it was precisely Wendy's absence that sparked what I can only call our chemistry. My narrowly oral interest, this flatline focus on Another, was the only way I could release the thing in me that needed to exist—and that coupled precisely with Wendy's need to not be imposed upon, so that the thing that *she* might be could be hers alone to build. She could only reverse her damage by crafting small assertions of freedom out of her sexuality, which had been, since its debut, the agent of her enslavement. Thus were we a fit: my vanishing enabled her materialization. So perfectly did we understand one another, after our first sessions, that no words were exchanged. As Wendy entered and moved the two steps to the Danish Modern, dropping her rag-doll teddy, kicking off her heels, the silence was complete.

As she stripped, I took out the first of the five individually wrapped grams I'd tucked beneath the mattress and, sitting up, tapped a mound of rocks and powder onto the glass top of the night table. (This system served the end of convenience, not paranoia, and ensured that, even whacked, I might keep track of the status of my stash.) Wendy made no objection—indeed, the appearance of cocaine remained a signal moment in the transaction: the drug gave me something the girls wanted other than money or control, it created a genuine interest. Absorbed as I was in crushing the rocks, cutting the lines (using my health club card, being as bereft, inevitably, of a razor blade as was Scarlett O'Hara, in crisis, of a handkerchief), I could feel the usual quickening: Wendy's joy at the appearance of the origami-folded package, our satisfaction as the granulated waterfall cascaded onto the glass, her anticipation as she lay belly down on the bed, ankles crossed above her death-camp ass, watching with a student's absorption as I tightly rolled an ATM-crisp twenty—this was the hour's one true transit of shared, unmixed pleasure.

I lay back on the pillow, the twenty balanced lightly between my fingers. Looking at nothing, Wendy put a hand on my chest and rested her chin on it; then, moving closer, she put her alley-cat tongue in my mouth and used the tip of it to massage my own, rubbing the planes and edges of it as though she were an artisan restoring the luster to old wood. (I know: the conventional wisdom, that oxymoron, holds that whores don't kiss. This is no more true than the oft-repeated chestnut that whores don't come, that they fake it for the sake of les monsieurs. Some whores come and some whores kiss; it all depends on what they hold sacred, how interested they are in exploring certain emotional realms with their johns. Whoremongers like myself will be drawn instinctively to these venturesome girls, who will in turn be emitting sympathetic pheromones. Just like life.)

Taking her tongue back, Wendy's eyes shifted her eyes to the blow. It was time. Sitting up, I handed her the rolled bill; knowing my likes, she crawled over me, stretched her body prone across my lap as she leaned over the glass table. It was a standout turn-on, the first and best of the night: the naked girl—and faceless: hair, ass, legs—sprawled across my body as she did my drugs. The silence grew deeper, as textured as a field of Rothko black, ruffled only by Wendy's snorting, her small moans of animal pleasure; I stroked her ass, ran my fingers the length of its declivity, her thighs oscillating with their first stirrings of lust.

I had my routine. I'd begin by helping Wendy up onto her knees, narrow shoulders turned toward me as she faced the mirror. I would then step back and consider her defenselessness: how, with her tousled head lowered, as if in sorrowful anticipation of a blow, like a child awaiting punishment she seemed. Then I would set the mood by foreshadowing a different outcome: easing up behind her, enfolding her in my arms—aware of my weathered skin against her paleness—drawing her to my heat. Gently I would lay my left hand on Wendy's forehead, pulling her head back onto my shoulder, and then caress her throat as my right hand rested atop her belly. I'd do this until I felt Wendy relax, release her professional and primal tensions and, under the influence of tenderness and cocaine, give herself to me. When the cords of her throat had softened, the cheeks of her ass unclenched so that I could feel the musky humidity between them, I would turn Wendy around and embrace her, looking over her shoulder at my flushed, slack reflection in the mirror, until I controlled my own trembling. Then I'd lay her down on the narrow bed, and wait until she'd arranged her head on the pillow before lowering my own, my hands on her rising knees.

I'd make myself comfortable with a relaxing roll of my shoulders, on which her upraised thighs nestled naturally, one hand resting on her belly, the other free, as necessary, to raise the drape from her clit. Now my entire body commanded hers; yet by virtue of having let her come to me, I'd not so much taken Wendy's power as received, and promised not to violate, her trust. For Wendy, too, rubbing her itchy nose, shifting her shoulders on the pillow, it would be not surrender but relaxation, each of us knowing that privilege would not be abused.

Then I would simply eye her cunt, fill myself with the image: the twin mounds meeting in a tantalizing seam. And my joy in this view, inches from my avid eyes, would transmute itself into her in the hour's first erotic exchange; I'd feel it beneath my hand, in the focused rise of her belly. Encouraged, I would slide my tongue's tip the length of her shut slit, not with any intention other than a tactile version of my visual taking-in: slowly, stopping moment by moment to listen, to the charged silence of the whorehouse, as live with discreet action as the depths of the sea, to Wendy's first gasps; then resume, continuing upward, absolutely without opinion but with total absorption.

And because, I think, I didn't impose myself on that first pass of the tongue, Wendy built her own arousal, her own way; what came back as her lips began to swell, to open and glisten in the dim, distorted light, was the first wave of a pure carnal concentration. Which I took pains to purely receive: reaching the top, I'd pause, my tongue en pointe over the still hidden clit, and wait, pressing lightly, as the wave would crest; then down we'd come as the wave broke, spraying foam, and I began to open her in earnest.

Now I would speak to her, speak from my heart, respond to every response teased out by my tongue by acknowledging it and encouraging more. I'd commence with long licks that exposed her inner lips, and this delight, play mixed with a mindless hunger, set the mood. My pleasure would be apparent and deliberate, I richly enjoyed the tactile satisfaction, the *eating*, I wanted Wendy to know it and she did: desire stirred in the void of her, the unspoiled natural goodness of it; her hips pumped, once, like a wave's languid curl or the slow-motion crack of a whip. She'd make a sound—"Mm"—short and thoughtless, and that would inflame me, I'd get into it with an athlete's gusto, my tongue sliding deep into her, over spots so responsive that the slightest touch would make her writhe and twitch, running the tip of it along her cunt's upper ridge as though licking foam from my lip. My hands massaged her belly, her thighs; I put her in attitudes I enjoyed, taking her wrists in one hand, reaching back to grasp an ankle—gestures, poses, that by virtue of making me happily sexual, without hostility or menace, did the same for her.

And soon, always, I would arrive at that beloved object, that so amazed me with its capacity, like a central government, to wreak havoc far from headquarters. With a fingertip I would raise the hood, and there it would be, the pink clean oval in its wet slick swaddling clothes; with care, I'd separate it from its surroundings, draw my tongue around the side of it, beneath it, coaxing it forward into the air, attuned to Wendy's gasps and twitches as it fattened and firmed, my drenched chin halfway through her cunt's door, feeling it clench as the bolts of pleasure flashed up and down her canal, up and down her ass. With my eyes closed, as intent as a diamond cutter, her clit would seem enormous, these minute actions on this tiny landscape would feel like the motions of an army, such was my absorption in the transit of her come. I have experienced the loss of concentration in sex that arrives with age and familiarity. But never on drugs, never with Wendy. Eating her, I was a teenager again: lost in original wonder.

And finally, inevitably, the tree would start to topple. I would hear the echoes in the void begin to grow louder, as her belly rose and fell with the force of a saw cutting wood, as the rolling whip-crack of her hips grew regular and more swift, as her ears began to redden, her thighs tightened their muting grip. The coke would now abet us by shutting down my body's systems, as though the lights were going out upon a stage, leaving only a single figure bathed in a white-hot spot. All the skills of the rest of me would leave their posts and head for my mouth, responding like firemen to an alarm, turning my tongue, my sole functioning organ, into the absolute agent of my will. As Wendy's belly rose and fell beneath my palm, now high, now deep, now high again, as those minute attentions and violent responses began to form themselves into their final order, my tongue would become heroic: I would be like one of those folk with multiple disabilities, whose bodies seem the most pitiable prisons, and who yet manage a poignant eloquence in the single part of them that still works, a bright eye, a left foot; I would become, in those late moments of delirium, the Christy Brown of cunnilingus. My tongue was gentle, firm, pointed, reflective; geysering from my throat as Wendy's hips rose to their final plateau, its sensibility and purpose remained defined and directed. It opened a space in which she could be herself, and in so doing, revealed me.

And so the moment would arrive. I'd raise Wendy's orgasm almost to the point of detonation, then slow down enough to enable the most finely calibrated adjustments to her pleasure's pitch; use a completely focused stillness to hold her there, long enough for us both to consider the magnitude of the universe we'd made; and then, with every muscle in her body tight as wire—her toes pointed, calves in knots, ass and belly stretched flat, tits the same but for the rock-hard mesas of her nipples—flip her into the abyss.

Wendy's come satisfied me deeply. From this silent, remote girl, a girl so not with me (or with herself) in so many ways, I would elicit an orgasm that was a paradigm of abandon. Her hands shot into the mirror above her head and she jammed herself into me, face flushed and body convulsing as her hips twisted and she ground against my teeth, as she barked, staccato, as her pussy flatulated the air displaced by her contractions, a wrenching, involuntary seizure that was torn from her, flayed from her. We could not speak. But I could entomb her in the isolation of a come so complete that we connected, for half a minute we connected, to the extent that, more than once, she forgot a whore's life of lessons about letting down her guard, she would expire in my arms and—like a child—go to sleep.

Usually at this juncture, there would be an intermission of sorts, in which our creation would unknit, and what might be described as our social selves would reemerge. I would lie with my head on her thigh, shifting my jaw, feeling the slight irritation of tissue beneath my tongue, the rug-muncher's version of tennis elbow; Wendy would stare at the ceiling, her mood returning by degrees to its usual exhausted remoteness. This is not to say that (so far as I knew) Wendy disliked me. After a minute or so, she'd raise her head and look at me with a small, very particular smile—not one of gratitude or affection, but a smile that belonged to nothing but itself. That independence—the suggestion that our sex had returned to Wendy a part of herself that had been lost—that was my reward.

Or should have been. I would smile back with a like neutrality, but less sincerely, as I'd want some acknowledgement that I had reached her. That was a question, however, that one could never ask. To attempt to elicit an expression of feeling, I knew, was to awaken the whole dispiriting

Godzilla of male-female relations, with its cankers of power and control and, above all, misperception.

So I had to take it on faith. And in so doing, I would think, invariably, of my wife—who, finding herself in tears at the end of this or that cinematic turd, always said, "I was crying at my own movie." Perhaps, *enfin*, it was all in my head. The question is, Does it matter? What is *any* human exchange, except the hope, by a fatally narcissistic organism, that it is being truly perceived? The grace sex with Wendy earned me was the beginning of the ability to not ask for what was not mine to have, to proceed on faith. Here at last was true intimacy, for the way it respected what it gave, for what it did not pretend to be.

By now, a good chunk of the hour would have passed, and rather than recrank the apparatus and risk the interrupting "time's up" knock, more lines would be done, and Wendy would apply herself to me orally. I did not, to be sure, want a blowjob. But I would let her try, because I sensed that, just as I had something I needed to do, so did she. And since Wendy understood that I had no expectations, she might take to her task in a way that provided, like drugs, comfort via the restoration of a familiar state of being.

But not always. Sometimes intimacy begat intimacy and—I am thinking of one visit in particular—the gates swung open to Nirvana. It was the night that Wendy opened her purse to get a smoke, and accidentally revealed a joint: fat and misshapen, crooking me toward vice. She looked at me, saw that I saw; and with what, in my condition, was remarkable dexterity, I reached across her downy thighs and plucked the joint from its nest.

It was an interesting moment. My action introduced a potentially souring element of the hooker/john dynamic into our pristine cloud. But—let me say it—*our history as a couple*, the license facilitated by our mutual respect, not only saved the moment, but deepened it. By invading her purse, that sacred place, I violated the rule that states that the john must never be construed to win. Except that the excitement of what to me was an uptick in our intimacy—I had not snatched the joint, but *removed* it—produced a near-miraculous result: it caused my cock to stir, to turn and thicken like a worm after a rain. Seeing that, Wendy saw that she still controlled me, to a far greater degree than either of us realized, and the combination of successes—on the transaction's surface and beneath it—created something like true feeling.

Our bodies touching, we sat side by side on the bed's edge, and she watched as I put the joint between my lips. It torched up nicely and drew thickly, crackling like a Yule log, a boiling ring of resin appearing almost immediately; the smoke ripped at my savaged throat, but I held the hit and passed the baton. Wendy took a deep drag, and then we each did one more (a third, and we ran the risk of being discovered. That was another of coke's virtues: the dental-office aroma didn't travel).

Two hits were plenty. Wendy and I fell back on the bed, as whacked as a pair of pachyderms who've been hit in the ass by tranq darts. Here, I blubbered inwardly, was something new: it kept the coke's focus and thematic accuracy, while filling me with an exquisite pornography of sensation that I'd never before experienced. Those two hits tipped us into the erotic ether: Wendy and I flopped toward each other, her nipple appeared in my mouth, my finger touched down lightly in the coke on the night table, it did a zero-gravity bounce and landed atop her clit, awash in the liquors of an arousal every bit as dirty as my own. That one worm-turn of tumescence was the whole story for me, but the pot-and-coke combination lent me new license, to explore Wendy in a way that, while still evoking her presence via my absence, epitomized male sexuality, the drive to plunder without excuse. My tongue on her tit, my finger on her clit: I balanced Wendy on a wire strung between these poles, and my pleasure derived from seeing just how long, how variously, I could rock her on the seesaw of her sexuality. It was different, Wendy was more of a woman to me this way: we were pressed together, my chest to her belly, and I rattled her as though shaking a cookie sheet, bringing out her comes differently, until they began to run together, boom, boom, piling up like cars colliding in a fog. It let me feel like a man, Mr. Macho Man, to rattle the little rag doll senseless, her legs kicking spastically as though she'd been shot in the head. Aware, as I was, that to use Wendy this way was to be akin to her abusers, I didn't care. With each come, I felt the restoration of my honor, the lessening of my humiliation at the hands of my wife.

Finally, I'd shaken it all out of her, I rose up and pulled her close, my chin at the level of her eyes. Wendy's hands were on my chest, half pushing me away, half steadying herself. Either her head was jerking or she was shaking it, to tell me, No more, no.

I picked up my tightly rolled twenty, scooped some snow, and put it to her nose. Then I dosed myself, and dropped, and into that wet divide I put my face again, and realized that, for all that had preceded, Wendy had not truly finished, nor had I achieved my objective. For now we were both of us finally, deeply, mindless, we were there, we were nude, I was eating her, but these were the only certainties, and they mattered as much as the train matters to the traveler lost in reverie. She came, wide open, hips pumping absently on the arc of my tongue, and we were with ourselves entirely: transported on a river of feeling and emotion that shimmered like silk beneath the moon.

That come was the one that changed me. When it ended, and my head lay stone-heavy between her legs, a part of me had been freed definitively. Wendy. It was she who addicted me to this transformative act of intimacy without penalty. It was through Wendy that I discovered— and became addicted to—love.

The rapping of the heels, the knock-knock at the door; "Okay," Wendy half-called hoarsely, the heels went away. Slowly we unbent ourselves, rising like audience members in the afterglow of introspection following a play.

"Wanna see another girl?"

I stared at myself in the gilt mirror (to which, when the

drugs ran out, and the horrors descended like thunder, I would add a "u"). "Send in whoever's not working. And I'll pick."

Wendy dressed, did a line, kissed my cheek, and went away. The experience left me the moment she closed the door.

XXXX

Wendy, of course, was unique. But it might be possible to spend an entire evening in a similar mode, seeing a series of girls who delivered comparable pleasures. It was better, I found, if she were followed by someone who knocked me off-stride: forced me to look at what I was doing from a different, even unwelcome, perspective.

On one such challenging night, the door flew open almost immediately, it seemed, after Wendy's departure. The girl caught me unawares, she strode up to the bed without slowing, as though it weren't there or she didn't see it; I almost put my hand up, whether to catch her when she fell or protect myself, I couldn't say. I needn't have worried. She froze the instant her shins touched the bed frame.

"Hi, I'm Sinclair?" The accent on the first syllable, a slight vocal uptick at the end. Which made it seem less like an introduction than a question.

"Mike."

"Hi, Mike, I'm the only girl available, would you like to see me?"

I looked up at her—aware that my head had involuntarily turtled. Sinclair was watching me with avid eyes: utterly still, but with a nearly radioactive air of predation.

I wasn't sure I believed her. I hadn't noticed the door buzzer, I didn't sense any fucking going on, I *thought* I heard, over the dim rhythmic fart of Barry White on the waiting room stereo, female chitchat. But I couldn't be certain: the hour with Wendy had been conducted on a distant planet. Glancing at Sinclair, who continued to regard me with a charged neutrality, I felt she understood my predicament, and was drawing a certain pleasure from it.

Still, she turned me on, no question. A big showgirl, Sinclair wore a bikini-cut leotard and red heels that made her legs, long and shapely, ascend with the humbling majesty of sequoias. Her breasts drooped—she was a mother, as were most of the girls—but Sinclair drew your eyes upward with a cascading mane of chestnut curls, styled specifically to express pizzazz! to let you know she was fun! and wild! and up for anything! She had a wide mouth that didn't close, quite, that showed the edge of a line of Chiclets she could sink into your ass as easily as if it were a slice of angel-food. There was a sexy beak of a nose, too, with nostrils that flared with the regularity of a fish's gills, the better to stoke the erotic engine between her hips. Lastly, the pose: Sinclair's elbows were glued to her sides, shoulders upraised, forearms out, talons hanging. She topped it off by staring down with steady, frank, Aqua Velva eyes: "Hey, big spender," the look seemed to say, "I am Sinclair—I will give you the Real Ride."

So I replied—still a bit turtled—"Sure. I'll see you."

At which point Sinclair released an almost inaudible laugh—the faintest chuff, the slightest uptilt of her chin—followed by an equally cool half-grin, as she looked deep into my eyes: a look that dripped satisfaction, as though she'd known how I'd respond all along.

That's when I knew I was in for it. It was a look I had seen many times, and it always meant the same thing: that one had fallen into the hands of a girl who would, not only hustle you out of everything but your toenails, but take pains to reveal the sour obverse of all your smug notions about what you were doing. If Wendy addicted me to love, the Sinclairs of the game taught me that love wouldn't just come my way, I'd have to fight for it. And since they were real pros, I generally took a beating.

She went off to sign in, she was back in a flash—I heard her this time, red heels hitting the carpet with a boom (I saw them in a floor-level shot, the camera retreating from their mighty onrush). Sinclair came in, she dropped her bag, she sat on the bed, eyes bright with anticipation as she watched me do a line. Her hustle broke from the gate: "Do you want to give me a present?" By "present," she meant a cocaine doggie bag, a presumptuous request; but before I could take exception, Sinclair was bent over the table, demolishing my stash with her splendid schnozz as I watched her Medusa curls.

Before I could take exception to *that*, Sinclair turned genuine. Sitting up, she tapped the side of her nose, eyes bright and wide and a little scary—like, "Wow!"—she winked and blew a silent kiss and ran a red lacquered nail along my cock. "Wendy says you're a nice guy," Sinclair confided. "I'm thinking, a mensch, right? We're going to have fun to-*night*."

A *mensch*? *Excuse* me? Stick and dance, that was the style in the Sinclair division: before you were on your feet, she knocked you off balance, you stuck out your fist and hit nothing but air. Wendy, the silent cipher, had submitted to my routine. Sinclair hadn't even let me get situated, and that was deliberate: by the time I did, we'd be fighting on her terms.

She was nude, on the bed, on an elbow, on her side, my own posture her mirror image. Sinclair made her eyes sultry, I could feel her breath; her nose gently brushed my cheek. "Maybe you should give me that present now," she purred. "Before we get too distracted." There was, I saw, a dollar in her hand.

All right, all right. I pushed myself irritably into a sitting position, the better to express my displeasure, but this only elicited another of her spectral laughs, so I checked it; passive aggression wasn't going to help me any. I scooped some coke onto her dollar and Sinclair tucked it into a red leather change purse, looking pleased and absorbed. I found myself thinking, If she'd just be a little smarter, she'd get two hours out of me, I'd get her *so high*…But that was beside the point. Girls like Sinclair didn't expect the second hour: there was more joy to be had from making you feel like shit. Yet it was more subtle than that, it was the way they did it: Sinclair's greed and presumption played as commentary on the whore's hustle; and when you both accepted the abuse and showed chagrin, she stopped it and laughed, squinting as she looked at you, to make sure you knew she understood: as she played the whore, you were playing the john, which is to say the fool. Sinclair's ability to both act and editorialize, point to the thing as she caused it to unfold, made the hour feel almost like performance art, and the start-and-stop of her scenario fused style and substance with precision: I could not get a rhythm going, launch a satisfying narrative that might lead me to satori.

Determined to take command, I powdered my middle finger and reached between her thighs, but Sinclair stopped me with a powerful grip. When I looked at her with surprise, she released me immediately, then shook her head, wrinkling her nose with distaste. "I can't feel anything," Sinclair said. "I'll do a *freeze*," she offered, "and *then* you can touch me," taking my hand, watching me demurely as she sucked my digit clean. I let her continue, but only because I was out of ideas. My achievement with Wendy struck me as inadequate, effective only with a passive partner. The problem was that I'd yet to develop an alternate style, I had no other way to play it.

Extracting myself from Sinclair's inhalations, I tried to lower my head, but that, too, was a taboo, one she enforced with an edge of panic, by grabbing my hair—an embarrassment, as it cost her authority. Quickly, she released me, vamping: "No, honey, I—There was a bad experience…"

"What happened?"

Sinclair repeated the nose-wrinkle and head-shake. "That's not for here. Some other time."

"When?"

"We could meet at a party," she speculated. We faced each other, fists to temples. "Do you like music?"

"Uh-huh."

"What kind? Blues, right?" Again she gave me the bemused squint, this time with a more innocent pleasure, at her accurate reading of my taste. "Ever been in San Francisco?"

"While back."

"You came up there, right? We're about the same age."

Somewhere a car horn blatted, abruptly I tasted bile. *Who cares?* Sinclair was stripping my night of its lambent anonymity, dragging it into the realm of real people and things. But—I saw it clearly—this was *my* fault. When Sinclair had fumbled the advantage, I could have seized the moment. Instead, I had made myself interesting by taking an interest, given her time to take restorative pleasure by sussing me out. Glancing at her, watching the smile go knowing, I saw I was right: her signature response was my barometer. Sinclair's chin tilted up slightly, as if in challenge: waiting to see what I'd do with my knowledge.

I thought…I thought I'd use her roughly. Not with pain, but enough dominance to create the submission I needed to give pleasure. If I fed her enough coke, I figured, and asserted myself, I might turn the fake eroticism with which she tortured me to my advantage.

I cleared my sandpaper throat. "I love your hair," I said. (Dazzling smile, shake of curls.) Reaching behind her head, I ran my hand over her stiffly hennaed ringlets and, in a painless but commanding way, grabbed me some.

Sinclair got it: she tilted her head back, lips parting in mock-helpless surrender. It was quite a show, and she nearly ruined it by making it so, but the coke, my corner man, hardened my heart. I put my free hand on her spine and pulled her close, pressing us together, bellies, groins. Giving her hair an extra tug, I scooped up a breast—it was like trying to catch oatmeal as it ran down her chest—and as it puddled in my hand, gobbled the amoebic nipple. Sinclair offered a few soft, leading moans; then, just as I found my groove, lengthily scratched an itch, the better to telegraph her lack of interest. Sighing audibly, I fell back on the bed, arm on my forehead as I stared at the wall.

Soon she was giving me head. "I'm *very* good at this," she said, before frenching on the condom (ah, archaism! Is fellatio still "frenching" to anyone?) and she was: no acrobatics or teeth, only the fluent administration of high-end pleasure. Sinclair took cocksucking seriously, and what struck me as I lay there was how smart that was. Most girls, if inclined to show contempt, did it hard and quick; but by reducing themselves to angry machines, they lost face. Sinclair's contempt for me was like a true line, it had neither end nor beginning, but she was too much of an artist to disrespect her own talent. *That* was power, and even as I stopped her bobbing head, I admired it.

We dosed ourselves and lay back, heads side by side on the pillows. "Married?" Sinclair asked, picking something out of her pussy and examining it.

Oh, brother. Now my wife's spectre had joined us in Bleak House. Who says, I thought, they can kill you but they can't eat you?

"Hey, you know," without waiting for an answer. "I say, if you're gonna get it, get it here. I mean, an affair is like having a second marriage," she laughed, "and one's bad enough, right?" I felt her head turn toward me. "Are you a screenwriter?"

I'd been staring at the ceiling, holding very still, as though I were having a tooth drilled. Now I looked at her. Sinclair, I reminded myself, was a professional. If she was fishing around, she was up to something.

"How did you know?" I asked.

"*Isn't everyone?*" she replied with a punchline leer, and resumed picking her pussy. A perfectly timed pause, and: "Jewish?"

I was watching her, trying not to look too gaga. "Why do you say that?"

"You seem smart."

I had to hand it to her. It was amazing, how she'd contrived, not only to neutralize my intentions, but to drag in the miseries of marriage and the pathetic ubiquity of my profession, *and* to insult my faith (and me, by hinting that I was the exception that proved the cliché). She even added a note of symbolism, by flicking whatever she'd found between her legs onto the rug.

I had to do something, Sinclair's sportive mutilation of my corpse was intolerable. Ending the hour was not an option. I was being challenged.

"'If Marxie Heller is so fuckin' smart,'" I blurted, "'how come he's so fuckin' dead?'"

"Huh?"

"It's a line from a movie. *Prizzi's Honor*."

"What's it mean?"

"It means, if I'm so smart, what am I doing here?"

Sinclair smiled richly. "You don't like me, Mike?"

I rubbed her ringlets reassuringly, kissed her tit, and showed my rictus of a smile. "Men," I began, and gasped, violently—the signal that I was approaching cocaine overload. "Men," gasping again, beginning again, "*Women* cheat because they're not getting something. Men, because they're not *taking* something."

Sinclair squinted again, this time with confusion. "Hah?"

"Men. Don't. Want to. If they're with somebody, they don't want to," gasp, "want to get trapped. Buh—By their *feelings*. So they hold themselves back."

"Their feelings…" Sinclair watched me with interest, unconcerned by my condition. She turned her eyes back to the ceiling. "You mean," she said, "guys protect themselves. From, like, getting trapped…"

"And then cheat. So they can have the feelings where it doesn't count." I had, I noticed, regained near-normal speech.

Sinclair nodded. "Is that how *you* feel? With your wife?"

"I think every man feels that way," I said perfectly, "and will, instinctively, if he finds himself in a situation where he's feeling trapped"—I hesitated, then understood, all at once, where I was headed—"will *get* pleasure by *giving* pleasure…"

There it was: struggling to take command, I explained the gambit I'd perfected with Wendy. I droned on, Sinclair nodding, commenting, the both of us stopping now and then to get higher; listening to myself—the well-formed sentences, the sensitive observations—I began to sour on my nature so desperately that not even coke could block it out. Giving myself to a prostitute by passing on the conventional receipt of pleasure had worked, with Wendy; when pushed to take action, however—to bravely send my embryonic self out to do battle—I chose to use my sexual construct as a feint, so that I might gain control by gaining Sinclair's "respect." Most telling: I'd done this by playing my old character, the dead identity I'd come precisely to bury: the smart-boy writer, incapable of intimacy or authenticity, too cowardly to admit his intentions.

It was anguishing, galling. I was here to be myself, wasn't I? Yet look how easily I succumbed to the desire to impress, to impress the dumb girl with my smarts; and look, look how I'd managed, as we spoke, to slip a finger into her, and how she was responding, I heard her breath steady with arousal as she drew it in through her nose, and look, look most of all at how I smirked, how I could not keep that expression—that of a kid getting away with something—off my face. Alas, the joke was on me; when I saw Sinclair's narrow-eyed, telling smile, I knew that she knew, she had me yet again. Here it was, that sour obverse: the moment in which one's act is peeled like a piece of bad fruit, and the black banana of self-deceit is revealed. Sinclair was a genius, she'd been onto me from the start. She came, grinning, and I felt like shit: the coward, with nothing to show for his money, self-destruction and attitudinizing but a cunty finger.

Ah, well. It was, as the saying goes, all good. If the construct enacted with Wendy enabled me to begin to be someone new, getting belted around by Sinclair showed me that, as quickly as possible, that new person had better take form and reveal himself, use what he'd discovered and take a real emotional risk. I was grateful to the Sinclairs I met, invariably at just the moment at which I'd become too pleased with myself, for teaching me this lesson—one that, like the others, I could not learn often enough.

Meeting Sinclair's eyes, I saw that she'd read my mood. There was a moment in which we really looked at each other, I conveyed my understanding of what she'd taught me, and she acknowledged that there might be something in my sorry self worth saving.

"So," she said, resuming her ironic profile, "I hope I made it good for you."

"Very. And I hope it was nice for you, too."

"It was. Really. I really mean that." Her eyes, as she spoke, were on the snow pile.

"Go ahead," I drawled. Sinclair took a few more pulls on the mound, dipped in a finger and rubbed it on her gums, took one more pull and one more dip, and went off to get me some more loving. In the wake of her departure, I actually, audibly, groaned.

XXXX

At this juncture – the clock hovering typically around 2 AM—I would begin to feel, tearing away from me, the last tattered remnant of my dignity. I was heading into the end zone, in which the coke ceased to work, it became, simply, toxic waste. Not that this made a difference. I had never known, in any context, when to leave the party; if things began to curdle, I just pushed harder. So it was still: I was approaching the moment when I would commit to continuing until circumstances, rather than will, made it impossible, until the money ran out, my nose could no longer inhale, until they closed the place up and the whole decimated lot of us went home. I was slipping, tumbling, into an implacable compulsion to continue, I could feel the need to keep snorting lines, licking pussies, the whole frenetic program, become everything and nothing, the universe and the void.

But I was not quite there. The sky remained dark, I could still consider that the onrushing horror belonged to my education (without reflecting that I'd repeated this grade three or four dozen times). Indeed, often as not, coming off a frustrating Sinclair-style encounter, everything chemical and existential clashing within me would come into balance.

Despite all evidence to the contrary, with the right girl, I could experience transformation.

On one such night, the door flew open and three girls marched in, displacing nearly all the room's air. I had to blink nonstop to clear my contacts as I gasped and ground my jaw, but even so, I chose instantly: not the Asian (not my type), nor the ugly one (teeth like shetl gravestones in a liverish mouth), but the third, a soft-faced blonde in what looked to be her early thirties, big in the shoulders, with a persuasive come-hither smile. I nodded at her, and the others, casting regretful glances at the coke, eased out.

"Hi. I'm Michelle."

"Mike."

I met her smile with my own—the moment of selection being, for both parties, largely an affirmative one—and waited for her to leave. Instead, Michelle turned her chocolate-eyed gaze on the place where the floor met the wall; her expression inward-looking, as though marveling at the astral turns that had carried her to this moment.

She looked at me then, eyes gentle and wise. "Be right back," she said.

I knew the type. Michelle was a Girl on a Mission: someone who sees in her life a highly particular narrative playing out a fundamental theme, and to whom a session represents a chance to step out of the story, to elucidate her drama and—critically—have you validate its significance. Such hours could demand more than one cared to give. But, I understood, my instinctive selection, at the night's hinge, of a Girl on a Mission (the unpalatability of my other choices notwithstanding) was cocaine's most important gift to me: Michelle wanted to connect, she would give me an opening and wait for a response. My failures with Sinclair and others like her demanded that I give life to my changing self, jump the chasm of infernal reticence and *act*. That night, I saw—as Michelle again came through the doorway— I had my chance.

I watched her undress. She looked good. Her skin was like tawny silk, her breasts capped with tan nipples, satisfyingly quarter-sized; her legs strong and shapely, her ass the prize, a matched pair of volley balls, dished at the sides. A big girl, with large, expressive hands, Michelle moved with somnambulant deliberation as she posed on the bed's end like Copenhagen's mermaid, regarding me with vivid, needy eyes.

"So," I found myself saying, "how you doing tonight?"

I was only trying to break the ice. But hearing that line as I uttered it, a bell dinged in my head: it was a whore's line. A wave washed through my mind, and when it receded, I found myself watching a short film I'd seen as a child—its black-&-white imagery having remained, for thirty years, in the aspic of my unconscious—about a fisherman on a beach. In this film, the angler wolfed down sandwiches as he pulled fish after fish from the sea—until, with shocking abruptness, he bit into a slice of bread, a hook tore through his cheek, and he was reeled, writhing, into the waves.

Watching Michelle, I understood the mnemonic visitation. Though it would appear to be self-evident, I'd not perceived that there were whores who, as I needed them, needed me, to achieve a depth of intimacy not possible in the real world, where the price was the loss of oneself. Michelle wanted to enact a ritual that delivered primal comfort, for which she required, as I did, someone to be the agent of its facilitation. She needed, in short, a harlot—and from the look on her face, she believed she had one. Me.

Never too deranged to practice cheap psychology, I thought of the hook in the film, and how interesting it was, that my brain should have made this connection as I found myself being *fished* for by a *hook*er, one of many in my prey-filled sea. Yes: even as I responded to the *lure* of a doppelganger, my higher brain warned me: rather than eating seafood, I might wind up as catch of the day.

Yet I realized my opportunity. Though powerfully driven to continue, I was too stoned to arrange my impulses into a lucid choreography of desire. I needed to be at once more active and more myself, and the drugs had left me, physically and imaginatively, nearly inert. As Michelle's whore, no more would be asked of my active self than that it discern and respond to her fantasy.

This could be a tall order, even for someone with the proven talent for it. But being a whore, I knew—embodying a fantasy—bestowed enormous power and intensified one's selfhood; even now I could feel Michelle's greed for me, and the excitement flowed like adrenaline. I felt it with certainty: if I let go, this would prove my epiphany. As for the fear of the hook, I didn't understand it—and that, I reminded myself, was why I was here. The only way to define a fear, finally, was to give in to it. To give in, finally; finally, to give in.

And so, fearfully, I did. Feeling both thrill and trepidation, I chose to simply look at her, put my openness to being in her drama into a frank, unwavering gaze. (This was boldness only in part. My eyeballs felt cemented into their sockets: staring, at the moment, was once of the few choices I could credibly make.) Reading me, Michelle half-grinned with sexy knowingness, then let the grin melt into a speculative shift of the jaw, looking at me sideways from beneath her brows, tracing a line languidly along a fold in the sheet.

She was, I realized, with her smile (sidelong), glance (molten), gestures (suggestive), telegraphing her femaleness. I understood now why she'd arranged herself that way, the weight of her buxom torso on her straight left arm, hips rolling outward, knees slightly bent, slender calves tapering into high-arched feet: it was a pin-up pose. This was how she saw herself, and wished to be perceived.

To my surprise, it was easy. I found that I wanted her badly, I glanced at my cock and hoped for a miracle. Reading my mind, Michelle met my gaze, lips parting as those vivid eyes radiated a suffering emotionalism; we looked at each other, a man and a woman with nothing intervening between us, and I felt my heart lurch with the moment's intensity. There is nothing, I saw right then, so seductive as understanding. I flooded with an irresistible impulse to cross the bed, take her by her broad shoulders and kiss her, slip the tip of my tongue between her parted lips. Desire shook me.

And with that inch of distance I never lost, I observed how exciting it was, to surrender to a role, to experience extremes of emotion ordinarily beyond one's reach. Washed by these fugues of feeling, I grasped the attraction of prostitution, how compelling it would be to make a job of this intensity. And yet I also had a hint of the whore's great problem, the attrition, over time, of intuiting men's desires and placing oneself at their center. It was why, despite the power of the urge, I did not kiss her. The price of receiving a whore's pleasure, I sensed, could be a truly uncontrollable addiction—that is, to being the object, with the ability to discern human desire, to become desire itself and thereby intensify one's own objecthood.

Understanding this, I understood my fear of the hook—and, just like that, made a leap: I connected it to my surpassing terror of myself. In the years since moving to LA, I'd been in a fury at my need to please, I had flogged myself for believing I was unworthy, and so had to disguise myself to be accepted, to be loved. Realizing that giving pleasure like a whore would be a fishhook into my narcissism that I might never extract, I saw, quite suddenly, the arrogance of that self-hatred. One could speculate that a prostitute chose her profession out of a profound sense of unworthiness. But I recognized, from this tiny exchange with Michelle, that a whore could as easily feel like a goddess—and my true problem might be the opposite of what I'd always assumed: that rather than not loving myself, I loved myself too much. My terror—at least a facet of it—was that this self-love would consume me.

Understanding *this*, I understood as well that this was not the kind of man I wanted to be, and stoned as I was, I recognized the moment as one of significance: I chose not to kiss Michelle so as not to encourage a narcissism that would leave me less able to cultivate the maturity—the sobriety—I would need to make a better life. Lying to my wife, I learned that being nice and getting one's way were not always compatible. Driving to the whorehouse, walking up the stairs, I'd experienced the pleasure of being comfortable with desire. Now, in thirty seconds with Michelle, I realized that, while I wanted to *be* myself, I did not want my life to be *about* myself. Thus did I begin to define the one-celled organism that had emerged with Wendy, and retreated under Sinclair's assault.

It was the right choice for both of us. Michelle, I could see, was relieved: a kiss would have been too much too quickly. The choice proved smart in another way: my restraint created trust and released her from her pensiveness.

"I came straight from the airport," Michelle said, taking a bit of the starch out of her pose. "Just got in."

I disappeared a line, then settled back on the pillow. "From where?"

"New York."

"Ah, New *York*..." I smiled, extending the rolled bill. Michelle laid a steadying hand on my thigh as she knelt before the night table.

"Yeah, I don't know," she said, sniffling, sighing, waiting for the lines to take hold. I could see her clearly now in the lamplight: her golden-brown hair, the Nestlé of her eyes. "I felt like, you know. *This night*..." Again, the look of amazement. "I just felt it was something I had to do."

Michelle sat on the bed's edge, close to me now, her body charged with a new avidity. She was ready. Whatever she'd hoped to achieve in New York had not materialized, and Michelle needed to drive out the resulting anxiety with a consoling buzz: acknowledgement, from men, of her sexuality.

I was ready, too. My twin desires—to please, and be pleased—had seldom been more in balance. "Get on your knees," I said, touching a finger to the coke (careful to keep my pitch below middle C).

"On the bed?"

I nodded, then added a corrective: "Your knees, not your *hands* and knees." Michelle complied, irradiating me with her gaze. Carefully—being sufficiently stoned now to crash to the floor—I got into the same position, facing her. We were close enough to feel the heat off each other's bodies; I could see the down rise on her thighs, sense the exquisite near-touch of her belly as she breathed in, witness the time-lapse flowering of her nipples. I tucked the coke-whitened tip of my finger into her declivity.

No clit.

I looked at her. Michelle's expression remained the same—excited, encouraging—but almost imperceptibly crusted with apprehension. Instantly, I understood: whatever I thought—and I didn't know what to think—I couldn't express the slightest surprise or, worse, discomfort. And so, after only a nanosecond's pause, I stroked her pussy from its uppermost to the start of her canal, grinning with a touch of vanity—precisely, I hoped, like a guy who thinks he's doing real well, but doesn't, in fact, know what It is, and certainly not where It's supposed to be (such men, goes the whorehouse scuttlebutt, are more numerous than one would believe).

Michelle, of course, wasn't fooled. She recognized my gallantry. I saw again, in her eyes, the suffering vulnerability.

"Let's," she said—and then, with sudden, unexpected brightness: "take a bath!"

In a jump cut she was on her feet, leaving my pussy finger to writhe in midair like the head of a confused turtle. Bending at the waist, Michelle pulled open a drawer in the foot of the bed and removed two towels. "It's okay," she said, as infused with can-do purpose as a kibbutznik, "we'll start timing the hour when we're done."

Well. A free bath, now that was something. A thousand dollars, and they give you a free bath. Michelle extended a hand to me, but I was spaced and confused, lost in reverie. The moment she'd sprung up, I thought I'd found a nubbin a centimeter or so north of the urethral orifice. But what could it be? Where *was* her clit? And why a bath?

I looked at the night table, the drugs spilled raucously

across the glass. "S'okay," she reassured, "nobody'll come in."

"My wallet," I gasped.

"Bring it if you're worried."

I was, but it was too complicated. What if I dropped it in the tub? Drugs, disappearance, derangement, all this I could lie away, but a wet wallet? What possible excuse could I make? Michelle shook her extended arm, rippling her fingers, waiting. The choice, as it were, had been made. I did a line, and in a moment found myself as I'd never been: nude, being led by the hand (Michelle, I now saw, was much bigger than I, a real linebacker), stumbling stiff-legged and grinning my rictus grin, past startled whores and mortified johns, an idiot child of sex, with big mama, at bath time.

Despite the evidence of a filling tub (the moan of the pipes more genuine than any similar sound I'd heard all night), I could not quite believe what I was doing. My drugs, my money, my ID, were strewn in a distant corner of this dismal ruin, my wife—my wife! I was married!—was waiting. And I was lowering myself into a filthy tub—practically a horse trough—powerless to influence what was happening to me. Simmering in the grey liquid, staring at clitless Michelle as she prodded my nuts with a toe and sang "Here we are/Out of cigarettes" in a voice from the planet Boop, it occurred to me that, overboard as the previous hours had been, things might actually have gone too far. Pushing away panic, I determined not to linger in this soup excessively, and assigned one of my hypersensitive ears the task of listening for assaults on my grubstake.

Returning to the moment, I found Michelle sliding a sliver of soap back and forth between her armpit and the underside of one breast. Seeing that I was with her, she began to speak. "There was this man," she said carefully. "We were together—I mean, we started *out* together." She looked at me meaningfully. "And, you know, it felt right for a while. But more and more"—she put her palms together, then arced her hands away from each other—"there was this separation. And, like, the more he pulled away—"

Michelle stopped, looking at me guiltily. "That's not fair. It was like we were being pulled apart, you know, *unstuck* (and it was so *pain*ful…). And the more that happened…"—she scooped water beneath her arm and watched soap suds stream onto the surface of the bath—"…the more I lost my balance. Like I didn't know *what*, right?" She gave me her sideways grin, and her eyes, which had gone black in the dim light, blazed toxically. Exhausted, I simply listened; sensing my sympathy, Michelle eased toward me, and now we had that kiss, suffused with a private tenderness. "Until," she continued, "the man died. Which I knew had to happen, but it was like, I thought everything was going to *change*…" She rolled her eyes and made a flicking-away gesture above her head, as though to summon the chaos that followed her loss. "And then I was here." She grinned at me. "*Farshtay?*"

What was it, I wondered, that caused these girls to find me so Jewish? She waited for a response, but the coke held my tongue, and Michelle went a little fluttery behind the eyes. Recovering, she pinched my cheeks. "You're so cute, you're so *cute*! C'mon," she said, rising, water streaming off her as from a submarine emerging from the depths, "let's go back in."

Standing with the care of an osteoporitic crone, I reflected that my silence, which I laid to the drug's side effects, was fortuitous: as with Wendy, communion with Michelle required that certain things go unsaid. The knowledge, of course, was simple: the man who had died was Michelle. I considered her as she toweled off: the big shoulders, the over-vividness of the face (so like a female impersonator's), the absence of a true clitoris. Michelle had undergone a sex-change operation—and yet, as her parable revealed, the emotional transformation had not materialized with the physical one. Though her new identity was irrefutable, Michelle didn't believe in it, and so she found herself selling her body to men—posing, flirting, joking nitely—in an attempt to gain the self-acceptance she'd hoped would be hers when she awoke from beneath the knife.

Emerging from the bathroom, I confronted the

improbability of whores and johns seated decorously on the furnishings, more interested in watching us promenade again than in feeding on one another. I couldn't have cared less—my decoding of Michelle's subtext had bonded me to her, *it was my story, too.* The fact that her outside belied her inside, that she characterized the loss of her former self—the "I" that was her—as a death, most of all her decision to go to extremes…My manner had become a wall-eyed stiff-leggedness, I was in fact blubbering, but I clung to Michelle's hand with both of my own. God, *God*, we were the *same*, we were *both* trying to molt a vestigial fraudulence, to inflate the balloons of our new identities with the helium of truth. And: using the same pump. Sex, change. God, *God*.

We reentered our box, my eyeballs scraping like rusted guns in their turrets as they inspected: good, the drugs were there, my wallet still filled the faded square on the back pocket of my jeans, good, good. I staggered to the coke and drew in two big hits, fumbling my fifth gram from beneath the mattress, crushing new rocks ineptly as I licked clean the package that had held gram number four. Standing, turning, I crashed into Michelle, we gripped each other's forearms. "Oh, honey," she moaned, "maybe you could pay me for another hour, they'll, I, I could get *killed*…" So she was a hustler, so what? Didn't she need that, too? I paid her for two hours, she left without dressing, I drained my dinky beer and rubbed too big a chunk of chalky rock onto my gums and goggled at myself in the mirror as I gasped and shook, bang, bang, in rhythm with my thrashing heart. My mood roared back, my fears abated, whatever concerns I'd had about the woman to whom I vaguely recalled being married had been booted out the door. I'd found the perfect girl, one who could only be satisfied by a transforming fusion of understanding and imagination. My moment was at hand, and I was ready.

Michelle returned, I kissed the top of her head as she knelt and snorted with a pleasured moan, a sound I loved, the Coke Moan, I crushed another two rocks and Michelle did them and tongued the residue and touched her tongue to my own. "Wow," she said, "I am really high," and it was true, we were flying as Michelle went to the fireplace, folded both arms on the mantelpiece and presented her ass, the reflection of her face watching me as it floated in the ovular, gold-rimmed mirror.

Immediately, I understood. Struggling to my feet, I stood behind Michelle as she pushed back into me, eyes glazing as I put her on the bed, face down.

Michelle looked back at me discreetly, waiting, open legs extended off the bed's edge, toes touching the floor. I got on my knees between those legs; ran my hands along the backs of her thighs, and placed them on her ass, feeling the tension as the muscles clenched. I breathed; and then, parting her cheeks, laid the flat broadsword of my tongue on her clean, quivering bunghole.

A low moan, a *masculine* moan, came out of the depths of her, Michelle leaned her forehead on her fists as her body stiffened and shook. All it took was a single sweep of the clock—total traction from noon to midnight—to release the rapid, involuntary contractions. She went off like a spastic cannon, banging her ass against my face (cracking my nose), slamming herself into the bed; I slipped beneath her as she rode her ass, her cunt, over my mouth, the moan a kind of anguished lowing now, an unabated low-register ululation, like a steamship whistle. Until, finally, Michelle heaved me onto the bed, threw herself atop me, and kissed me sloppily, murmuring over and over, "How did you know?"

I just knew. That before becoming a woman, she'd taken it up the ass, as a she-male, and that had been a more workable identity (being clearly about transition) than the one with which she'd been struggling. I knew that the past was past, and that to treat her asshole like a cunt was to coax her into change, recognize and retire her history with a sweet kiss goodbye, the same kiss that, with tenderness, welcomed in the new. I just knew, and acted, and I had never been prouder: It was the first time I'd ever divined a woman's secret, and found the imagination to return it to her with love. Yes, I thought, holding trembling Michelle in my arms, love was not too strong a word for this unity of understanding, imagination and sex, and suddenly I found myself in a zone that was entirely new to me. Recognizing that, owing to the affirmation embedded in its meaning, Michelle would always find a rim job the ultimate turn-on, I found a truth that applied to myself: that I couldn't change the things that turned me on—my nature was set—but I could change the way I felt about them, and thereby change myself. That was my path—my breakthrough.

It was at this culminating moment that the existential problem presented itself. Even as we enjoyed the peace of post-coital afterglow, a certain tension was making itself known. I was still in a whorehouse. The clock continued to tick. The time had to be used, the money well spent. Having found each other so dramatically, we now felt compelled to retreat to neutral corners while—as hooker, as john—we considered our next move. We could not just lie there, and this reflected my larger dilemma, which sprang from the baldest of facts: the lesson had been learned.

Another mnemonic wave now struck, and I was carried back several years to an acting class, in which I'd hoped to sharpen my dramatist's skills. The teacher posited two concepts: the objective and the action. An objective, he explained, was what a character wanted *overall*. An action was the way in which the objective played out in a given moment—that is, the action the character took to *achieve* the objective. The difference was important to grasp because, while the objective remained fixed, the action changed constantly in response to events. Thus, if one wasn't playing an action, our teacher declared, one wasn't doing anything, and could neither realize the objective nor credibly convey the journey.

Feeling a growing anxiety as I rested in Michelle's embrace, I thought of this acting challenge, and how it applied to my situation. My objective had been to collapse the distance between my desires and my reality—to be myself—and my actions, over the hours, had been in pursuit of it. With Michelle, the objective had been realized, and I now had to take what I'd learned and use it to remake my life. *Whorehouse: The Movie* was over, and if I did not play my final action—which was to leave—I would be doing nothing.

This much I could admit. What I could not admit was that I did not want to leave. My detachment had long since evaporated, I found myself screwed tightly into a drive at once carnal and emotional. Cocaine had flogged me into sex to experience emotion, to achieve a raw unity of feeling with another, and with Michelle, I'd found that experience; now, faced with the choice of going home or pushing on, something turned in me, I felt to this woman a desperate closeness, I wanted to drown in this sex-and-drug-induced but nonetheless real emotional fever, to sustain and sustain the pitch.

And so I drew back from my final action, a weak choice I justified by believing in the value of staying in a frenzy. By so doing, however, I was committing what my teacher cited as the worst of the actor's sins: playing the mood. Playing the mood is the sine qua non of both bad acting and addiction, and leads to the same result: a self-indulgent stasis—destructive to participate in, oh so boring to watch.

Playing the mood, I kissed Michelle's fingertips, I put my hand on her ass and pulled her to me. "Where do you live?" I gasped.

"The Valley."

"Where?"

"Studio City." Good, straight over the hill. I could never pilot a car down Laurel Canyon Boulevard, my brains would be splattered from Mulholland to Ventura, but I was confident that Michelle had the wits. She watched me, interested. "Why?"

"Cause…" I struggled to put words together. "Could go back to your place." It was on the table.

"How'd you get here?"

"Car." I realized I'd left something out. "Got a *gram* left…"

Her eyes glowed like coals blown by a bellows. Michelle,

I could see, was going to go for it—until, incredibly, we heard a knock.

I looked at my watch. Somehow, it was after four.

"Okay," Michelle called. She sat up, looking confused. "What do you want to do?"

"Do you…?" I began hopefully.

"Oh, honey, I'm here til six, I *gotta*. Can you go 'way and come back?"

This I assigned to the Fat Chance Department. We were not in New York, where at 4 AM the desperate and disreputable might find hidey-holes in which to coop for a couple of hours. I was in, essentially, a *residential suburban neighborhood*, and cursed inwardly the so-called city, its lack of even the most basic demimonde hospitality.

Michelle wiped each nostril with an index finger. She was getting a little desperate. I understood: The deal is, when the knock comes, the girl withdraws, monsieur dresses, the girl returns and escorts him to the door with much thanks and assurances of a good time had and exhortations regarding a timely return.

Unless.

I still had 360 bucks. But I did not want to buy Michelle again, I wanted to run away with her. Considering this, the two of us eyeing each other suspiciously, I had also to admit that the moment, the mood, had paled. Such was the fickleness of cocaine: one could reconsider one's entire life in a heartbeat and, with the slightest narcotic fluctuation, shrug it all off in the next. If we'd flung on our clothes and run, our improv might have evolved into an entirely new theme. Instead, I found myself looking beyond the Bonnie-and-Clyde-on-coke scenario to its arrant impossibility.

We heard the milling of heels in the hall, as though there were a herd of buffalo out there. Michelle faced me impatiently. "Do you have any money left?" she asked.

"Who else is working?"

Silence. I could feel the coldness come off Michelle as palpably as if I'd entered a meat locker, the stiffening in response to Man's bottomless capacity for dishonesty and betrayal. Alas, I could muster only so much sympathy. I knew that it was as much lost income, the who's-the-most-popular-girl-in-school mentality that pervades most whorehouses, as injured pride. I thought: Fuck her. Hadn't she hustled me? She got a free hour, plus dope. I had nothing to be ashamed of. We'd had our moment and, as was our wont, life had failed us.

"I'll send someone in," said Michelle, leaving.

"Good," I replied, just as hard.

XXXX

By now I would be bored, well and truly. What was left to do? I couldn't speak, couldn't get hard, had eaten enough pussy to last until Doomsday, and was half-dead besides. Fluid rattled in my lungs, my drug-induced hemorrhoid felt gecko-sized, crumbs of bloody snot freckled my chest. Why not call an end?

At such times, I could feel oppressed by my addict's need to continue, like an Old Testament figure who's been tasked, by his god, too excessively. Once established in my routine, however, I knew better. Hooked though I might be, this went beyond addiction, this was—to revisit the religious reference—a calling. Bored, scared, disgusted, even sick: I had drugs. I had money. I was not going home.

The night now took on a brute aspect. I was not the only geek bearing gifts: All the girls, even the ones I hadn't seen, were as packed with coke and blank-brained determination as was I, and the place became a live wire of want. I could hear it in the slamming doors, the hopped-up thud of *Thriller* humping its way through the walls, the accusations and bitchiness and the laughter akin to a snarl. Those who've not had the experience might presume that even mid-level houses run with precision, but in the wee smalls, there comes a point when discipline breaks down and chaos rules—girls poach each other's men, sex is exchanged for drugs, johns stack up in the waiting room and the mix of liquor, testosterone and embarrassment drives them to throw drinks and punches, to peek through keyholes. Such riot can be unnerving but has its charms. It is not unlike the moment when a rock band, after hours of jamming, suddenly finds its groove, and the rush of commingling vibes blows the roof off.

This energy crashed through my door with the next series of girls. In truth, this passage of the night, as packed with indelible flashes of imagery as an Eisenstein montage, is the most difficult on which to report. I crushed rocks carelessly, girls watching foxlike from the shadows, we zipped up crude, pebbly lines and dropped crumbs on each other and licked them off. Bodies were prone and supine and facing the mirror; I buried three fingers in a girl and they came out bloody; one grunted while another slid in a dildo and a third watched from the Danish Modern, smoking a fag. The gate rattled, the door slammed, the buzzer startled me so violently that I threw beer on myself with uncontrollably shaking hands. I was down to eighty bucks and half a gram. The sun rose.

And the end of the night would often go something like this:

Three girls. Two are talking, I'm not sure about what, because part of my brain isn't working anymore, and the voices are distorted, as though they came from a warped record being played at the wrong speed. This warp, this "off" quality, is reflected in my confusion, my agitation, I am unable to focus on anyone, any one action, for much more than a moment. Bug-eyed, shaking, the last of my body's fluid leaking from every pore, I am muscling the girls around, gasping fragmented instructions, try it like, yes, here, you, turn on your side and face the, now *you*, no, put your arm *over*, the while scampering about like a demented troll who has swallowed a particularly toxic toadstool. The girls, I can see, are equally agitated (and drugged), but whereas I am plaintive in my desire for fun, to still, somehow, sort and stumble through my confusion to find the last gems of pleasure, the girls are *transparently* sick and tired and fed to the *fucking* teeth with my puling, addled shenanigans. They've been here for eleven hours, they've fucked thirty-plus guys between them, they want only to do my last lines, polish off my cash, and get the hell home. But no. *No*. *God forbid* this *ass*hole should just *pay* them and not root around for his pathetic perversions, *God forbid* it should be that simple. No. They must endure my little number if they would end the night on a win.

The girls, the girls. Who's here? A fattish girl, dark-skinned. With a Caesarian scar like a vein in a well-done piece of meat. Ungainly, unsexy, she would yet be tolerable were it not for her Shirley Temple ringlets, which have somehow, despite the night's onslaughts, kept their spring, and make her look, poor thing, like a pig in a wig. Who else? A skinny girl, skinny in a caved-in way, like she's had the guts vacuumed out of her, skin cadaverous and grey. And…Ah. *Ginger*. Short, sultry, curly-haired, beak-nosed, Ginger is Mediterranean, Italian or Greek, she has flawless olive skin, round, high breasts, a low, narrow waist, and a perfect, spankable pear of an ass, she is amazing, down to the last detail, to her thick, clean bush and elegant, expressive hands. Looking at Ginger, who is in absolutely the foulest mood imaginable, I manage a philosophical smile at the eternally springing hope of the male, I try to pull my staring, clench-jawed fright mask into something more debonair. I am thinking, It's a new day, I've got a clean slate at the ATM, if I could get my hands on another eightball, I could, well, hell, I could begin all over again. I am actually, truly, thinking this. Ginger, however, sees it, and she is avoiding me, when I lay my hand on her saucy rump she *throws* it off with an extravagant geshrai, she springs off the crowded, unruly bed as though it were a trampoline.

This has all, I think, been going on for some time. And now I am trying, as I fuss befuddledly with the fattish girl, to make out, despite my undependable ears, this new thing, a private conversation between Ginger and the cadaver, whose name I have forgotten, if I ever knew it. Seated face to face at the head of the bed, they are murmuring, they are looking at each other meaningfully, and I see now (and how

I could have failed to see this sooner I cannot imagine) that Ginger has a strap-on dildo slung over her shoulder, hooked on a crooked finger, saddle-bag style. These women are reaching a Lesbian accommodation. It's Ginger's play, I see. And I see as well the cadaver's equivocation, not because she's not attracted (though I sense she is more of a laissez-faire Lesbian than an active one), but because Ginger, the cadaver knows, is seducing her for reasons having to do with power rather than sex, to achieve a control over the cadaver that will give her, within the business environment of the house, a strategic edge. Whether Ginger has been planning this or is availing herself of an opportunity, I cannot say, but what is clear is that, quite apart from her whore's compulsion to loot me, she has maneuvered us all into our present circumstances precisely to seize this chance. And the cadaver, I can see, coked up, horny, aware of her susceptibility, is not sure that letting Ginger *do* her is such a smart idea. And she's right: Even in a whorehouse, sex between coworkers can be problematical.

I take this all in, of course, in what would be the blink of an eye if I could blink. It is obvious. And just as obviously, the fattish girl, with her sad ringlets, has only been pressed into service, with God knows what promises, to distract me.

A souped-up blast of Eisenstein, compressing five minutes into seconds, and this is what we have:

Ginger, who has buckled on her appurtenance, has got the cadaver flat on her back, Ginger is kneeling over the cadaver, she is putting all her weight on her left arm and stroking the cadaver's face with her right hand, as she speaks to her soothingly, her voice a hypnotizing buzz, the cadaver is watching Ginger, she is listening, nodding, her will to resist is re-forming itself into a powerful desire to give in, and I, half-sitting between these two and the fattish girl, facing the fattish girl but with my left hand behind me, I am holding hands with the cadaver, I am helping her hold a part of herself in reserve, so that when she submits, as she will, to Ginger's ministrations, she can pretend it is part of the "hour," that we are doing all this for me. I am observing this in the guilt mirror (the "u" has now been added), it is happening behind me, I am facing the foot of the bed, across which the fattish girl is draped on her left side, her right leg straight, her left knee bent, and my right hand, the one not engaged behind me, is between the fattish girl's legs, I am, with stiff, fumbling fingers that have lost all subtlety, I am attempting to get her off. The left side of the fattish girl's face is flat against the bed, she is very still, she is so still in part because she is so tired, but also because I have shaken out my last sprinkle of cocaine onto her right cheek, so that I will not have to get up, I can't get up, so that I can, as I finger the fattish girl, as I preserve the cadaver's necessary fiction on her transit into workplace slavery, so that I can, by leaning over, snort and lick and try, as best I can, to avoid the horrible depression, the epic crash, toward which I am hurtling with frightening velocity.

This anxiety accelerates my breakdown, and though my mind is racing, from the fattish girl to the cadaver to Ginger and back again, a million things are tumbling through the tornado in my brain (my car! my wife! my alibi! my 3:15 at Disney!), I am arrested by the previously unnoticed presence of…a television. Staring at the box at the foot of the bed, I suspect hallucination: it seems inconceivable that I could have spent nine hours in a room this small and not have observed so major an appliance. But the television lingers, an oversight more profound than my failure to notice Ginger's dildo. Henry James's famous remark about being someone on whom nothing is lost pinwheels through my mental weather—obviously, I am seeking to be the opposite—but, really, I am past this kind of irony, so flat has my affect been ironed by the drugs. Very quickly, the TV becomes one more fact, of no greater or lesser meaning than anything else unfolding in the room.

It is only now that I notice that the TV is on—that an "erotic" video is playing, the image partly obscured by the horizontal white lines produced by the malfunctioning VCR. The volume, moreover, is low, so that I can hear only dimly, through the grind of acid rock, the sobs and moose-calls of the participants.

Immediately my mind responds with drear predictability, expulsing an editorial fart regarding the bottomless capacity for self-delusion of the bourgeoisie. Of course: the video is an *amenity*, like the beer and the threadbare old stroke books, the whorehouse equivalents of the sewing kit and the sippy cup. Amenity, meaning freebie: that which makes us feel that we have come out "ahead" (thereby implying that the thing for which we have paid is not worth the price), the booby prize for which we so gratefully relinquish our judgment and self-respect. Yes, I think, giving my circumstances the once-over, just as a dirty, smelly hotel room, with cigarette-braised furnishings and a shower that dribbles as intermittently as an old man's pee, can be converted in our minds to luxury by the discovery of a thimble-sized bottle of shampoo, so can a dirty, smelly whorehouse full of hostile, predatory skanks reinvent itself as a maharajah's harem by introducing, for the gentleman's delectation, a few yards of garbled videotape. Quickly I pass more mental gas, a great satisfying stream of it, regarding the soul-killing effects of television, the loss of quality implicit in a medium like video, the extent to which the agreed-upon meaning of things has been separated from how we feel about them, a condition accepted so unquestioningly that the offer of a dirty video as prelude to paid sex—the introduction of a marital aid into a situation that is itself a refuge from marriage—could be presented completely without irony, without so much as a wink or a nudge or a smile.

I drive these thoughts away, they are, I know, common-place, the dross of an ordinary mind. But even as I beg that mind to stop, stop, its reflexive spinning, I recognize, between the horizontal lines produced by the unclean heads of the VCR, the star of the video: it is S_____ G_.___, an erotic ingénue—elegant, intent, her unenhanced breasts proof, seemingly, that for her porn is a "choice"—and I remember, with a jolt, that this girl is a recent suicide; and reluctantly, reflexively, I begin to scrutinize the screen, as she wraps her mouth around the outsized cock of some faceless stud, trying to find, between the lines, a sign, a hint at a misery so desolating that it could only be stilled by self-annihilation.

And as I ponder her misery, my hand rooting between the thighs of a stranger, my tongue slopping its way through the residue I've spilled across her cheek, my mind once again throws off its narcosis, and recognizes the on-screen doings as a commentary on the moment. Yes: in this tiny, stifling cell, the four of us are killing ourselves, we are in a cold, remorseless death-embrace. Gripped by this recognition, I experience a brief, frightening inversion, I am not sure, for an instant, who is watching whom, if I am alive or exist as particulate traces, flickering at the whim of a cathode ray.

Unnerved, I jerk my hand from the cadaver's, creeped out by the name I've given her, and wrap myself around the fattish girl, with my right hand still between her legs I lay my left against her forehead and pull her violently into me. I arch my body, she arches hers, my fingers dig, clawing; and with her sad, tired eyes on the TV, on the dead woman— her pretty ass now being penetrated by a second hung stud, her arousal obvious—the fattish girl begins to moan, making a final effort to drive herself into the moment.

The moment. I, too, want to embrace it; I do not want the night to end. I have, in fact, been fighting to sustain the labile hysteria I achieved with this or that Girl on a Mission for what now are numberless hours. But as I marshal my forces for one last effort, I am clinging, I realize, to a woman who will never kiss me, smile at me, help me to release my most ardent, unguarded self, a woman who is, to me, as blank as a television—who is indeed going through her own experience not with me but with the girl in the video, who is now, at the drama's apogee, being fucked orally and anally in violent rhythm, eyes wide with amazement, barking with each jolt of two cocks so long that one imagines them meeting at her center like a transcontinental railway. Watching this spitroasting, considering that the girl is so thin, the cocks so enormous, that it is almost as though there is nothing else within her, she is *all* cock, I realize suddenly that I have found what I am seeking: evidence of her suicidal misery. Whatever S_____ G____ had hoped to gain, she stayed too long at the fair, her essence has been exorcised by the brutality of the trade, she is, even in this Dionysian moment, already in the grave. The woman in my arms is having sex with a corpse, and this is, I realize, the source of the attraction: my plump companion has been as cored by experience as her counterpart on the screen. The fattish girl has overstayed her purpose, she will soon perhaps be with her vanished video sister, and the more I clutch and flail and attempt to make my yearnings known, the more remote she grows.

I realize—because now my mind, focused by the crash, is all realization—I realize that this catastrophe is the outcome of my original intention: to give pleasure to another without being trapped. I could not have achieved my objective more perfectly than I did with Wendy. Yet I have continued to batter at the door, to try to have a thousand perfect prostitution experiences, in the hope that they will, collectively, make up for the absence of a single exchange of true love. I realize that, though Michelle has shown me how I might reinterpret my pre-marital romantic yearnings in a new, realistic way, I am afraid to do so, and so have remained stuck in a static moment, repeating, repeating, the limitation of my premise becoming ever more glaring with each passing hour; until now, struggling with the fattish girl, my stratagem collapses under the weight of its own insupportability.

As I come face to face with my miscalculation, the fattish girl at last begins to come. Her hips jerk rhythmically against my stiff, aching forearm, I fold my fingers into her as she squeezes tight her thighs, as she closes her eyes and moans, not with joy or enthusiasm but exactly, I am sure, as she has moaned on a thousand smog-fragrant mornings, with an equal sum of men. I realize that helping a woman to orgasm under these circumstances is meaningless, it is no more a guarantor of connection than helping her across the street. I look down at the fattish girl and, as if in confirmation, she is still coming, coming and coming, she is coming in fact with the two studs on the screen, who have pulled their cocks from the suicide and, jerking off, are shooting ropy jets of sperm, ivory flumes of jism arcing past each other like something out of an aquacade. The fattish girl, the studs, even the suicide—pelted by a rain of pearlescent globules of seed—everyone is coming, and I have never felt so mocked. Orgasm. A spasm. A bodily function that, devoid of emotion or connection, amounts to not much more than exercise. Desolation, depression, close upon my heart, and the coke, which has dealt out lesson after lesson, now plays its most pointed card. If I do not take the next step, if I try and fool myself into thinking this repetition is anything other than fear, I will go the way of the fattish girl and the girl on the screen, indeed I am already doing so. I remember a line from a song heard long ago, and its meaning has never been more plain: "He not busy being born is busy dying."

The scrims of the fattish girl's come finally part, she turns on her stomach and thinks of the time, her discomfort, of a score of life details that have not to do with me. I am feeling a shiver of emptiness that is akin to horror. There is work to be done: I must take what I've learned, scrape off half a lifetime's worth of emotional callus, and release that original innocence, in a form appropriate to who and what I have become. There is work to be done and I've been busy dying: because I have no template for what comes next, because I am so utterly alone, because I'm afraid.

A catch of breath, a sharp intake of breath behind me, I turn on the bed to apprehend the heroic spectacle of Ginger and the cadaver in the throes of fucking: slowly, slowly, Ginger is easing her fake cock into and out of the cadaver with the utmost subtlety, the most discerning sensitivity, she is hitting every note in the cadaver's pussy, and she, the cadaver, is helping her, she is raising and lowering her hips, tightening, clenching her ass, her cunt, there is a mist of concentration on each woman's brow, and by God they are doing it, crossing the divide and wading into each other's lives with a fearlessness that is intensely erotic. Ginger's cock goes in to the hilt and their pubic bones meet, their bellies meet, the cadaver's eyes roll back, turning white—and two white droplets appear, like a second pair of eyes, on the spaces beneath her breasts. I look up at Ginger's breasts and realize that her body's perfection is the more remarkable for her being a recent mother, she is lactating, her breasts are full of milk, and she, Ginger, is so consumed by this climactic moment that she is brimming over.

I am mesmerized, for a moment my crash ebbs, the cadaver has absently taken hold of my cock, my hand is atop her head, I am so close to both women that Ginger's foaming breasts are just above my eyes, I am feeling the pulse of their orgasm, as consumptive as the throb of a jet engine, feeling it with a humility and a respect and a jealousy that are heretofore unknown to me. Flushed, Ginger stares blankly at me, her dark brown eyes rimmed with black, until she focuses, turns instantly to stone, and snaps, "*Can't you relax?*"

Ginger's question, I confess, threw me. Men went to whores, I knew, for many reasons. My own research—that which I'd seen in the waiting room and heard through the walls—suggested that the majority wanted to enact self-flattering fantasies of power: they were tough and aggressive, such johns, they liked to be told how Big It Was, and how it hurt but, oh, it hurt good, baby, oh, oh, etc. Ginger's blunt question, therefore, was simply amphetamine-fueled irritation with me for not being able to *get into it*—to act like a john.

Unlike Sinclair or Michelle, however, Ginger was incapable of certain subtleties of understanding. Thus she was unable to imagine needs beyond those of the john genus with which she was familiar, and certainly not my own—which I now, analyzing my surprise at her question, understood to be nearly the opposite of her experience: whereas Ginger's typical john sought to distance himself from women by punishing them, I wanted to belong to women without them punishing *me*.

This was why I couldn't relax: I'd been confronted by the spectacle of that which I wanted, and could not have. What caused me such a pang of longing, upon seeing Ginger and the cadaver fucking so intently, was the recognition that their ability to do so derived from a special camaraderie. Working in a whorehouse—wasn't it like being a soldier? You and your buddies were thrown together beyond the perimeter of civility, every encounter was a test of fire, and only personal and collective valor kept you alive. Whores, like men who together endured combat, might know each other with an intimacy born of the extremes of experience, and when they came together it was with a complexity of understanding and hard-won maturity— indeed, with grace. Yes, I was envious. I envied, not only the guts and wisdom, but the sense of community that enabled the profundity of their coupling.

And I envied, too, how easy they seemed to be with sex, their workaday normality. What I understood in this stunning moment was that, in the course of my experience, I'd unknowingly conflated these longings, so that what I wanted was to live normally and unthinkingly in an unbroken condition of fearlessness, with an identical other. And though I'd convinced myself that, doing what I was doing, this was the case, the spectacle of Ginger and the cadaver showed me otherwise. One gained a certain community, a certain condition, through the assumption of risk; having not done so, I was entitled to neither, and here—in an intimacy that was beyond me— was the proof. Ginger's question struck me to the marrow. I could not relax because, though I had, repeatedly, walked right up to the line of transformation, I remained afraid to cross it. And challenged, unstrung, for one brief instant beyond caring, I snapped: I found it in myself to act on impulse, to do as I felt, for me, for no one else but.

I took one of Ginger's nipples into my mouth and sucked.

It is worth reflecting, for a moment, on the nature of pure action, and its aftermath.

There are those who believe, and I am one of them, that acting on impulse accrues strength and power to the actor. Such purity of action, however, must be consistent, so that each success builds upon the last and opens the way to the next. Impulsive actions undertaken by the preternaturally hesitant, conversely, often end in disaster, as they spring from frustration and are devoid of judgment. To those who suggest that the essence of action is judgment's absence, I would answer that only the habitual self-gratifier has the wisdom to know when to hold back. The habitually hesitant has no such wealth of experience. When he lets his arrow fly, it goes wide of the mark.

Ginger clawed at my head, rearing with such force that the dildo shifted violently in the cadaver, causing her to shout and buck free of the shaft as I fell against the fattish girl, nearly knocking her to the floor. Ginger drew back, hands upraised in the manner of a pianist's poised above the keyboard—except that she seemed ready to bring her talons down, not upon the eighty-eights, but yours truly.

"I, uh, didn't," I began.

"Don't even try, motherfucker," voice acid-etched with hatred.

Motherfucker. I sighed at the irony as the girls got to their feet. Too late, I understood the impulse: to receive the gift of nurture from a woman, as unequivocally as suggested by this particular mother-and-child reunion. It was an expression of my desire to reclaim my innocence, to find the kind of love I'd yearned for as a youth, before everything changed. But as I sat up and put my head in my hands, feeling the women's hostility beat down on my back like rain, I understood that my method was, in contemporary parlance, inappropriate. This I had not realized: that even on drugs, even in a whorehouse, one can act inappropriately. One does so, in this situation, in the same way as in any other: by permitting one's actions to transgress the boundaries of another's humanity.

I stood, the girls surrounding me with wary authority, like prison guards. Ginger unbuckled her dingus, let it slide to the floor, and stepped out of it.

"You want to see another girl?" she asked, still tundra-cold.

The money, the drugs, the night itself: all were gone. I shook my head.

"Get dressed. Someone'll come back for you." The girls stepped into their heels and fled, so anxious to get away that they barely bothered to cover themselves. I heard the contemptuous murmur of their voices as they rapped off down the hall.

What, I'd wonder after the night's last session, as I struggled into my clothes, what do I do now? I'd begin these nights with a fantasy of myself and a vision of my mission. But when it was all, all over, and I apprehended my blanched and sagging visage in the guilt mirror, I would be left, not with what I'd fantasized or learned, but with what I was: a junkie. That was not an identity that permitted much in the way of a future.

And yet this could prove the most useful part of the experience, as I would have to deal with the world from the perspective of my condition. Given that I'd be absolutely shattered, facing a daunting range of challenges, this was not so easy. Yet to do what was necessary to change would require a toughness that I did not believe that I possessed, a toughness equal to my wife's. There was no better place to look for it than in the ashes of the night.

Hearing, for the last time, the rapping of the heels, I began composing myself. It would require everything I had to make it home, but I was ready, ready as I'd ever be.

The door opened and, to my surprise, Ginger appeared. She was, I could not fail to notice, naked—more naked, it somehow seemed as she faced me frankly, than she'd been previously. Shame, however, had inoculated me against such blandishments. I smoothed my jacket with shaking hands, then folded them before me, as resigned as a fallen preacher on the way to the gallows.

Quickly, Ginger began stalking around the tiny room, straightening the sheets with a violent snap, banging the ashtray into the trash and, pointedly, snatching up my empty gram packages and licking them clean. At this— dreadfully—my interest began to rekindle. Ginger was attempting to make me feel like the baddest of boys, to inspire a degree of contrition sufficient to compel me to do "anything" to make amends. This meant that she proposed to hustle me. An offer would follow this dumbshow.

The pump primed, Ginger strode up to me. Her fury seemed to increase a notch, as if in direct proportion to her self-disgust at what she was about to do.

"You got any more blow?"

I shook my head. Ginger's hands went to her hips, she clicked her tongue contemptuously. A yawn seized me, and I convulsed with the attempt to suppress it.

That got her in gear. "You want to score?"

"Off you?"

"I'll give you an address. You go and get a gram, bring it back. You smoke?" Crack, she meant. I never had, but I nodded. "Bring it back and we'll do it. You and me."

"In a session?"

Ginger's eyes were focused on some indeterminate point on the wall. She put her hands lightly on my chest and leaned in; I could taste her sweet breath as she spoke. "I'll suck your cock without a rubber, the other girl and me'll—"

"I go down on you?"

She nodded, eyes still on the wall. Ginger was lying, though I didn't much care. The fire bell had clanged, I was stomping in my stall. And yet my high had waned sufficiently to make a space for hesitation. We were heading toward noon, in my book the very worst time to find yourself getting stoned: it meant that you were in danger of blowing an entire *second* night. It was, most certainly, time to go home.

Feeling my ambivalence, Ginger turned her head and, still with her eyes on the wall, kissed me. It was, despite the ocean of bad faith in which we swam, a pretty interesting kiss. At first she only brushed my mouth with her own. Then she nudged me more firmly, enough for me to feel the texture of her lips. Finally, our tongues moved languidly against one another, like a pair of snakes getting comfortable on a hot rock. Elsewhere, the traffic abated, the waiting room radio was switched off; the kiss sustained its cool through a sudden, startling quiet. It was as though we were the only two people in the world.

Ginger withdrew and looked at me, thumbing a bit of moisture from my cheek. Yes: her kiss held sex, freedom, the joy of dissipation, in a restrained balance, but it had spoken above all of realism. Certainly, Ginger hated me as much as she had ten minutes ago. But she was an addict and a whore, she knew what she wanted and what she needed to do to get my cooperation. I nodded; I understood. We were who we were, and we had things to do.

I watched, my eyes tracing the elegant line of her flanks, as Ginger bent over the night table and wrote down an address. My acceptance seemed blessed by the light, the quiet, most of all by Ginger's classical beauty. The situation neither frightened nor depressed me.

Ginger handed me the paper and I stared at it, eyes narrowing, widening; I was, I realized, swaying slightly. "You go down Sunset," pointing at the paper with the look of a terrorist forced to entrust a dangerous mission to a neophyte. "When you get past Vine," Ginger continued, then looked at me. "You know Vine?"

Annoyed, abruptly, by this nursemaiding, I pushed aside Ginger's rudely pointing finger. "I know Vine," I said. "I get the picture."

The location was that transitional zone known as East Hollywood, a neighborhood that mixed faux chateaux with motel-style structures set back from parking lots. The bleak promise of these latter places troubled me. Their balsa-wood doors bore the marks of irrationally expressed anger, a hole where the steel toe of a boot went in, a dent from a fist; behind their sagging curtains, mercy was a scarce commodity. I could find myself mounting poured-concrete exterior stairs, knocking twice lightly and, perhaps, scrambling on the carpet with the taste of blood in my mouth, before my eyes could adjust to the dark.

I said, "Who am I meeting?"

"Tiny. I told her you wanted two."

"You did, huh?" I looked down my nose at the woman cooly. I was a little sick of her machinations.

"O*kay*?" she said, with her signature pissiness.

"Who's Tiny?"

"What?"

"You heard me," I replied, our bickering taking on a familiar, marital cast.

Ginger had hoped to finesse this one. But she could see that I wasn't going to walk into anything without information.

"A transsexual. Pre-op. She's weird," Ginger admitted. "You okay with it?"

I confess that when Ginger described the person I was about to do a drug deal with as weird, it gave me pause. My Judeo-Christian upbringing had instilled in me the concept of *Judge not lest ye be judged*. But I would have been foolish not to think and think again about meeting someone a woman as weird as Ginger thought was weird. Still, quite apart from my sober commitment to further derangement, I was curious. In the netherworld, I was no longer such a tourist.

"Yeah," I drawled. "I'm okay."

My partner gave me a sidelong glance, then kissed me quickly. "Come straight back," she said.

In the waiting room, Wendy, the last girl remaining, lay dead asleep on the couch, face mashed and damp, a child in a fever dream from which there was no awakening. I made my way past her and down the stairs, pushed open the heavy gate and—some fourteen hours after my adventure began—walked out into a Los Angeles morning.

XXXX

I felt myself flung into the brute chaos of the city. Through clouds of exhaust, I beheld a warping vision: acre upon acre of motionless steel, a traffic jam nearly Godardian in its proportions. I had a ticket, of course, a summons that, as I wobbled to the curb with the caution of a Wallenda, became two: one for an expired meter, the second for parking in a traffic lane (for which miraculously I had not been towed). With unresponsive fingers I worked the car keys from my pocket, squinting myself nearly blind against the insult of the glare. Suddenly I felt it, as though the door to a forge had fallen open: *the heat.* So aggressive was the burning poltergeist that it left me terrorstruck, I staggered back alarmed; the amphetamines clutched and squeezed at my heart, my throat, the sweat slid viscously down my bottle-green flesh. A motorcycle rolled past, between lanes of autos still as gravestones, the cop astride sizing me up, deciding. There is nothing like the threat of arrest to deliver that all-important tool of the actor, motivation. I plucked the tickets from beneath the wiper, snapped open the door smartly, turned the key in the ignition.

The natural and man-made environments now conspired to extract a punishing toll. So dormant was the traffic that it took me five minutes to pull out of my parking space; the Nissan's transmission bumped and strained, I had to throw it into neutral and cut the A/C to keep the cheap piece of junk from burning up entirely. The cloth seats, fire-hot, turned black with sweat as the grams and humidity emptied me, I could feel myself beginning to panic, the anxiety of confinement, whipsawed by my fears about the car, the police, the outlaw times I would shortly be having with the hopefully-not-ironically-named Tiny, undid my reason completely. Here, now, I would have a heart attack, a stroke, I would begin to scream and never stop. I emitted hysterical peeps, of the sort released by mourners when, at graveside, they are attempting to control their grief.

Fifty-eight minutes later, I pulled up across the street from Tiny's (having stopped to withdraw $1000 from an ATM, an act of which I had no memory), and fell out of the car. I had traveled, perhaps, three miles. The trip had escalated from hysteria to hallucination, an urban collage I did not experience so much as witness, like an actor who appears to be driving, but is seated in a prop car before a rear-projection screen. It was a transit entirely different from the one that had brought me to the whorehouse. Then, I had charted with detachment the journey from hope to desperation, to get myself in a mood, become a certain kind of player in a highly particular place. By mid-morning, however, I could not have been more genuinely desperate than I was. Detachment—editorial, ironic, or analytic—was inconceivable.

Thus was this second drive constituted out of absences. It combined withdrawal, an out-of-mind condition that provided enough distance to keep me from cracking up, with a physical auto-pilot, in which my nervous system used the memory it had compiled during half a decade of LA driving to follow the best route to Tiny's. I was abetted by the East Hollywood landscape, a catalogue of brand names that, on this infernal morning, blazed with such ferocity that they seemed to be decorating the main drag of hell. It was these to which my nerves responded: they formed a cultural third rail that, by delivering a steady current of low-grade reassurance, kept me on track and moving forward.

Escaping Sunset, I'd headed north to the next major crosstown road, Hollywood Boulevard, comparatively traffic-free. I went east, crossed Vine, and within a few blocks—once I'd passed Gower Gulch (onetime gestating ground of the low-budget Western, now a mini-mall), the Old Spaghetti Factory (and whether the adjective reinforced the product or the plant I could not ascertain), KTLA-5, with its antiquated broadcast tower (original home of Warner Bros.), and crossed over the arroyo through which the Hollywood Freeway fumed and raged—the corporate-America montage began to play at the wrong end of the telescope that constituted my vision. I passed Arby's Roast Beef, Midas Muffler, 7-11, Denny's (then Fluff'n'Fold); Home Depot, the Wherehouse, Carl's Jr. (then Tae Kwon Do Museum); Pep Boys, McDonald's, Savon Drugs, Thrifty Drugs (then Food 4 Less, No Membership Required); I turned the wheel and pressed the pedals, the movie in my mind made a right and got back to Sunset, now changed: plazas and centres, Dental Arts and Auto Parts; and now I was passing the Bucharest Market, where despite the million-degree heat it was winter in Romania, women in woolen kerchiefs and sweaters and heavy black shoes from which their feet overflowed as though squeezed from tubes; nude, nails, dialysis, tacos, 99-cent, babaganoush; another right and I sensed the movie coming to a close, the coin in my private nickelodeon running out; cypress, palm, magnolia, pine, Now Renting, All Utilities Paid, courts, manors, empty bird cage gnarled in the street like a squashed Calder, smell of fabric softener ventilating from basement laundry room, jalousie windows, Astroturf stairs, my nickel ran out, my time expired, I was at Tiny's.

The drive, on which I had been, essentially, a passenger, had rested me, or so I believed. My near-collapse upon exiting the vehicle, however, suggested otherwise. The supreme physical effort required to execute the trip had taken everything I had, and now, finding myself *not* home, *not* twenty stumbling steps from a short explanation, a shower, fifty glasses of water and sleep, but facing new social demands (meeting Tiny), new mathematical braintwisters (counting money) and, of course, a new crime, followed by *more* driving, whores, carpet-munching, narcosis—facing all this, the trip's restorative results vaporized and I melted down as cleanly as a sand castle struck by a wave. Stumbling back, falling back, I plastered against the side of the car bonelessly and lay there, as depleted, I was sure, as an organism could be while still laying claim to life. I felt the desolation of the cop who, having just finished dealing with the aftermath of a terrorist bomb, hears another explosion.

Drugs, I thought. *Drugs.* If I can just peel myself off the side of the car and score, they'll pull me together, like a fillip to my blood sugar, like food. It was that, I thought, raising my head from the burning car roof and surveying the street (noting the trio of Craftsman-style bungalows near the corner, fine examples of the genre), or spend the rest of my life stuck to my Nissan like a wet towel. I checked and rechecked my pockets, I reread the scrap of paper I found there and stuffed it back down deep. I made sure I had my keys in my hand before I locked the car door, I put my keys away and took them out and looked at them again, I looked at the helicopter that swooped and whopped over my head, searching, I was sure, in response to my wife's demand for an APB, I took out Tiny's address and reread it, I had forgotten it in the fifteen seconds since I'd last seen it, that smeary little scrap to which I clung as though it belonged in a reliquary. Then I crossed the street, moving with the slow, robotic unnaturalness of a Claymation Godzilla who has eaten one too many Japanese.

Tiny, it transpired, lived not in Motel Desperado but a Bazooka-pink bungalow not much bigger than a dog house (I wondered if Tiny were named for *it*). My diminutive connection awaited me in the doorway, she took one look and rolled her eyes. "You want two?" she asked. I nodded, gape-mouthed, dying. In response, Tiny looked unaccountably pissed—were all women pissed today, I wondered, even the fake ones? And what the *fuck*, I thought garrulously, was *she* staring at, this doll-like Filipina with tits and (presumably) a dick? "Let's go," she said, putting on lipstick the same shade as the house (and her angora jumpsuit) and grabbing her keys.

"Where?"

"The rock house."

The *rock house*?! "Don't *you* have it?" I sobbed. "I thought—"

"You want it or not!"

I shut up and looked contritely at the junked Hyundai on her front lawn, a lunch box with tires that, next to the house, seemed as big as a stretch limo. Tiny took my hand and we walked up the street, past people who sat on their lawns and stared at us openly, the incredible spectacle of a drenched, middle-aged maniac and a transsexual midget, out for a stroll. We covered half a block, Tiny pulling me in a huffy silence, before it occurred to me that something was off.

"Where are we going?" I managed to ask. Tiny simply looked madder, she chuffed and fumed like the Little Engine Who Could. "Is it in walking—"

"We're gettin' in a cab!" she yelled.

Again, my mind italicized. A *cab*?! In *LA*? You didn't *walk to the corner* and *flag a cab* in *LA*. And—I almost laughed—even if there were freely circulating taxis in Los Angeles, what driver in his right mind would stop for us? Surely, I thought, there was a cab *stand*…But no. We reached Sunset and, before my violently resisting eyes, Tiny stuck out her tiny hand.

This was the limit. Of everything that had transpired during the half-rotation of the planet since I'd left home, this was the most bizarre, it made not even the slightest gesture toward a governing body of knowledge.

"Tiny," I croaked, "there are no cabs in Los Angeles."

Tiny ignored me, eyes barely visible behind Jackie O-sized shades as she scanned the dense, steady traffic. For laughs, I watched the faces of passing motorists, which returned, with their expressions of grave shock, a precise reflection of the image we presented: they first slowed, then sped away, as though avoiding a particularly grizzly traffic accident. I looked back at Tiny and found her mute and stiff as Barbie, arm up, expression fixed, stirred only by the wind of passing cars. I thought: *I will be here forever*.

In response, a cab pulled up, South Asian behind the wheel, the only guy in LA who didn't know he wasn't supposed to be doing what he was doing. We got in, nyah-nyah music on the radio, reek of car deodorizer, Tiny snapped out an address, she turned to me and stuck out her hand. I gave her $200. Tiny's eyes rolled and she fumed again, she jabbed herself and mouthed, silently, "Me! Me! Me!" I threw her another $60. The rest was for Ginger: I was going the whole route, no doubt about it.

We stopped, Tiny told the driver to wait, she leapt out and stalked like a little volcano into the middle, not of a rock house, but an auto-repair lot, a pink-clad figure with big hair amidst mounds of agonized fenders and mute stacks of tires. Immediately Tiny began screaming at a trio of Hispanic grease monkeys, who first stared, then exploded with laughter. One was her connection, it seemed.

Watching this, sitting primly with the equally unruffled driver (who clearly assumed that missus, with her excellent temperament, did the negotiating in our family), I began to reflect on the nature of reality, and how it gladly suffered the committed fool. I could see, not merely how people got into messes like these, but how welcome it was to remain in them. The ludicrous escapade with my director, the nervous breakdown engendered by a Nissan hatchback—all this passed, in my life, for normal, and every second was luminous with pain. Whereas here, in the mysterious taxi, observing a transsexual yell at a garage mechanic while I awaited the arrival of my drugs, everything seemed so peaceful. Perhaps the simplest lessons take the longest to learn, but as I sat there, I finally got it: if one's life isn't working, then it's the wrong life, and one shouldn't lead it. Better to go with the flow, and forget the world's opinion. The world, after all, had seen it all, it was not going to be surprised by anything one did. It was why, when I lost every illusion and began to deal realistically from my depleted state, I started to do better. Being a whoremonger and a junkie, apparently, suited me more than being a husband and screenwriter—indeed, when I put it that way, it didn't even seem strange. Why not accept it?

No lifestyle, of course, comes without penalty. Sure enough: the moment Tiny produced my cash, the mechanic I'd pegged as her source punched her, with a downcoming right that popped her shades like a lightbulb. Before her ass hit the blacktop, he'd snatched the money from her hand and they were strolling away, this Wild Bunch minus one, back into the garage's inky depths as Tiny wailed like a baby, the other mechanics and bodywork guys watching impassively.

That, as it were, was my cue. The driver looked at me, a changed man: however little he knew of our customs, he seemed clearly to apprehend that auto-shop disputes were not settled by intra-gender fisticuffs. I told him to wait. Then I blinked the trash from my eyeballs, climbed out of the car, and commenced my Sergio Leone walk toward my fate.

The wrecking crew obviously assumed that Tiny had come alone, and my appearance threw them off-stride. But only for a beat: I was not, I knew, an especially threatening figure, and sneers began quickly to play about their oil-smeared lips. Even Tiny, scrambling hysterically on the ground, launched a series of warning looks that would have been overstated from the seventy-fifth row.

It wasn't her honor I was defending, however, but my viability: if I let the theft pass, I would never again take myself seriously in such a situation. Luckily, I was too exhausted to feel fear, indeed I did not even especially care about the outcome; and my fatalism, along with an overall lack of affect, played as unnerving cool. I could see my opponents' bravado congealing as I came closer.

Passing Tiny, I leaned over and, without breaking stride, took a snaggled shard of metal from the pile of fenders. Thus armed, I stepped into the shadow thrown by the garage roof and stopped, waiting for my eyes to adjust before I spoke.

"That's my money," I said, looking with blink-proof orbs directly at the guy who'd thrown the punch. "Let's have it."

The mechanic took a step toward me, and I pivoted slightly, setting up the first stroke of my makeshift sword. However muddled my mind, my nervous system was thinking clearly, and it stopped the man cold.

"*Fuck* you, maricon," he said, too loud, juicing himself up. "Take your pussy boyfriend and get the fuck outa here. 'Fore I *kick* your ass."

"Try it," I replied, staring with my fixed and dilated cocaine eyes.

Now the others stepped forward, warily. I was, after all, armed, drug-crazed and effectively in the right. "Get the fuck outa here, man," one said, his tone placating. "This a place of business."

"Give me my money," I said, "or I'm gonna start swinging this."

At the edge of my attenuated peripheral vision, Tiny writhed imploringly, attempting to get the mechanics to back down. Her connection looked at her, something intimate in his glance, and I had a useful realization: she'd sucked his cock. As the look quickly became furtive, I understood equally that this remained a secret, one he did not wish shared in present company. I narrowed my eyes merrily and grinned (a la Sinclair). *I* was not the maricon in this drama.

That ended it. Without a word, the guy threw my money on the asphalt and walked away. I picked it up, tossed my weapon back on the pile and, pointedly turning my back, took Tiny by the bicep and walked her to the cab.

I opened the door and Tiny sprang in; the instant I settled myself beside her, she pressed her face against my shoulder and began to sob. "I cannot be a party to," the driver began, but I cut him off with a gesture. My eyes closed; for an instant, I actually dozed. Opening them again, I found the driver staring at me, anguished, in the rear-view. If I did not do something, we would all be here indefinitely.

I slipped an arm around my cohort and tilted up her chin with a finger. Tiny, a bruise rising beside her eye, looked at me with childlike dependence.

"Where do you live?" I asked her (having forgotten), voice barely audible.

She murmured the address and I repeated it for the driver. "Know where it is?" I asked.

"Yes! Yes!"

I nodded solemnly, though this Talmudic gravitas was in fact the drooping of my chin from fatigue. "Go there," I intoned.

The cab started forward; my arm still around Tiny's shoulders as she snuffled and swore, I gazed out at the wastes of Sunset Boulevard; the horrific seesaw of anxiety and depression at last began to abate, and I started to feel more normal. It was as though, having leapt into the night's waters in my own skin, I'd emerged finally as a man comfortable on the far shore of the underworld; and the ease this delivered relaxed me to the extent that I allowed myself to be a little outré. I'd been idly looking down Tiny's semi-open top at her breasts, which seemed to comprise half her total body weight, and found myself attracted to this chromosomal centaur, half-trapped as she was in the body of a man; turning toward her, I slipped my free hand between her legs and fondled the confused cornucopia I found there. Tiny looked at me gratefully—she needed a little positive reinforcement right then—the cabbie nyah-nyahed along with the radio, we caught the lights. At long last, I was good with the situation, it was precisely what I'd been seeking. I was completely myself, and completely in control.

XXXX

And with just such a mixture of relief and release would my experience come to a close. Typically, I'd drive out to the beach, stopping just past the 405 to call home and explain to my hypervigilant wife that, after a drive that had taken me almost to San Luis Obispo, I'd dozed off in a roadside parking lot and just awakened. My profound exhaustion, which expunged the anxiety from my lie, made me credible—credible enough, that is, for my wife's own credulity to make up the difference. Near-hysterical but mollified, she'd accept it, even take it well; I'd apologize for having frightened her. Did she have a ride to Al-Anon? Good. In future, I promised, I'd try not to tie up the car.

And yet however suave my handling of the moment might be, the need for it—for the lie, and for its acceptance—mooted everything. Hanging up, returning to the car, I'd be swept by a sense of hopeless so consuming, it would take everything I had to turn the key in the ignition. In the course of a night, I'd be exposed to every manner of human behavior, I'd gain insight, even revelation. All it took to blow it away, every bit of it, was my wife's approval. It was the most profound of the night's truths: Despite all my exertions, I remained trapped in my pathology, I could not change. Thus it was that every experience ended with a consideration of suicide.

This is not a confession published posthumously. I came close, though, once; very close. I'd traveled the length of Wilshire to Ocean Drive in Santa Monica, where the boulevard that divides the city ends, at the bluffs overlooking the Pacific. There is a park strip there, and even on the stickiest days it retains the capacity to soothe. A path, edged by a wood-slatted fence, follows the contours of the bluffs; from its vantage points, the eye travels north along the coastline to the canyons that terminate the Santa Monica range, or else southward to the honky-tonk pier, with its slowly turning Ferris wheel like an upside-down bicycle tire. There are eucalyptus that quiver with squirrels and crows, flower beds, lawn for those who eschew the benches, temple-like structures open to the sea. Most charmingly, one sees all kinds: individuals seeking beatitude in meditation, groups picnicking extravagantly, all the classes and races.

Yet there can be a coldness about the place, literally when fingers of fog comb the treetops, but atmospherically as well. Parking the car that day, crossing the street, I felt it sharply as I walked northward and encountered the shade of the town's irreplaceable bard, Raymond Chandler. In the thickening swirls of mist, I saw ancient men agog in wheelchairs, heavily robed, tams arranged crookedly on their translucent skulls—the sort of men who, in Chandler's oeuvre, are referred to as "the Colonel"—being pushed by mute muscle boys or mannish dames, deferential and, behind dead eyes, scheming. I felt the coldness again as I settled on a bench and considered the family of Russian émigrés, seated in the grass in their plastic shoes, all of them smiling gamely at this pretty, end-of-the-world place, smiling to drive off dislocation and loss. I had, I realized, always experienced a certain melancholy here, which I'd laid to the sense of conclusion that comes with the continent's end. But that day, alone on a bench, hearing the creak of wheels as menace-shrouded spectres rolled past me in chairs and sons of Odessa spoke in voices which seemed to shrug and shake their heads, that quality of conclusion felt more final. We had come to this public sanitarium in the hope of feeling better, and were instead infused with the outcome of all human endeavor. We had found, in the land of movies, THE END.

Gazing at the broken fence rails, feeling within and without me the overwhelming presence of death, I understood that my bad character had beaten me, I had not beaten it. Rather than responding to my wife's crippling manipulation by leaving her, I had anesthetized the pain; rather than using what I'd learned from drugs and whores to change, I'd become addicted to the lessons. Rather than ending my misery, I had doubled it.

Feeling all this, at that literal and figurative end of the world, the deep desire for a true end overwhelmed me. For how long had I despised myself, for how many years had I been sick and tired of my evasions and lies? And for how long had I wanted, so desperately, to just switch it all off?

I stood up, walked to the fence, and looked down. I estimated the distance from where I stood to the Pacific Coast Highway below at about 75 feet. The drop, however, was not sheer: the vegetated bluff flowed outward, I could not simply lean over and let go. This upset me, I almost sobbed, thinking Not even this goes right, but I shook it off, I found the resolution that had, more often than not, eluded me. I spotted a declivity, a crease in the hillside that might enable me, if I climbed to the top rail and propelled myself outward, to plummet straight down to the blacktop. I focused on the fold and made for it.

Coming toward me, trotting pell-mell on the path, was a dog. It was a West Highland terrier, spry on its stumpy legs, its facial fur short enough to reveal the breed's blank yet friendly expression, that endearing mixture of befuddlement and cheer. I barely registered the animal's presence: having reached my destination I owned an athlete's focus on pure action, on stepping up, bending my knees, and flipping into oblivion. I put my hands on the rail, elbows extended outward, and prepared to lever myself into position.

The Westie broke into a run, its round black eyes on me, a ball of some sort gripped in its teeth. I scanned the area for an owner, and it was perhaps the fact that I did not see one, combined with the urgency of the dog's approach, that compelled me to hesitate. The animal seemed as intent on getting something done as I was, and its objective clearly involved me.

Abruptly the dog was upon me. Still in my fugue state, I watched as it dropped the oddly-shaped ball and looked at me, tail wagging slowly, almost thoughtfully, it seemed. How sweet, I thought, this friendly critter, carrying none of the complexities of human misery in its soul, sees only a man—a friend!—and, in the wise way of the dumb animal, reaches out. There was a catch in my throat at this, I mourned for a nanosecond all that I was bidding a fond aloha, farewell, sweet dreams.

And then, repositioning my hands on the rail, I took a second look at the thing the dog had dropped, and realized that it wasn't a ball at all. It was, in point of fact, the severed head of a dildo. Someone had been roistering too strenuously, broken his or her tool, and the dog had picked it up (drawn by God only knows what scent).

The Westie sneezed with glee, tail switching madly; and I understood that I'd stepped into my own version of a Bergman film, in which I am visited by Life, not Death, and he comes, clad not in black and bearing a chess set, but disguised as a dog with a broken sex toy. I nodded, dryly, and the Westie brightened, it positively lit up. "Yes!" its expression seemed to say. "You thought I was an icon of purity and you have been confounded, I am a disgusting dirty joke, one you can perhaps uniquely appreciate! I am your version of existence, a fuzzy ball of sentiment wrapped around a nugget of perversion! Ha! Don't go!"

I rubbed the dog's head and put the boot to the slobber-covered glans, which bounced away, Life tumbling after. It was a moment that seemed specially crafted to appeal to the darkly comic sensibility that had arisen from my experiences. Whether or not this rose to the level of "sophistication," I couldn't say; but what seemed indisputable was that, while my life might make me incrementally miserable, its admixture of elements gave it a savor that, *enfin*, made it worth living. It was true as well that the dirty joke, its maudlin wrapping concealing a nasty surprise, delivered a message: to sentimentalize my unhappiness with considerations of suicide was to be as dishonest about my longing for death as I was about everything else—which suggested that, if I went through with it, I'd be making a mistake.

Thus it was that I stepped back from the brink. Exhausted by the thought of going on but with the crisis passed, I returned to my Nissan, unable to imagine what I might do but willing to see things through, at least for a while.

It was precisely that failure—of my imagination—that goaded me into true and lasting change. Getting in the car, I recalled another morning, on which I'd attempted to get a rise out of a whore by tormenting her, and in the most infantile ways: sniffing her armpits, poking my fingers in her mouth. Seeing her woe, sorry for the both of us, I abruptly lay back and blurted it all out, my unhappiness, my desperation at being trapped in cross-addiction. The girl remained silent; but later, as she let me out, several others at her back, said, "We'll pray for you."

I thought, at the time: Have I fallen so low that *whores* are praying for me? But later, and on other mornings, I thought about those words, about the power and inde-structibility of faith. In the transit of my addictions, I experienced a heartsore melancholy that felt like mourning—I presumed, for my wasted life. Yet as I repeated my experiences, I began to see that this was less addiction than striving, and that I was mourning, not the lost years, but my inadequate imagination. I had imagined my way into a situation that would enable me to tell myself different kinds of stories—the Wendy story, the Sinclair or Michelle story—stories with meanings and outcomes that delivered different kinds of illumination. But was this really so different from the life I'd lived pre-wife, when I'd fantasized that I was another Miller or Mailer, screwing my way through New York womankind, in pursuit of satori? My new existence was more extreme, perhaps, but as an act of creativity it was regressive—*that*, rather than my wasted life, was what broke my heart.

Of course, I reflected that near-death morning, as I pointed the car toward home, an inadequate imagination and a wasted life were not unrelated. My unwillingness to do a certain kind of work on myself blunted my creativity—as an inventor of new stories *and* new selves—caused it to collide repeatedly with the lies by which I persisted in living.

And yet, I wondered, as my car passed under the 405 and into the logjam of Westwood, if the whores could pray for me, could I not pray for myself? This inadequate but nonetheless illuminating life I'd invented *had* taught me some things, one in particular: I was doing a version of that for which I'd always criticized my wife. She did not really want to do the hard work of change, I believed, and so had remained in therapy for decades, re-raking the same old ground, kidding herself that, if she'd yet to change, it was only because she'd not had the right kind of "breakthrough." Was I not, with my endlessly repeated, near-identical nights, doing the same thing—continually rephrasing the question because I didn't like the answer?

Drugs and whores constituted my own brand of home-grown analysis; and what became increasingly apparent, as I re-raked my own terrain, was how deeply embedded was my need for approval. I saw that with the advent of my time in Los Angeles, this need had burst like a psychological appendix and contaminated my entire emotional life. Indeed, I felt increasingly—consumingly—*invaded* by the desires of everyone I encountered. It was one thing to have shaky boundaries; it was quite another to be, as I was, *porous*.

I knew this, of course, just as my wife knew what her own problems were; but—as she could not *feel* her knowledge without the repetitions of therapy—I did not perceive the size of my struggle to draw a line between myself and the world *while still remaining human* until I watched myself dramatize that struggle in a whorehouse. Every girl presented me with a chance to be as giving as I wanted so desperately to be, and without vaporizing—to be, as I was with Tiny, completely myself and completely in control. And the more I repeated the experience, the more I understood both its difficulty and potential.

So I found myself challenged, and I understood where the knuckle of that challenge lay: in the meaning of the night's inevitable conclusion, the call to my wife that restored the status quo. The dread that my revealed self would be unacceptable—that compelled me to seek my wife's effective forgiveness—could be described, very simply, as shame. Shame was the demon I did not wish to confront.

And yet, as my problem became ever clearer, I became privately—murderously—obsessed by my shame, and my inability to conquer it. Cocaine killed shame, but not lastingly; it might lead one to the water of one's nature, but could not make one drink. This conundrum—that I could not unify the halves of myself, that I remained *ashamed*—maddened me. I would ask myself Ginger's pointed, penetrating question: *Can't you relax?*

No, apparently. Not yet. But I could pray for myself. This was the place to which I came that day, as the Nissan bucked and sputtered up the street; as I lumbered down the courtyard path, to shower, drink Brita water and go, in the afternoon, to sleep. There was self-hatred, hopelessness, a longing for an end, but there was something else, too, there was a spark to the challenge, there was—yes—faith.

It was decided. Until I had a more imaginative attack, I would go back, I was not done, far from it. There was murder, not suicide, in my damaged heart. It would murder me, or I would murder shame.

THREE

Finally I murdered shame by embracing it.

Six months had passed, approximately, since my first whorehouse visit, and the experience had become routine. Indeed, an apathetic somnambulism had oozed its way into every part of my existence. As my wife and I no longer had a struggle to keep us close, our dealings were cordial, remote: she enjoyed Al-Anon, I my drugs and girls, and the pursuit of our separate programs (each cloaked in anonymity) left little to discuss. Though it remained my intention to reinvent my fate, this aspiration became something to which I paid little more than lip service. It was analogous to my professional desires: though I was going broke and not writing, I remained optimistic that "something would happen," one of my scripts would sell and joy would reign. Thus was a lack of realism spread over every part of life.

Occasionally—as it did on the cool late-winter evening that changed everything—my epidermal apathy would peel back, to reveal the unpretty facts of my condition. Driving down Sunset, I found myself, not pondering the iconic Hollywood plummet from hope into desperation, but cursing the traffic and checking my watch. Where the *fuck*, I thought, was everyone *fucking* going on a *Wednesday* fucking *night?* Why did everything have to be infused with this infuriating overlay of control?

Pulling up before the whorehouse, I thought of a meeting I'd had the previous week. The producer was intelligent, well funded, open to ideas. Yet the moment he opened his mouth, I began disagreeing, turning a potentially productive alliance into a misery of ping-pong. Finally, the guy sat back in his chair and smiled. "Why are you fighting with me?"

"I'm not fighting—"

"Yes you are, you're *still* fighting. You're fighting about fighting with me."

I smiled back, unable to offer a response. But not for the lack of one: my conviction that my environment's assertions of control had spoiled everything, my aggravation at nothing ever going my way, had left me a reflexive mechanism of disputation.

Well, I'd fucked *that* up, I thought, walking up the whorehouse path. Hands in my pockets, checking to make sure the drugs were in place, I elbowed the bell, then shouldered open the gate as the buzzer rattled. It was remarkable, I considered as I mounted the stairs, how that disputatiousness—my belief in the inevitability of disap-pointment—had made it impossible, really, to feel.

Such were my thoughts when the door opened, and I found myself face to face with a man.

The guy was about my height—medium—but skinnier, with thinning hair roostered upward, a row of poorly capped incisors, and body fur that stopped at the base of his neck only because he shaved it. Naked, I knew, he would resemble a man in a bear costume without the head on.

"Ever been here before?" said the guy, voice syrupy with insinuation.

"Yeh."

"Who'd you see, man?" I caught the edge of the habitual stoner's whine.

My hands were still in my pockets, and like a customs agent with an instinct for the smuggler's guilty tell, he glanced at them. I was glad that the coke, which by now would usually have rendered me speechless, didn't seem to be working.

Holding his eyes, I answered the question: "Wendy. Sinclair. Bonnie, Linda—"

"I get the picture." He sneered, revealing the pimp's contempt for his patrons, his own professional tell. Without turning his back, the guy stepped aside. "You're in," he said.

I walked past him into the waiting room. It was like entering a habitually unruly class during a visit from the principal: I found Sinclair Windexing the coffee table, Wendy emptying ashtrays and Ginger, of all people, running the vacuum (as well as an appealingly pissy Latina I'd never seen before, swiping tendrils of cobweb off the ceiling with a broom). Treating whores like maids, I knew, amounted to especially cruel punishment. I felt their hair-trigger fury, a twin to what I'd left in my car.

Perching on one of the cleaner but no less ratty chairs, I was startled to find, opposite me, a fifth girl, seated with lowered head on the loveseat. I couldn't gauge her appearance, however, in part because the lamp, behind her, flooded my dilated pupils, more pointedly due to a cascading, glaringly fake blond wig that covered her completely. Oddly, though the girl was idle, none of the others' hostility seemed directed at her. This I laid to the likelihood that her weird presentation inspired, not resentment, but sympathy.

Ginger cut the vacuum, and the stereo, playing Donna Summer's *Last Dance*, reasserted itself. The girls took seats but, shifting from a janitorial staff into objects of desire, they ground the gears: Ginger, who could smoke a vial of crack without breaking a sweat, wiped her flushed face, and Sinclair sniffed at her hands.

I pretended not to notice, and this small mercy had almost restored the groove when the pimp leaned in, presumably to make sure his chattel had assumed the position. Irritated, I tongue-clicked and flopped in my chair. This moron was cramping my style.

He didn't take the hint, though (or, good narcissist that he was, didn't notice). Rather, the pimp once-overed the room, rolling his eyes at the vacuum.

"Don't leave that there when a guy comes in," he said to Ginger. She shot her eyes at him murderously. "*Don't* look at me like that. Get it outa there."

Ginger rose with elaborate precision and picked up the Eureka Mighty Mite. As she walked past, he gave her a relaxed crack on her perfect ass that smacked of droit du seigneur.

Ginger turned, slowly. The pimp folded his arms and lounged against the wall. "Something wrong, babe?"

"Big time."

The pimp laughed, silently. He nodded at the vacuum. "Cut the radio when you're running that. Waste of power."

"And you don't got power to waste," Ginger snapped (making me smile). She strode off down the hall and, after tossing me a laconic "Enjoy," the pimp followed.

"*What*," I said. "An *ass*hole."

"There is nothing worse," declared Sinclair, "than a bad manager." We all nodded: as usual, she'd hit it on the head. "I mean, look," getting up to get an ashtray. "Five girls, nobody working. Know why?"

As she paused to light a Merit, the Latina supplied the answer: "Cause a guy don't wanna see a guy when that door opens, and they all took off." Adding, bitterly, "Never to return."

"Ed," Wendy croaked, invoking one of the departed. The others looked glum. Whoever Ed was, he'd be missed.

"Not Mikey, though," Sinclair said, gripping my chin between thumb and index finger. "Nothing stops Mike," she leered, "when he's on a *mission*."

"It's certainly not to his advantage," I said, biting her wrist (to make her let go).

"See, Mike, that's just it," Sinclair said. "He doesn't care."

"He has to bend you to his will," the Latina snapped, folding herself into a tight origami of resentment.

"Bob," Wendy foghorned, drawing, from her sisters, audible moans of despair. Despite myself, I smirked: I'd come to get laid, and wound up at a Sicilian funeral.

Ginger returned, as ever as perfect a product of the Mediterranean as a ripe olive, and silently took a chair. No comment necessary: her je m'en foutisme said it all.

We sat there and burned for a bit, in a silence loud with grievance. Seeing my own feelings on every face in the room, I had an epiphany: I was attracted to prostitutes because their emotional lives were identical to mine, we had all been traumatized by the destruction of our belief systems by those to whom they'd been entrusted. The girls' traumas (I knew by now) had been experienced in childhood, mine was the product of marriage, but the result was the same: we had lost the hegemony over our dignity that is every creature's right, and our bitterness arose from the fact that, no matter how much control we might gain over the externals, it could never restore what had been taken from us.

Considering this, I again forgave my wife for her interminable psychotherapy: it had taken me multiple whorehouse visits, after all, to understand why the idea of control was so important, and so useless. I had dwelled among the whores long enough to know that their default equation—taking from a man without giving him anything—did not compute. Now I saw the hopelessness of my own variant of this endeavor. By controlling the kind of sex I had, I hoped to achieve emotional satisfaction without paying an emotional penalty. Looking at myself and my companions, I was reminded—in a way that only repetition could have taught me—that the antidote I'd chosen was as pointless as the anger it was meant to cure.

"So, Mike," Ginger said, bestirring herself from the communal reverie. "Who you want to see?"

Ordinarily, it would have been Wendy, but—either because of the coke, which I realized had been overcut with some blunting toxin, or the fact that Wendy, in the decomposing teddy that seemed to be all she owned, seemed so sad—I could not decide. I looked from face to face and back again, the idiocy of my grin increasing in direct proportion to the girls' annoyance with me.

I found myself turning toward novelty: the pissy Latina. "I don't think I know your name," I said.

"Angel."

"Jessica."

The second pseudonym had emerged from beneath the polyester wig. I looked at the girl, a little surprised (I'd begun to fantasize that she was artificial, placed there to fill out the room), and realized that she'd been, throughout the preceding dramatics, *reading*. There it was: a folded-over paperback, resting on her closed knees.

I blinked, rapidly, as much from amazement as the desire to see her face. The spectacle of a whore reading while waiting to be picked was so unusual, it nearly qualified as a manifesto. Viewed from this perspective, Jessica's bizarre peruke seemed an act of pointed concealment: the desire to see, given the statement she was making, who might be moved to peek in.

It was, at the moment, more than I could deal with. But something had passed between us. I saw that Jessica, unlike the others—unlike myself—had not let the situation squelch her nature; and she—with the slow, deliberate turn of a page—noted my recognition of this.

Then I picked Angel: big mistake. I laid out my habitual dozen lines, but she declined and, fearing a spot check from management (or so she claimed), insisted that I put away what I didn't snort. This meant scraping eight lines back into the package; then, as the stepped-on coke wasn't working for more than five minutes per hit, pulling out the leaky wad again and again, recrushing and cutting, etc. Plus, my paid friend proved standoffish: she would not let me go down on her, neither would she be fingered; I could not, of course, get an erection, and a dozen tugs of toothy head put an end to our escapade altogether. We lay side by side, staring at the acoustical tiles above us, I anxious, she bored.

And, not very secretly, satisfied: Angel, I could see, was taking out her anger at the pimp on me. This I found depressing: it was as though our shared trauma penned us in a behavioral ghetto, in which, instead of rampaging through our psychological equivalent of Beverly Hills, sacking the legacies of those who abused us, we looted our own storekeepers.

"Do you want," Angel said, "to see another girl?"

I sighed, aloud and unguardedly. "Pick me a couple of winners, Angel."

She was up and dressed in a jump cut. "I'll send

someone in," she said.

I noted the singular with rue: since Angel was not nice, I did not expect a good result. Yet as I dumped out an extra-large mound and started cutting lines—I didn't buy the business about the pimp, Angel had just been making my life difficult—I shrugged it off. No one was going to make much of a difference in my mood.

Then the door opened, and I realized that there is something to be said for having no expectations: it increases the pleasure of the surprise. The new girl—who had not been in the waiting room when I arrived—was in most respects Angel's opposite: petite, just over five feet, and with a vaguely crabby expression that owed itself, I guessed, less to disposition than an unlucky confluence of features. Her body, however, ignited in my brain the full panoply of potboiler clichés—jaw-dropping, brick shithouse, va-va-voom. A redhead—her fuscia bob broke just above her jawline—she owned the best of the breed's peaches-and-cream complexion, and this edible coloration overspread a form comprehensive in its near-perfection. Traversing the three steps to the chair on cork-soled platform shoes, her gently rounded calves quivered tantalizingly; when she turned, briefly, to peek out the window, I saw that the meats of her inner thighs tapered at the top, to reveal, just beneath her vulva, a diamond of light. The girl turned toward me, then gave me her back again as she set down her purse, showing the tiniest of G-strings, a mini-triangle of black held in place, it seemed, by nothing, and exposing a high, firm, faintly boyish ass, the twin creases formed by the bottom of the globes sweeping out, up and away from each other like wings. And when the girl kicked off her shoes, knelt on the bed and, setting her perfect ass atop her perfect calves, pulled off her tie-dyed tank top, the prize of prizes was revealed: a pair of perfectly circular breasts, capped by eye-popping (sometimes only the cliché will do) nipples measuring, I guessed, two inches in diameter, the enormous aureoles colored a rashlike red. Perfect, the girl was perfect; and this inventory of prime parts so delighted me, there escaped from my mouth the brief, embarrassing but heartfelt sentence, "Oh, boy."

The girl looked at me and smiled, smiled as though she knew me. I felt her body's compressed erotic energy. It was like a keg of dynamite the instant before it goes off.

I reached over, slipped two fingers beneath the eye patch at her pubis and, with a flick of my wrist, tore it off. I saw now what had held it in place: a pair of nearly invisible elastics, that twanged like guitar strings when they broke. This, I knew, was a too-aggressive move. But the girl had inspired the kind of warping lust that makes its own rules.

I hesitated, expecting an admonition. But she only clenched her ass slightly and showed her teeth, as though enjoying the elastics' sting.

I cleared my throat. "What's your name?"

"You don't remember?"

"We've met?"

"Before." I shook my head and shrugged. "I'm Jessica."

The wig! "*You're* Jessica?"

"You looked right at me."

"I couldn't really see you."

"You did, I felt," looking at me with eyes glinting.

"What?"

"See me."

There was a pause, in which I saw, with my own variant of Mr. Shakespeare's mental oculus, the word "beat." The word, appearing in a script, typically signifies a moment of subtext, in which what remains unspoken is so meaningful, it demands special acknowledgement. So it was now: *You are right*, said Jessica's beat, *I am in this situation but not of it, I have found a way to be in the world at its worst without losing myself, you saw that about me, I saw that you saw it.* Beat: everything two people can mean to one another, acknowledged in a caesura of silence.

I reached for her tits. There is no other way to put it. Without taking her eyes off mine, Jessica pulled back her shoulders, the better to meet my hands. Such girls, I knew, received an inordinate amount of devouring attention. Yet like the pimp's petty torments, Jessica took it in stride, it was all part of the job description. The independence I'd seen in the waiting room, the unwillingness to be controlled by circumstances, was something she'd extended to her body, she maintained its boundaries no matter what was done to her.

This intensity of understanding, which flowed between us as we watched each other—as I caressed her tits, my palms tingling—was the reason Jessica had maneuvered in to see me. I was certain of it: Angel hadn't just picked her. Neither, I realized, had Jessica been electrified by the current of *my* lust: feeling appreciated for the right reasons had flipped her own switch, more than business informed the calculus clicking behind those emerald eyes. Jessica wanted something; and as she laid one small hand on my thigh, she seemed to collect, mentally and physically—to prepare for her event.

"Are you an athlete?" I asked.

"I work out. But no. Why, do I..."

"You look—'great' doesn't begin to describe it. It's more your sense of focus."

Jessica laid both her hands atop my own, encouraging me to squeeze harder. "I'm not sure I understand."

I gripped her breasts tightly. Jessica held my wrists and gasped, eyes narrowing. "Do you watch the Olympics?" I asked.

"Sure." Breathless.

"It's like the moment before a routine. The ice skater or the gymnast. When you see them concentrate."

"Review all the lessons," she said, voice tight as my grip. "Before throwing them away and just *doing it*."

I grinned. "Exactly." And released her.

Jessica stroked the tops of her breasts, soothing them where I'd left marks. Then—as a kind of cognitive accupressure that distilled and released perception—she massaged her left palm with the middle finger of her right hand, a gesture that (I was to discover) accompanied many of her mental sortings.

"I'm an actress," in a cozy, resonant voice. "You're right, I treat this—it's kinda an exercise. You know: You have sixty minutes. These are the given circumstances. Here's your scene partner."

"And...*action*," she might have added. Jessica climbed astride me, I took her face in both hands, feeling the prominent points of her jaw. We were beginning in earnest, and though her desire remained as yet unrevealed, I knew precisely what I wanted: information.

"That pimp," I said. "He doesn't bother you?"

"Stan? He's not in that often." The T in the last word, pronounced, scratched at my ear appealingly. "From time to time he gets a wild hair up his ass. I read."

"That's allowed?"

Jessica grinned a rabbity grin, stroking my forearms as I caressed her throat. "He doesn't always see it."

"The *wig*..." I smiled. "It *is* like a tent."

"The wearable hideout."

I could feel the wet heat as Jessica leaned her hands on my chest and began to grind against me. I was surprised, but it made sense. How to assert the right to life in the face of soul-death: this question lay at the core of our common trauma, and my curiosity regarding Jessica's success at it was unmistakably turning her on.

"Only thing about Stan," Jessica murmured. "He 'samples the wares,' as we say."

"Isn't that sexual harassment?"

Jessica shot me an amused, slit-eyed glance. Her chin jerked rhythmically, beating time to her arousal's inner music.

"How do you deal with it?" I said.

"I detach," she murmured; then, opening her eyes wide, looked down at me drolly. "I do *this*," she said.

"Here you're the boss."

Jessica drifted in and out, chin jerking steadily, on the beat with the roll of her hips. "Guy like that," she said suddenly. "'Gimme a BJ, babe,' he says."

"A *BJ*?"

"'I'm the king, babe.' Elvis, he thinks he is. So you give it to him." Jessica looked at me lucidly. "You don't win with a guy like that."

"What then?"

"You make him dependable."

That hit home. I'd never been able to stop my wife's behaviors, but they were predictable. Rather than struggling with her intrusions, I'd do better to circumvent them.

"Then you put it aside," Jessica murmured. "Stick to what counts. *The work.*"

I'd heard that before. The charged phrase, the sharp way in which she spoke it, invoked the black-clad boho art girls I'd met in New York. True believers: sustained, committed artistic endeavor—"doing the work"—was all that mattered.

It had never occurred to me, considering Jessica's comment, that there were methods of winning other than getting my way. Yet even as a part of me opened to this with gratitude and relief (how different it was from the dead-end bitterness of the waiting room!), I could feel myself resisting the implication: that one's freedom remained encased in a larger enslavement.

"It can work for you," Jessica said.

I looked at her, startled. She'd read my mind. "How?"

"Better shifts. Flex time, in case I've got an audition." Jessica kissed my chest twice quickly; cantilevered over me, inches between our bodies, she watched herself in the mirror. "You'll notice *I* wasn't cleaning. *And* I didn't sign in."

I felt her thighs tighten as her thrusts became urgent. Even now, as she sprinted toward the precipice, I could not resist questioning her: "How," I gasped, "did you get in to see me?"

"Angel likes me."

"You're friends?"

"When she talks, I listen," she said in a slurry burst. "Sinclair—you know, right? No one's doing *her* any favors."

"She's that way with the girls, too?"

"Sure."

"What's her real name?"

"Patty."

"What's yours?"

"Jessica. What's yours?"

I told her. We were pressed together, I was nearly sitting up, Jessica's arms loosely enfolded my head. I inhaled the aroma of her hair, the humid zone of her bosom felt glorious.

"What about Ginger?" I said into her ear. "How'd you get past her?"

"Ginger's mostly gay. She likes to do doubles."

"And Wendy?"

"You saw."

"How do you know?"

"I watched you." The moment was at hand, and as her wet mouth covered my own, she said it again: "I watched you."

I held Jessica, my hands on her rounded, shivering back, and she came: quietly and breathing hard, as though her release was a wily creature she'd chased and caught. Finishing, she lay atop me, shivering as she recovered. I continued to hold her, my head filled with everything she'd said, wondering what was next.

Jessica pushed herself up and, still astride me, looked in the mirror, considering the effects of sex on her body—her mottled skin and swollen lips, the fuscia hank that fell across one eye—as though they were proof: that her belief in what she did was so profound, it had imprinted the terrain of her flesh.

"Do you always jump in like that?" I said.

Jessica smiled at me blearily, drawing the hair off her face with a finger.

"So many questions," she replied.

I smiled, blandly, and waited.

"Well, yeah," she said. "If I want to establish trust and, you know. A basis for continuing." The last of Jessica's post-orgasmic fog lifted, and she looked around. "May I do some drugs?"

"Be my guest."

Jessica climbed off me and knelt before the night table. She picked up the rolled twenty, then hesitated. "Also, you know"—she did a line, sniffed, then did another—"after I've been *handling* things all evening. It's like a sprint, that first one. Refreshing."

I took the twenty from her and did a line of my own. "So even if you've got control of the situation. You feel its effects."

Jessica looked to one side, thinking, then looked back at me. "Sure," she said.

We'd arrived at our first silence. The impatient idle of Jessica's engine, goosed by the drugs, filled the room. As for me, I was yet nagged by my resistance to her lesson, and wanted to confront her with it.

"Do you work a lot?" I asked. "As an actress."

Jessica shrugged, and I saw, in her gaze, the whiteness of mind that so often covers disappointment. "Mostly little stage-y things," she said, retaking the twenty. "But in a way, that's good, because my *ideal*. Would be to do movies *and* theatre." She snorted and sat back on her calves. "I have some friends and, you know. Everyone's an actor but also…"

I sighed. "Writing."

"Out of self-preservation," Jessica said. "So we do readings, and lately there's been talk of maybe formalizing it. Getting a space." She cocked her head and sniffed, gazing at the drugs dreamily. "To be part of an acting group that was really, you know. Committed…And we'd all keep it going with film money."

"Ah, youth," I blurted.

Slowly, Jessica looked at me, her smile tinged with surprise. I knew what she was thinking: she'd trusted me with her dream, and I had made light of it.

"I don't mean it that way," I said. "It's just I forgot what it's like. The hopefulness of having it all ahead of you." I reached for the twenty. Jessica stopped my hand.

"Don't do too much."

"Why not?"

"You'll lose it." I followed her glance to my cock. To my surprise, it was hard.

I felt the uptick in Jessica's drive as she stood, sleepy eyes glinting, and dusted carpet fibres off her knees. "Lay back, lay back," pushing me flat onto the bed and snuggling beside me, fist to temple as she leaned on an elbow. Jessica placed the middle finger of her free hand on my breastbone and massaged it, waiting for her moment.

"You're one of the guys who likes to play wise," she said mischievously, the words pouring out with the slow syncopation of clotted cream. "But the truth is, you don't even seem especially *mature*."

"Well," I said, "regarding my maturity, the facts speak for themselves." Jessica gave my breastbone an extra nudge. "But there are some things I've learned, and…" I thought for a moment, considering her. "When I was your age," I began, "the wise men around me said, 'Pay your dues.' I've never had worse advice."

"How is it any different from 'do your work'?"

"It was coming from guys who'd paid twenty years of dues, and had nothing to show for it except a lot of failure. I know, because twenty years later, I'm in the same position, and looking back, I can see it was a kind of treachery."

"What do you do?"

"I'm a screenwriter."

Jessica nodded: to those in the know, "screenwriter" was its own explanation. "What would you advise?" she asked.

"Make it young. There's always the chance you'll burn out or people'll get tired of you. But more likely you'll rise to your success and become a professional. *That's* 'doing the work.'" I turned on my side and faced her. "Make it young, because that excitement you feel is very hard to sustain, if at some point your dreams don't start coming true."

Our faces, our bodies, were very close. Jessica's eyes were downcast. "What did you mean," she asked, "when you said that professionalism was doing the work?"

"Don't bullshit yourself."

"About what?"

"Prostitution. *This* isn't the work."

Jessica considered me, searching for an agenda. "Did you bullshit yourself?"

"I got sidetracked by my fantasy of myself."

"Having that fantasy became the work."

"Yes," I said, and we looked at each other. This, I suspected, hit home for her.

"Do you think that's what I'm doing?"

"I'm not *quite* sure *what* you're doing," and we grinned, Jessica waggling her eyebrows wickedly. "I just sense we're similar. And…" I'd arrived at my question, the schism Jessica had created in my mind: the desire to be released from my anger, and my resistance to winning that release by accepting a larger imprisonment.

"Yes?" said Jessica, waiting.

"You're good at this. I mean you've really got it aced."

"And?"

"Is it really something you want to *get* good at? Why not leave, rather than putting the best of yourself into making it work?" I looked at her. "You know?"

My frustration had caused me to say this with some heat. But Jessica showed neither defensiveness nor hostility: she understood that I was, not berating her, but wrestling with the ur-question of my life.

Jessica turned away from me and lay on her back, staring at the ceiling as she again massaged her palm. "I'm not ready yet," she said.

Of course: One did not have to use one's knowledge until one was able to do so—indeed, to use it prematurely was to waste it. Right then, I understood: if I ever hoped to leave my marriage, I would have to prepare myself, emotionally and behaviorally; I could not change my situation until I changed myself. I glanced at Jessica, who was studying her hands. She was, to be sure, no more ready to quit prostitution than I was to part with my wife. But it was this understanding—that she could not depart before packing her emotional baggage—that had enabled her to do so well at the task that I, and her sister whores, found so difficult: being human without paying a penalty.

Abruptly, I remembered something. "'Cease to struggle and transformation will follow.'"

"Is that a quote?"

"A shrink of mine used to repeat it. He said it was a Chinese proverb."

Jessica turned her head on the pillow and looked at me. "Did you believe it?"

"I'm ready to believe it now."

There had been moments, such as the one with Michelle, when, positioned at the nexus of strong drugs and provocative sex, I'd been seized by a frenzy of emotion. Now I had arrived at a moment that felt the same, but I knew to be quite different. Here was understanding devoid of fever—insight that, if respected, might result in change.

Feeling the force of my belief, Jessica's own sense of moment, already at high idle, revved compellingly. "Have you ever," she said, holding my eyes, "been fucked in the ass?"

"Fucked in the...?" *This* was what she wanted?

"Have you? By a girl."

"Not by anybody."

"Tsk, tsk," said Jessica, enjoying herself immoderately. "What are you, forty? And never been booty-busted?"

"Who you callin' forty?"

"Want to give it a shot?"

"With what?"

"Show you," excitedly, as though talking about a new dress. Jessica rolled onto her back, reached down, and slid open a drawer in the bed. She fished around momentarily, then slowly raised her extended arm, stopping when she'd achieved a 45-degree angle. Caught between Jessica's middle and index fingers, pointing downward, was a replica of a five-inch-long, erect penis, crafted from some sort of creepily lifelike latex, and dyed a rich cobalt blue.

"Ta-da," Jessica sang.

"It looks like a dick."

"*No.*" Shifting her position, Jessica held the object, still downward-pointing, above my face. "Catch," she said.

Suddenly the dildo was in my hands. It was amazingly realistic: wide, thick and, for want of a better word, dicky. When I whacked it against my palm, it revealed a satisfying heft.

I glanced at Jessica, who watched me with a predatory sexuality that felt distinctly male, leavened by the humility needed to lay one's most private desires before another. In the silence, I considered how absolutely unreal this all seemed, yet how appropriate—I was in the right environment, in the right state of mind, with the ideal Other.

"It's small," I said.

"You haven't been fucked yet, and already you're complaining?"

"Well," I said, "size matters."

Jessica smiled tolerantly. "It's a starter dildo." I laughed, and she snuggled up to me coaxingly. "I'll do it real gently," with nursy reassurance. "Plenty of lube."

"*Oh.* I feel *much* better now."

"Tell me why you're hesitant. Are you afraid you'll become gay?"

I didn't reply. I was trying to figure out what it was about sodomy that she found so exciting. And she *was* excited: for Jessica, the prospect seemed to hold the same promise that cunnilingus did for me. What was clear, however, was that her pleasure's nature would only reveal itself in the transit of the act. Some things are beyond words.

I took Jessica in my arms, feeling the exquisite softness of her skin as I held her close. "Do you want to fuck me first?" she murmured.

I looked at her body, the warping lust overwhelming me again. "Let's do some 69," I said.

I lay on my back as Jessica put her knees on either side of my shoulders and lowered herself, as she sucked the head of a member than had become shockingly erect: her mouth moved imperceptibly, it was as though a wet, soft pulsing enveloped me, slid down my shaft and drew together an explosive tension in my balls. Her tits daubed at my stomach, her belly pressed my chest as I held the twin globes of her ass and ran my tongue in her; Jessica seemed to draw me in, I lashed my long muscle as she grabbed and gripped it, her fat and very hard, fully exposed clit bumping my chin.

Oh, boy. Dirty, filthy. My cock bulged like an overfilled sack of cement as Jessica wormed a finger into my ass—clever, sneaky girl—and began to palpate this nest of feeling from beneath, as her pussy Chinese-handcuffed my tongue, her hips began to thrust as I eased my own middle digit into her puckered bunghole, lubricated as it was by her spreading liquors, and Jessica came, barely moving as she thrust, releasing a "muh…muh…muh" before freeing my traumatized mouth, my stone cock and electrified ass, and falling sideways, stupefied, against the mirror.

It was smart of Jessica to give herself first, on my terms; by letting me get her off, she trusted herself to me before expecting the same. But it was unnecessary, and we both knew it: Jessica had what I wanted, and I was prepared to pay any price to procure it. Her mixture of openness and independence was precisely what had always eluded me; what was more, Jessica had achieved this state of being in a situation in which she was at the mercy of others who were, at the least, undependable and, at worst, amoral. She had even, I realized, as I watched her push herself into a sitting position, managed to use her circumstances imaginatively, to craft a scenario that enabled her to actualize, via the gratification of a profound turn-on, a vision of life.

That tied it for me: Jessica's imagination. Where I had stumbled frustratingly, she had triumphed. The struggle for approval, to keep control, to be myself while still being human by winning the world's regard while holding it off—none of it had worked. I felt ever more *invaded*: so infused with the needs and wants of others, I might as well have been a sponge.

Jessica's need was quintessentially invasive. But because her means of satisfaction didn't depend upon my destruction,

I saw that it might work to my advantage—my transformation. If in the course of playing my part, I could resolve my struggle the way she had—find a way to be in the world at its worst while remaining myself and not going dead emotionally—her beatitude might be mine, too. So I decided that, in the time remaining, I would give myself to Jessica entirely, I would take her request and make it my own transforming act of imagination, I would let her bugger me.

Because—I saw it clearly—*if I hoped to murder shame, this was perfect.* Having failed to avoid invasion, I would take the opposite tack and invite it, I would surrender ownership of my body in the way that a heterosexual male defines body ownership, I would invite humiliation and accept the world's terms and subvert its control by making the terms and the control my own. Instead of arguing with Jessica about whether or not it was better to resist a bad situation—rather than saying, as I always did, *no*—I would cease to struggle, and hope that transformation would follow.

Jessica followed my cogitations, a tube of K-Y in one hand, a pair of foil-wrapped condoms in the other. I found myself moved, as I often was, to wonder: Were all whores like The Amazing Randy? They lay in your arms, nothing up their sleeves—indeed, no sleeves—and presto! Prophylactics, lubricants, playthings. But I pushed these thoughts away. Seriousness might smack of pomposity, but equally did jauntiness feel like a dodge. I wanted to be present for the experience.

Thus did I decline any further coke, though I wanted a hit desperately. Jessica felt no such constraints. Emptying her hands into mine, she shook the contents of my package onto the night table and polished it off. Then she tore open one of the foil squares and unrolled the latex over her middle and index fingers. Kneeling on the bed, Jessica separated my knees, took the K-Y from me and began to unscrew the top.

Again I reached for her tits, those tits, but things had changed: setting down the tube, Jessica firmly grasped my wrists and crossed them above my head.

"Your hands are *tied*," she said.

I searched her eyes. Jessica's gaze was severe, but neither hostile nor threatening. This admonition was meant to make sure I understood: the drama had begun.

Again she took up the K-Y and lubricated her latex-wrapped fingers liberally. Then Jessica positioned herself between my knees.

"Wrap your legs," she said, "around my waist."

Of course: she wanted the experience of being a man. I encircled her waist with my legs, resting my crossed ankles on the high shelf of her ass. Jessica was looking at me, lips parted, breathing shallow. Whatever she'd expected, reticence or fear or equivocation, I had met her on the wire as an equal; whatever I'd anticipated, Jessica remained absorbed and deliberate. We were not there to impress each other. Or ourselves.

Digital insertion: Jessica entered me slowly, as—like certain exponentially increasing forces of nature—the effect of two fingers was greater than twice that of one. She pushed in to her knuckles, her other fingers digging into my flesh as she leaned over me; my belly rose to meet hers as her face loomed over mine. Jessica looked down to observe us fully united.

Abruptly her head snapped up, she looked me hard in the eye; fingers buried deep in me, she began to bang her pubic bone into the back of her hand, with a pure, free drive, unfreighted, it seemed, by a victim's history. Remembering Jessica's admonition, I "strained against my bonds," as they say in the bodice-rippers, grimacing as I gave in to the pleasure I felt despite my captivity. A silly act, but my own imaginative contribution: summoning the woman in me, who wanted to be tied up and fucked, permitted me to give up the control that had served me so poorly, in a way that felt safe because it wasn't really "me." For Jessica, too, it was an act, equally consuming: she groaned and sweated as she folded and unfolded, biting at my Adam's apple like a rabid cat. Finally, I closed my eyes, let my head slip to one side; I felt a flush go through me as, again, her mouth closed over mine.

Jessica withdrew her fingers and lay atop me heavily, the both of us breathing into each other's lungs. I caught a glimpse of my eye in the mirror: it was wide and wild.

I looked at Jessica's watch: we'd reached the eight-minute countdown. She saw me looking, looked at me; staring at nothing, I listened to the rattle of Jessica's harness as she stood and buckled it on. I felt the numbness one experiences on the brink of doing something, not merely out of character, but so in violation of one's nature that it inspires the belief that "things" will never be the same. And yet, beneath the anesthesia, I experienced a keen pleasure: it was like building a dam as a child, then watching as the stream eats away at it, the whole construction dislodges, and everything one has created is gloriously swept away. Watching Jessica's back as she fussed with something at her waist, I understood why it was that the destruction of one's dams seemed to provide more satisfaction that the building of them. It is the pleasure of watching nature take its course.

With four minutes to go, Jessica turned around, sliding the second condom over the plaster-caster's dream that stood out from her with the springy firmness of a diving board. Anatomically correct, it also delivered psychologically: not that it was long (though anything that is going to be inserted into one's rectum outside the confines of a specialist's office is, ipso facto, *too big*); rather, there was no pretending it wasn't what it was.

Jessica put one knee on the bed and, like a chambermaid about to flip a mattress, tucked both hands beneath my back.

"Turn over," she said.

She wanted me face down. So be it. Everything, I realized, had been leading up to this moment. It was appropriate that salvation should surprise me at the end of an angry night, on which it seemed that nothing could get through to me. It was my reward for having put in the time—for showing up, as my wife might have put it. Jessica was my double; yet had she appeared two months, or even two weeks, earlier, I might have lacked the wisdom to embrace her. I might still have been too afraid of losing all that was not working for me.

But now, as I turned over and lay my head sideways on my folded arms, I was ready. And if that numb bit of distance enabled me to think, It's nothing, in my heart I knew: this would change things. Not sexually: after the months of extravagant deviance, the taboo barely registered. No, it was the commitment to Jessica—the certainty that we were, if only in the space of these rooms, becoming entangled—that was momentous.

Using a flowerlike wad of tissues, Jessica cleaned her fingers; then, climbing onto the bed, placing her knees on either side of my hips, she reached for my wrists and, crossing them at the small of my back, held them in one hand.

"Ready?" she asked.

I nodded, my face half-buried in the pillow. She lay the head of her apparatus against the pinched mouth of me.

I could feel myself pucker against it, but that was an involuntary reflex; I forced myself to relax. The door had opened and, whatever it took, I proposed to walk through it. Jessica entered me gently, waiting until I relaxed into one step before taking the next; but she drove the last distance sadistically, with the velocity of a guillotine. I shouted, ripping my hands free and grabbing the damp, soiled pillow, my eyes squeezed shut as Jessica collapsed atop me, her back humping as she jabbed me again, gripping my wrists with amazing strength, with *my* strength, it seemed. "Oh," I blubbered, looking up from the pillow, trying to meet her eyes in the mirror. But Jessica was watching herself: she had the look of the brute, all cruel pleasure; but also the inward, dreamy gaze of the hero, one who has indulged myriad permutations of savagery in the pursuit of victory, seen her terrifying pronouncements go unchallenged, take on the sanctity of law. I saw the face of conquest, saw it as the bar set high; for, before all else, it was a conquest of oneself.

Jessica raised her hips and drove into me again, groaning with pleasure as I bleated and shook. I wondered: Was it her humanity she'd conquered? Did Jessica's true pleasure derive from the infliction of pain? I didn't think so. There had been nothing about Jessica's behavior throughout the hour that seemed insincere, as though she were setting a trap for that most hated of beasts, Man; and even now, as she nearly split me in two, there was a tenderness in the way she nuzzled my ear, ran her chin over the back of my neck. Jessica was enjoying herself, this was not a whore's revenge, at least not the conventional kind. The truth was that Jessica had sought a purity of sexual pleasure; and because she'd seen and felt that purity only in the drives of men, she'd re-sexed her own desire and found ecstasy in enacting the masculine part. Jessica's allure had turned her sexuality into a prison, and so to escape it she'd written a script that stripped that sexuality of pain and restored its freedom and dignity. That was her conquest: Just as Jessica had maintained her focus in the crushing circumstances of whoredom, she'd reclaimed the joy of her sexuality despite the experience of having it used against her. This was, of course, the ultimate assertion of life over death, the powerful motor I'd felt racing the moment she'd appeared. With pain-glazed eyes I gazed at the reflection of her ass as it pumped and stirred salaciously, my head sloshed with her pleasure-sodden moans. Jessica was not ready to leave because she was still stocking her emotional storehouse. That was the work, and it was worth doing: without it, there could be no other.

As she drove and drove at me, and pain began to be joined by an extreme of pleasure, I thought of Wendy: of how going down on her had been the key that turned in my lock, and how the experience encouraged a similar release in her. Buggering a man turned an identical key for Jessica and, like Wendy, I too was receiving a benefit. I'd always defined love as "giving" myself, and yet I'd struggled to maintain boundaries because of my propensity to become my partner's emotional prisoner; I did not want someone to really "get" me. But Jessica "had" me now, with each of her strokes I felt those boundaries shattering; and what I was discovering was that, rather than enslaving me, the experience imparted an unexpected power: the sense of relief—of release—that arrived with the laying down of the burden of self-defense was unspeakably satisfying. The source of my shame, I saw, was my failure to successfully protect myself—and, ceasing to protect, the death of shame transformed me. I did not feel owned; I was not a slave. I was free.

I gasped and groaned but we were moving together, Jessica and I, like a pair of spooned adders, we moaned together in our blessed release. Jessica could not imagine how grateful I was to feel shame shatter, to feel the shattering, too, of the carapace of anger around my heart, the undamming of the river of generosity in my spirit. And perhaps I was wrong about her too—could we ever really know how the other person felt? What was unmistakable was that we'd been brave, and the result was an extreme of sublimity, the recognition of which inspired nothing short of love. Yes: in the final tick-tock of my transforming hour, we loved each other, Jessica and I; and when the rapping of the heels and the quick double knock ended things (just in time, for the agony of this medieval proctology was threatening to nudge aside the benefits), I went home and—despite the coke and a lifetime of dedicated insomnia—went to sleep. My last thought, as I fell into oblivion, was that Jessica was the partisan come to life—the defender of hope that had survived within me.

XXXX

The first thing to go was the coke, followed by coke's pimp, drink. The latter proved tolerable; the former, far from it. The craving would persist for a year. What I came to understand was that the physical anxiety was an intensity of mourning, for the counterlife, the body freed to chase inchoate need heedlessly. Having cauterized shame, however,

I no longer felt so oppressed by judgment, and the removal of coke's raison d'etre compelled me to remove the drug as well. While I still felt guilt, anger, remorse, these became aspects of a free nature rather than its jailers, and that was fine. I needed to formulate a picture of my life that held everything, a picture that was real.

Clarity, alas, delivered bad news: I hadn't been paid in years, and my addictions had cost—I blanched when, sitting at my desk, I did the math—nearly $30,000. Confronting my bank balance on the same morning I tabulated my tuition fees at Whore U (punctuate to find the still-unanswered question), I called my agent, hoping the town's touts had upgraded my rating from "nonstarter" to "worth a look." No luck. "We really are trying to get you a job," he said, with his usual bulletproof self-satisfaction. Hanging up to the sound of golf strokes in his mind, I turned in my chair, my office crowded with truths long held in abeyance. First among them: I needed a new profession. Second by a nose: I had to get out of town.

The question of what to do with my life proved more sobering than sobriety. Reluctantly, I faced up to a fact I'd kept even from myself: the idea machine in my brain had fallen silent, killed off by the capriciousness of Hollywood, and the emotional catastrophes that had irreparably damaged the equipment. This recognition was sufficiently traumatizing to drive me to the window, to face a squirrel so stuffed with avocados, it resembled a fur volleyball with head and tail. The beast's rusticating complacence, so typically LA, offered a segue to my less overwhelming problem, relocation. The plan had been for two years. Now it was nearing five. If I did not just pack up and go, I might be here forever.

The same might be said of my marriage, which was problem number three, and inextricably braided with the relocation issue. I exhaled sickly through the window screen; the squirrel, scenting my anxiety, waddled discreetly down his branch as I returned to my chair. What to do about my wife was the gun that had been drawn at rise and now, in act three, was presenting its trigger. Yet though the problem looked the same, the soil in which it was planted had been many times turned over. I had been away, as it were, and though my new knowledge had neither been fully processed nor put to use, it had impregnated my nature. More interesting was that, subtly but undeniably, my wife had changed. Having raced unimpeded through the initial wilds of Al-Anon, her transit had ultimately described a circle, passing through ever more familiar stations, to arrive at last at the one from which she'd departed: The Past, where her issues, rusted into immobility, blocked the tracks. This outcome, after half a decade of meetings, finally began to break down the furious, offensive defense that had enabled her to survive, but prevented her from living. My remoteness abetted this: Encouraged by the fact that expressions of self-criticism, voiced typically at dinner, passed without hostile rejoinder, she began increasingly to probe the limitations of her methodology.

My wife's utterances, dropped like stones into the pond of our evenings, could be startling. "I'm a slow learner," she said one night, and we laughed. On another: "It's so difficult, you know? This resentment whenever I feel like I'm being pressured to *do* things for people." And, from a woman whose credo, it had always seemed, was "Why act when you can talk?": "I've been thinking of taking Prozac. *Any*thing to get un*stuck*."

I was indeed only half-listening. But it was not lost on me that both of us, in our programs, had confronted the same condition: the long-term ravages of misguided self-defense. Our discovery, moreover, was coaxing us toward that most difficult of truths: that loss was inevitable when one lost control.

This softened my hostility toward my wife; more usefully, it eased my attitude toward myself. I had taken Jessica's lesson to heart: I could not leave until I'd packed my bags. For so long, I'd felt that every minute I stayed with my wife was a reproach, to my manhood, dignity—the paradox being that, as my marriage made me *look* so bad,

I'd become paralyzed by what I perceived to be the world's judgment. Of course, as I'd learned on my adventure with Tiny, the world could have cared less. But it was Jessica who showed me how counterproductive was this auto-flagellation: it did not promote change, and depleted my self-regard.

In fact, Jessica had revealed herself to be my therapist (though our hours were not, alas, reimbursable under the Writers Guild health plan); and as with any therapeutic relationship, I proposed to take what I'd learned "in session" and apply it to my life. Looking out the window, seeing my wife, her busy face florid and streaming, smile up at me as she returned from her run, I considered that this meant avoiding the anger and accusation that produced false drama and were their own wrong end.

I began that night at dinner. I'd squandered the afternoon phoning my remaining contacts, prodding them unsuccessfully to help me find attachments (actors, director) for a script, and felt arid with resignation.

"What," I said, "am I going to do now?"

"You'll try something else," said my wife, mopping up the viscous pool at the salad bowl's bottom with the end of a baguette.

"I don't mean about the script."

"What then?"

"My life. What am I going to do about my life?"

My wife sighed, her eyes mournfully bored.

"Every career has its ups and downs, I know that. But this is…" The admission was difficult. "On a very basic level, this isn't working anymore—I mean really *not working*. I can't just keep doing it."

Whether or not I'd intended to bake a needle into this cake, I couldn't say. But my wife felt jabbed. She inserted the dripping wad into her mouth as though stuffing a sock into a mouse-hole. After an epic mandibular battle, she swallowed hard and spoke. "Have you looked at *why* nothing's working for you?"

"Practically," not taking the bait, "I've got enough money to last about another six months." My wife looked at me with surprise (and for good reason). "Whatever my feelings about the movies, I need to generate some income. I can't do it here."

"Where did your money go?"

"It went to life, okay?" I answered disingenuously, defensively. "I haven't worked in an age, I never intended for things to go on this way." I could feel the outrage in my eyes, fueled by the furnace of self-pity; I heard the note of blame. I took a breath. "I don't mind having spent the last two decades writing unproduced screenplays," sticking to the facts. "I would mind *very* much if I spent the *next* twenty years doing it." Better.

"It's the business," my wife replied.

"And I am *tired*," I said, with an edge that, it seemed to me, was appropriate, "of being at the mercy of everything. To the extent that I can, I want to control my life."

"You know," my wife said sharply, then stopped. She shoved back her chair and went into the kitchen, returning with another heel of bread, which she tossed into the salad bowl. "Instead of trying to *control* what you can't *control*," she said, screwing the bit of baguette into the dressing's dregs, "why don't you look at *why* nobody wants to work with you."

"Why, in your view," I said evenly, "doesn't anyone want to work with me?"

She mouse-holed the sock of bread again, licked her fingers, spoke as she chewed. "You fight with *everyone*—"

"I make *every change*—"

"Every *change*?" she sang derisively. "You think Bob, Irving, they don't feel your hostility? Oh, yeah, in the end, you do it their way, but it takes three times as long because you make everyone's life a living hell first." A few drops remained in the salad bowl. My wife picked it up and drank from it, banging it down savagely. "Irving's made fifty movies, he's a *two-time Academy Award-winning producer*. He doesn't need your shit."

Listening to this diatribe—accompanied, as it was, by a Breughel-esque display of appetite—I felt a complex of emotions. My wife was, of course, voicing sentiments I'd recently admitted to myself. Yet she was doing so for her own strategic reasons—she'd seized upon my desire for control and twisted it, entangling it with the pernicious brand of control manifest in my reflexive naysaying. Thus—unconsciously, diabolically—my wife was trying to control *me* by recasting my desire to control my fate as professional self-destructiveness. What was more, she'd amped up the horrorshow of her manners, to bait me into criticizing her, the better to accuse me of dodging the subject.

This amounted to precisely the sort of false drama I was seeking to avoid. Yet, to my surprise, my wife's response provoked in me, not anger or despair, but tenderness. Here, nakedly displayed, was the problem we shared, that of misguided self-defense. No less on display was its poignant motivator: the fear of loss. My desire to leave behind that which had stopped working did not end with screenwriting, and my wife knew it. And so her attempt at control: to avoid losing, however unsatisfying it might be, our marriage.

"You're absolutely right," I said, setting down my fork. "I have fucked things up royally with my shitty attitude."

"*Fin*ally," said my wife.

"But as you say, I do eventually come around to doing it their way. I find the confluence of what they want and what's personal to me."

"You and your fucking confluence."

"But you know," I continued, "it doesn't do any good. In the end, it's another six, eight months of work, thrown on the pile and forgotten." My wife looked at me; I met her eyes. "I don't want to do it any more."

She returned her gaze to her empty bowl. On her face was neither anger nor disappointment but uncertainty.

"What will you do?" she said.

"For the time being, what I did, I guess."

"You're going to throw away a career as a *screenwriter* to write *car* brochures?"

"It's strange, I know," I said, still looking at her. "It's just very, very strange to consider a life without the movies."

"Then why quit?"

"Because there's something missing," realizing it as I spoke. "I know movies really well, I know what *quality* is. Nothing excites me more than experiencing it." I was thinking of the final moments of Fellini's *I Vitelloni*, in which the protagonist, departing his hometown for good on the train, imagines his conveyance passing through the bedrooms of his sleeping family and friends. I'd recalled the scene, I assumed, because it was just such a moment of quality. But as it played in my mind, I saw that I'd reached for it for a personal reason: it was what I was experiencing at the moment. I was departing the village in which I'd dwelled for all my life, that of the movies; and the sleeping figure to which I bade farewell was my own creative ambition.

"I know quality," I repeated, clearing my throat. "But when I do the work, that quality is not present. I don't have what it takes to do what I love—that's why I'm failing. I simply need to move on."

The moment was a delicate one. My wife could choose the status quo, by again marshalling her manipulations. Or else she could, in the words of my philosopher shrink, cease to struggle, so that transformation might follow. I waited while she chose her course.

"Well, I'm sad," she finally said.

"Me, too."

And that was that.

Yet the grace with which we'd managed to proceed expanded the moment's possibility. My wife seemed to hesitate, then decide. She moved closer to the table, sat up straight and—I had never actually seen anyone do this before—wrung her hands.

"I'm thinking of going to school," she said.

I stared. She'd trumped me. "To study what?"

"Writing."

Once the surprise subsided, this drew from me a smile of philosophical rue: even as I was setting down the mantle of a dream, my wife was picking it up. I was surprised to find my generosity of spirit so quickly—immediately—put to the test.

But if I expected her to avoid self-serving manipulations, especially of the jealous, resentful kind, I had better learn to do the same.

"Where do you want to go?" I asked.

"Uch. Who knows? I was thinking I'd apply for a workshop residency."

"Good idea," I said. Instinctively I felt my wife would benefit.

"I mean I have no." She shook her head and exhaled. "I don't know if I could get in. I just think, if I were someplace I had to *produce*..."

"Do this," I said, charged. "Go to the library, look up the different programs around the country—I'm sure they're listed. Do it right away."

My wife lowered her head. She had the look of a dog that has sensed that you wish to pet it, and is trying to tell you that this will be answered with a bite.

"Look," I began.

"I feel judged."

"It was a suggestion."

"It feels like pressure."

This was my wife at her worst, or the way I least liked her: pigheaded, retreating into the arrogance of "feelings" to avoid change.

"If you can't talk to me," I said, "find someone you *can* talk to. Don't just *give up*."

Abruptly my wife sobbed. "I have so much anxiety about the things I want."

"Everyone feels that."

"You don't."

At this, I could barely find the wherewithal to laugh.

"How do you deal with it?" she asked. "When you're writing."

I leaned back in my chair. "How do *you* deal with it? When you act."

"I suffer."

"But you *do* it. Because you *have* to. Two things I've found—"

"Oh, shut up." We smiled. "What, what."

"You learn by making mistakes. You have to be willing to make mistakes."

"What's the other?"

"If you can't do something that scares you, you can't do anything."

That was as far as we got—the phone rang and, grateful for the interruption, we both lunged for it. But something changed, between my wife and I, as a result of that conversation. Neither of us felt able to state it. But we understood that, if we could manage to avoid old habits, the marriage, against all expectation, might have a future. Alas, it was equally the case that—if my wife and I chose to be true to whatever truths we uncovered—the future might not be a thing we shared. Thus was our optimism tempered by the awareness of where it might lead. Inevitably, in the days that followed, she and I drew back a bit, poignantly like new lovers who find themselves confused by the emotions they've released. But we did not forget our discovery. What we had now to do was more of what we'd done: talking, and listening. The paradox that we might discover an intimacy the result of which would be divorce was something we'd have to accept.

Yet loss was not the whole of it. The benefits derived from my time with Jessica made me anxious to return. But before I did, I had an experience that reinforced what I'd learned at the big hands of Michelle: if I could not change my nature, I could change the way I felt about it, and thereby change my life.

It began with a supernatural occurrence: a call from my agent with good news. A director had been sent a script of mine by a producer, this director had actually read it, and now wanted—astonishment of astonishments—to have a discussion. I had, of course, kissed off the movies. But once again the cessation of struggle had brought transformation to my door, and it would have been a break of faith not to let it in. Plus, I was curious about the director, who'd had an unusual career, on stage and in TV as well as the movies, both here and abroad. So I agreed.

Martin—the "helmer" in *Variety*-speak—had been in residence at the Chateau Marmont for nearly a year when I arrived at his suite. His choice of meeting place surprised me—the initial powwow typically unfolded around the producer's table—but Martin didn't drive, and so it proved easier (and shrewder) to have the world come to him. Whatever the benefits, the concept of surviving in Los Angeles without wheels—especially given my own troubles in this regard—seemed amazing, and I asked him about it even as we shook hands.

Martin smiled as he closed the door. "Well, I learned to drive in Ireland, when I was a boy," he said very quickly, in a low, theatrical purr burnished by thirty years of Havana smoke, "but had three accidents in two days, so I decided to give it up."

"What happened?"

"I tended to aim at the car coming toward me," Martin said, walking to a baronial armchair and gesturing me toward the sofa. A tall man, possessed of a sullen handsomeness, he moved with an attention-getting deliberation that seemed at once practiced and offhand. "Did the same thing as a kid, when I played ball," settling into his throne, taking up an unlit half-smoked lonsdale. "Leaned my head into the pitch as it arrived at the plate."

Martin grinned with a mix of mischief and merriness, inviting me to participate in the comic-poignant adventures that comprised his life. "Do you want something," telegraphing his lack of enthusiasm, "coffee or posh water or…"

"I'm fine."

"Good," sounding relieved. "Because they probably wouldn't send it."

"Why not?"

"Well, when I'm *working*," purring swiftly, "*they* pay. Whoever 'they' are. But I haven't worked in six months so"—he paused to relight his cigar—"'so *nobody's* paid."

"How much do you owe?" I asked, caught up in his

elegantly cheeky mood.

"Oh…" He glanced at me with invitational lightheartedness. "About $70,000."

As we ho-hoed lustily at this, I looked around Martin's digs. He was residing in a Hollywood variant of Machu Picchu, a railroad of rooms overgrown with scripts, books and videocassettes, through which professional vegetation glinted personal accessories: gold fountain pens, marquetry humidors, mille fiore paperweights. Martin, too, was accessorized, with suede gaiters and an ostrich-skin watchband dyed a shrill red. Yet like his arresting walk, all of what had once undoubtedly been cultivated now seemed of a piece, and this was instructive. Like myself, he was professionally on his uppers and in rough financial shape. But this had not stopped Martin from doing what he did or, apparently, being who he was—indeed, everything about him seemed designed to buttress this individuality. Martin had turned his vulnerabilities into advantages, and one sensed that, once, those vulnerabilities had been formidable.

This gambit's value was obvious: the question of his commitment to himself long settled, Martin remained free to focus on work. On a desk the size of a rectory table, a script page sat in a typewriter carriage. Beside it, I saw a collection of Hemingway's Africa stories.

"What are you working on?" I asked.

"A thing that might go in Kenya, if we can cast it and get the money, which of course we can't get without a cast."

"Is it based on the Hemingway?"

"No, it's an original, not mine, good script, not all there. I've been fixing it up. Does this bother you?" Martin asked, displaying his cigar.

"It will if you don't offer me one."

Martin blinked, not getting it for a moment, then laughed, bizarrely—a grin, from which emerged, as though over-dubbed, a disembodied *Ah. Ah. Ah.* He got up and surveyed a collection of boxes—calculating, I could see, which stash was the least expensive.

"Unless," I added disingenuously, "they're fifty dollars a cigar."

"Well, they're from Fidel's little island," Martin said, retrieving a walnut-colored corona and feeling it judgmatically for plugs before handing it over.

"Where do you get them?" I asked.

"Place in Geneva. They take off the bands and ship them with a manifest marked, oh, 'Nicaraguan leaf. Rolled in the Netherlands.' Then a few days later the bands arrive."

"Do they fit?"

Martin grinned, settling back into his chair. "Not always." He reached for a vintage Pelikan. "Give me your address, I'll have them send you a catalogue."

I complied. Martin's way of life, like Martin, was seductive, and the thought of converting to it—to living *my way*, and letting the world fall in behind—was appealing. Striking a cedar match, I held the flame in place and took a puff. "So," experiencing a sense of well-being unlike any I'd known, literally, in years, "if you get the money, you'll do it?"

"Depends," Martin said. "On cast. They want such-and-such and I want so-and-so."

"Can you do it with such-and-such?"

"No point," crossing his legs, flicking a dust mote off a shoe. "Listen, at this point, I just want to work on my own things, or other people's if they're of quality, like yours. But it's got to be *right*," with quiet force. Abruptly Martin shifted uncomfortably in his chair, as though constrained. "And it has to be a certain *way*, too," he added petulantly. "Even if I *want* to do it. Otherwise they mistreat you."

"Creatively?"

"Yes, but that's the end of it. I have to be very particular about how I do things. I'm adaptable but not infinitely (and who wants to be, because what's the point), so I need to make them come to me, so when I *do* my work, they're already a little on tiptoes. So I don't get stupidly questioned and have to wastefully defend myself."

"It's like the not-driving thing," I said.

"How do you mean?"

"Making people come to you. Turning vulnerabilities into advantages."

Martin looked at me quickly, with a frown that, as one eyebrow rose, turned arch. "Well, I don't see them as *vulnerabilities*, quite. They're just my way. But yes."

I puffed my cigar as his gaze drifted to an open window. Martin's most distinctive characteristic was his voice, but it was the eyes that revealed him. When I arrived, after opening the door, he'd turned aside to let me pass, and I noticed that he abruptly looked stricken, as though defaulting to an inner charnel-house when not otherwise engaged. Yet when we spoke, Martin remained vividly in the moment, and this back and forth between desolation and sunshine amended the lesson of his individuality. Martin's eyes were a living demonstration of Beckett's I-can't-go-on-I'll-go-on principle, the revelation that no amount of real success and rigorously cultivated panache could banish the spectre of despair. Perhaps, I thought, my belief in an ultimate happiness through self-realization was naïve. If Martin still needed to stand by his choices, one moment at a time, to skirt the abyss, I would do well to readjust my expectations.

Shifting in his chair, Martin regained his poise, the lightness of spirit that was his own. "Now what about you," voice sonorous and swift, "how do you like to work? Do you concentrate on originals until you go broke, or find it stimulating to take assignments?"

About to open my mouth, I hesitated, realizing that I lacked an answer: it was a question no one had ever cared to ask. Intermingled with my bitterness at this was the recognition that it was largely my fault—hadn't I always put myself in positions of supplication, agreeing ferociously with one or another power figure, in the hope of getting a job? I had, in effect, always asked others how they *wanted* me to work.

I glanced at Martin, who watched me with the hopeful anticipation of a man who's proposed a night on the town. I felt embarrassed, but also challenged: if I ever expected to get my own way, I had best start considering what that might be.

"I've never turned down a job," I said, "even when I knew I should."

"Because you were afraid you'd never work again," Martin said impatiently.

"Right."

"And you've been sorry. Because no one has infinite creative energy and you hated to waste it on something unnourishing."

"Yes."

"And it's such a fucking slog when you're not engaged."

"Exactly."

"Mm." Martin puffed his cigar, thinking about this. "So now you won't work unless it's your own thing or you're desperate."

I wasn't sure what Martin was driving at, but this grilling remained especially useful. Only days before, I'd decided I couldn't go on. Yet if I resolved to do the work differently— in acceptance of The Business, but in accordance with my instincts—the idea machine might reactivate.

"No," I answered finally, "I'll work on almost anything, unless I can't find a way into the material. Or sense I won't be a true creative participant."

"You mean you won't take dictation, even from a star." He grinned. "Or star director."

"Those were precisely the jobs I shouldn't have taken."

Martin balanced his cigar on the edge of an ashtray. "So," he said mischievously, "you turn your vulnerabilities into advantages as well."

"Actually," I said, "I never have. Which is probably the source of all my problems."

"Well it's never too late," Martin said very quickly, taking up his cigar and puffing forth an obscuring cloud. "You're from New York, like myself, like all the best people?" he asked, with the exaggerated interest of the subject-changer. Here was a prime component of Martin's nature, and another lesson for myself: In the way that certain film stars refuse to do television, believing that it will diminish their cachet, Martin didn't commiserate—not from a lack of feeling, but because his buoyance of spirit could so easily crash to earth. Yet though he made a point of keeping things light—even the breathless speech seemed the equivalent of a man skipping over hot coals—this was not the same as keeping them trivial. Understanding the difference, I sat up, smiled, and banished my gloom: not only was being professionally depressed a distraction from work, it wasn't going to make me any friends, either.

Instead, we got to know one another. Martin had made his reputation directing landmark half-hours of rock 'n' roll television in Swinging London, and I looked forward to a nostalgic gossip-fest. The director, however, wasn't biting. "That's all lost in the mists of time," waving his cigar dismissively, leaning forward to knock off the ash. "Tell me," he asked, "which part of the city did you live in? Growing up."

"I didn't live in the city."

"I thought you were from New York."

"Upstate."

"The Borscht…Belt," with a dollop of wariness. "Mm."

Those "Mms," I was learning, meant a variety of things. There was the simple, short "Mm" that reaffirmed your point and encouraged you to say more. There was the more neutral, slightly elongated "Mm" that signified thought in process. There was the terse, imagine-that "Mm." And then there was the toneless one, which indicated disappointment. That was the "Mm" Martin had just delivered.

His reaction reminded me of something: I didn't, as a rule, talk about my past. In a way it was a correlative to Martin's disinclination toward commiseration, the fear that absorbing someone's miseries would undermine his confidence. One of the reasons I loved *La Dolce Vita* (Fellini again) was my intense identification with Marcello, the protagonist: the northern bumpkin who embeds himself in Rome's sweet life but whose insecurities clash with his aspirations. Like Marcello in the Italian capital, I had been attracted to the perhaps over-civilized but tantalizing artistic and intellectual milieux I discovered in New York, and yearned to fit in. I wondered if Martin, the student of character now considering me through a blue haze, saw the truth: that I'd spent years trying to turn the midcentury Catskills peasant that I was into an urbane aesthete, an identity I cultivated and yet—again, like Marcello—did not comfortably, entirely inhabit.

"What about you?" I asked, avoiding all this. "Manhattan?"

"Upper east," he said. "But not money. My mother, who worried about money, thought we should live in Brooklyn. But my stepfather was an entrepreneur, and he said you couldn't, as he put it, put butter and eggs together in the land of Whitman and Crane. So we were always in the best building on the worst block, or vice versa." Martin looked at me hopefully. "I'll bet your folks brought you in a lot, though. To the city."

"I used to beg them to."

"What did you like to do? Did you see shows?"

"I did. But what I liked best was to go to Patsy's."

Hearing this, Martin fell back in his chair. "On 56th Street."

"Yep."

"Mm. Hm. Because Frank would come in."

"*Everyone* came in."

"I was there one night—I was, you know, a very young, green fifteen—and it was an amazing cavalcade. Noel Coward, Burt Lancaster. Elaine Stritch. Each one coming in like this"—he extended his arms and leaned forward, as though rushing toward a table in greeting. "You thought, God, it's *great* to be alive in a time of…cufflinks. Glinting in pools of light. Snap of lighters. Gin."

"Spaghetti aglio e olio," I murmured. "Mozzarella in carrozza."

Stomachs rumbling, we sat in the present-day California light, dazed by smoke and memory. So, I thought, he *did* see: Martin had related his own history from the perspective of someone like myself. Very kind, also very smart: he was creating a practical intimacy, one that didn't involve the sharing of feelings, which wasn't his style. It was important for him to know that he had a means of connection beyond the work, to negotiate those moments when the work went sour.

"Good script," Martin said abruptly. He picked up his copy from the coffee table, shook the ash off its cover (as though it were a Pompeiian relic) and turned to a page. Martin read for a moment, then tapped a sentence with a finger. "I like the generosity you've shown your characters," he said. "Because one could just as easily hold them under," he coughed, "the microscope of condemnation. Instead, you're funny about your people. And sweet."

I wasn't used to this. "Do you have any thoughts?" I asked.

"What do you mean?"

"About what it needs."

Martin looked surprised. Then, understanding, he smiled. "Well, yes," he said. "It *needs* to go into pro*duc*tion."

"Mm," I replied.

"Now how do you like to work?" Martin had asked me that before. This time he meant it differently. "Are you like Tom Stoppard, who has very specific notions of what things mean? Or are you like Harold Pinter, who, when you ask him what something means, says, 'Well, what do *you* think it means?'"

Abruptly I saw why I'd decided to quit the business, or rather the reverse logic that had led me, for the right reasons, to what might have been the wrong decision. With the director of *Ovarian Cyst*, I'd been subjected to the process of development, an ordeal that began with the assumption that what I'd written was a failure. Martin, conversely, treated my script as a fait accompli, and like a drug, it delivered results: sitting there, smoking a Cuban cigar and pondering whether I more closely resembled Stoppard or Pinter in my preferences, I was not merely anxiety-free but powerful, entirely in command of my fate. If I felt like this more often, I thought, I wouldn't be so unhappy—and saw Martin grinning at me. Of course: It was right to detest my professional situation but, I now saw, wrong to solve the problem by giving up something I loved. Rather than quitting screenwriting, I might do as Martin had, and was prodding me to do: See things differently.

"I have a strong sense of what everything means," I replied. "But I'd rather hear what you and the actors have to say before I start talking."

"Good," Martin said sharply. "What about the ending?"

"What about it?"

"Why did you end on two minor characters?" His manner, as aggressive as a detective's, implied a test.

"Well," smiling cagily, "why do *you* think I ended on two minor characters?"

"Ha ha ha," Martin snapped tonelessly. He slumped in his chair. "It's a fun scene, funny, unexpected. And a metaphor for a new beginning, for everyone in the story, and men and women in general."

"Those were my intentions exactly. Is that a problem?"

Martin, holding his cigar between thumb and forefinger, took a pull, then exhaled thoughtfully. "I'm considering it from the studio's standpoint. Their little minds…" He shrugged and sat up. "We'll try it, and if it doesn't work, we'll try something else."

"Great."

Martin looked at his watch and crushed out the cigar. "All right, now I'm bored and want to get a pedicure," a remark that held a wink. "You'll call Harry"—the producer—"tell him what you really think of me?"

At this, I could not help but smile. Whether or not we worked together, of one thing I was certain: I wanted to be Martin's friend. Yet I felt compelled to recognize the double-edged nature of my attraction. On the positive side, there was everything Martin exuded: his independence and irreverence, lack of pretension and ready availability, most of all his commitment to his work and the life-wisdom he wore with grace, all of it encased, like a fine Havana, in an interleaved wrapper of emotional generosity and a nearly alarming degree of charm. And then there was my attraction's left hand: the fact that Martin's armor, and the success it had produced, had left him hugely self-involved. Any relationship we had, I reckoned, would be entirely on his terms.

But, you know—that was all right. There is a benefit, I considered, to accepting the things one cannot change. My needs were plain: I hoped that we'd make a film; absent that, I wanted the pleasure of Martin's company and the benefit of his experience. If I did not convert need into neediness—if I held onto myself, and did not ask for what could not be had, a lesson I'd learned from Wendy—any time we spent together would be satisfying.

"Can I ask you a question?" I said.

"You just did. What?"

"What motivated your career?"

"Meeting girls. What do you mean?"

"Why did you, ah…want to be a director?"

Martin frowned dramatically. "I'm not sure I *wanted* to be a di*rec*tor," he replied. "I wanted to work in some capacity in the theatre, because it was a refuge. I was a miserable kid, and nobody there found me stupid or awkward, or minded about things."

I nodded, waiting.

"As for *directing*," Martin said, grinning, purring, "as a director once said, the director is the person who says, I'm the director. I don't know," petulantly, "I'd had a job in TV sweeping up, someone said, there's this new rock 'n' roll show, who knows about the telly, and I said, I've *worked* in television, *ah. Ah. Ah*. I never had a plan. Just opportunities."

"But you can be ferocious about getting your way."

"Well, yeah, sure. You can only play the wide-eyed eager grateful sort for so long. At some point, you have to convert into a belligerent, self-centered cunt."

Martin grinned as I blinked at the 'C' word (before remembering that the English, actual and honorary, use it freely). He stood up and stretched. It was my cue to leave. "I was lucky," he said as I followed him to the door. "Right place right time, worked a lot, learned my tricks before I blotted my copybook." I thought of what I'd said to Jessica: *Make it young.* "So that when I'd go in and out of the wilderness…oh, I don't know. I guess I was expecting it. The axe to fall. So I was philosophical and resilient."

Martin opened the door and stood aside, impatient. Here, I understood, was the moment, not to be needy, but to insist upon my need, which was—as ever—for information.

"Because you were an outsider," I said.

Instantly a thundercloud loomed above his head. "*Outsider?*"

"It's sort of a constant in your work. Isn't it?"

"How?"

I put my hands in my pockets and leaned against the door frame. "Often your subject seems to be the good-hearted, well-meaning *outsider* who's invited into a world, is grateful he's there, and then is, as you say, philosophical and resilient when he's cast out."

Martin's eyes had taken on their death's-head gaze. "Mm," he said.

"Or else they become a part of things—"

"But always stand at a distance, right, right. As though not entirely trusting their luck." Martin looked at me gloomily. "So you've found a theme."

"Don't tell me you weren't aware of it."

"I've been too busy *making* movies to worry about what they might mean. Why are you torturing me with these questions?"

"To find out if you have a calling."

"What does it matter?"

"I'm thinking of quitting," I blurted. In the annals of self-destructive professional moves, this ranked as a front-runner: telling a director who hopes to make your script that you want to leave the industry.

Martin, predictably, was unfazed. "Oh, yeah, how come?" he replied vaguely, as though I'd mentioned that I was selling my car.

"I thought it was because I wasn't really good at the

work," I continued, nailing my career's coffin even more firmly shut, "though now that we've talked, I'm thinking I just haven't handled the business well."

"But you'll do better in future. So what else could the matter be?" Attentive now.

"I feel like a fraud. Like I became a writer to make myself seem special."

This was, I realized as I released it, an oblique way of talking about my past. If Martin sensed that, however, he didn't let on. "There was an actor I knew in London," he said, eyes on the middle distance of memory. "Good in a certain way—not a star, but interesting. He'd come from a family of theatricals, and his father, whom he detested, expected this actor to follow suit. Eventually, in a rage, he gave it up and became a horticulturist."

"And?"

Martin looked at me now. "I ran into him a few years ago, at an orchid show. And he said that he'd only just grasped, twenty years after the fact, that by the time he gave it up, he'd become pretty good and rather liked it." He half-closed the door, sagging against it; the mischief returned to his eyes. "Do you know the story about the director who gestures for an actor, who's far away, to run toward the camera. And the actor, being an actor, calls out, 'What's my motivation?' And the director yells back, 'I'll tell you when you get here.'"

I smiled. "I've never heard that one."

"The reasons don't matter," Martin said. "You'll find out when you get there." He grinned his needling grin. "Some stranger will come to your hotel one day, and explain it all in a few pithy sentences. But," he added, shooing me out, "*get* there."

"Nice meeting you," I said.

"Call Harry," eyes dying like embers as he pushed closed the door. "Good script."

XXXX

Shuddering, hands gripping her shoulders, I pushed deep into Jessica's ass and felt myself implode, as though my foundations had been dynamited; then, as the dust of my orgasm rose into the space I once had filled, there followed a consuming peace. I remained inside her, in a silence charged by the nature of our lovemaking and the implications of our connection. After six months, I had finally completed the act, and with someone who formed the portal of a new life for me.

From the moment I set out for the whorehouse that evening, I'd been in a fever to fuck. I had chosen to focus on my first impression of Jessica—the warping lust that made its own rules—and to use everything I'd learned to push my desire to its natural conclusion. Driving this approach was my dinnertime discovery: that if I avoided defaulting to my usual behavior, I might break through into a deeper intimacy. With Jessica, this would mean releasing the construct upon which I'd built my sexual life with whores: by keeping my needs out of the exchange entirely, I could enjoy intimacy without feeling entrapped. It was past time to slip this routine and stop hiding.

Pulling up in front of the whorehouse, empty of Dutch and Colombian courage, I recognized my anxious energy to be, in part, a pretense. This was due to an odd irony: for a man straight and sober, whoring was a new experience. Walking up the path, beholding the ruin in which I proposed to get naked, my middle-class squeamishness violently asserted itself. But that was okay, too. If my nerve (or anything else) failed, I had Jessica's lesson: Things would take as long as they took.

And my nerve, as I entered, nearly did fail. The tunnel vision coke induced had caused me to miss the unmissable, like the aged, dead refrigerator, big as a fullback, looming in a corner of the waiting room. I stared at the crooked hulk, its open door releasing a ripe sourness—how could I have failed to notice it? Equally did I find myself amazed by the filth. Entropy, nature's art director, had enhanced the room's cavelike quality by strewing mouse droppings along the edges of the floor, adding the intermittent guano of a larger rodent by way of accent. Mice and rats didn't mix, I'd heard. Here, every species did.

All of this paled before the reality—the hyperreality—of the women. It was hard to know if my shock stemmed from their appearance, or my realization of the extent to which cocaine had shaped my consciousness: Beholding them as they smiled with more than the usual whore's familiarity, I did not recognize a single one. Rather, I faced a trio of mean, hard strangers, their flesh a graphic-relief map of skin pops, cysts, and sores, their teeth the color of tea. Saddest was the odor that seemed to rise from them collectively: an inner curdling of body and soul, for which the vagina was the ventilator. As the three faces began to take on a familiar cast, I stiffened, realizing that I'd spent hours—indeed, whole nights—drinking from the infested ponds between their thighs.

Finally, my memory returned. Here was Wendy, whose face, shorn of its narcotic attraction, resembled an old sailor's, chin protruding and mouth sunken, teal eyes empty as a vacant sea. Next I identified Gloria, an easygoing tomboy I'd killed time with once or twice, from the elephant-hair bracelet I had slipped around her ankle. And, inevitably, Sinclair: eyes narrow, bright and scheming, her patch of the jungle firmly staked.

It amused me that Sinclair, with her hey-big-boy-wait'll-you-see-what-I've-got-for-*you* grin, thought I might choose her. Admittedly, this was my fault: after my humiliating first session, I'd given her a second go, on a night on which the alternatives were particularly unpalatable. Sinclair had played it masterfully, first whispering, "This time things'll be different," then (once she'd gotten my cash) disappearing for nearly the entire hour, taking first a shower, then a call.

Well, I thought, grinning back with equal insincerity, fool me once, shame on you, fool me twice—

"Mikey's changed tonight," Sinclair said suddenly, glancing with theatrical mischief at her sisters.

"Oh?" I replied, startled by the interruption of my

thoughts. "How so?"

Fiercely, she rubbed the tip of her regal beak. "You look like you've been getting more sleep. If you know what I mean."

Give the devil her due: Sinclair, with her finely tuned sensors, had observed that I was straight. More to the point, she'd grasped the implications of my condition, an understanding that imparted a twist of curiosity to her signature squint-and-smile.

"*So*, Mikey," she said with unwholesome appetite. "Who's the lucky girl?"

"Hi."

I looked up. Jessica stood beside my chair. We considered each other with an anticipation that was not uninformed. "Hi yourself," I said.

She wore traditional whore's regalia—fishnets, stilettos, the stupendous blond wig—and that was good: given my desire, a sex object was ideal.

"I'll see you," I said, observing the formalities. I sprang up, Jessica turned on her heel. We were stopped by Sinclair's broad and raucous, "*Well.*"

Actually, it was Jessica who stopped. She felt, I sensed, that it would cause less trouble, in the long run, than ignoring her nemesis. For that was Sinclair's identity: the enemy of anyone who challenged her primacy, not merely as a whore, but as arbiter of the meaning of being a whore. Prostitution, Sinclair decreed, was for beating men, and the possibility that a girl might use it to marshal her better instincts, cauterize her anger and pain, was intolerable. To Sinclair, the look exchanged by Jessica and myself was a breach of discipline, a mutiny in the making. As the Pasionaria of her movement—the anti-partisan—she had no choice but to declare *No pasaran*.

"Mikey's got a girlfriend," Sinclair said, grinning at me chummily. "Don't get *too* attached, hon," shooting Jessica a look. "She's engaged."

The others stared at Jessica with surprise. Then they turned their eyes on Sinclair.

"How do *you* know?" Gloria said.

Sinclair let her head fall back, then lolled it from side to side. "I'm the queen bee, *bay*-beh," eyes closed, smile mellow. "You think I don't hear the buzz in this hive?"

Jessica emitted a short laugh at this practiced retort. However much she regretted sharing with this most treacherous of confidantes, she wasted no apparent time on it. I glanced at her, not knowing quite how to take the news.

The girls seemed equally flummoxed. "That's nice," Wendy finally croaked.

"Yeah, mazel tov," Gloria said uncertainly.

Sinclair dropped her head forward and opened eyes and mouth wide, as if in comment upon the moment's absurdity, two hookers congratulating a third on her engagement to a man who might be most charitably described as *not very observant*. "You going to keep working after you tie the knot?" Sinclair said with exaggerated polite interest.

"That depends."

"What's it depend on?"

"My finances. That's the only reason, isn't it? That we do this?"

The exquisite modulation of Jessica's delivery impressed even Sinclair, who chose to cede the round. "Well," she said. "I hope we'll all receive invitations."

"Maybe I'll catch the bouquet," Wendy added, with a little smile that, for a moment, stopped our hearts.

"Now you kids run along," Sinclair said. "And make hay while the sun shines."

Jessica again turned on her heel. As I followed, I remembered Sinclair's real name.

"See you, Patty," I said.

Out of the corner of my eye, I saw Sinclair's face contort with an explosive rage. Jessica said nothing but, following her down the hall, I noted the tightness in her shoulder blades. "I'm sorry," I said when we reached the room. "That was a stupid thing to do."

Opening the door, Jessica tilted up her chin, at once forgiving me and motioning me in. The moment afforded a revelation: that every aspect of prostitution demanded the ability to decide what constituted a violation—as, since one was always being violated in new ways (in this case, by my betrayal of a confidence), the definition required constant recalibration. As Jessica had already done so, in the transit from the waiting room, I said nothing further. She went off to sign in.

The space delivered my next jolt. I had grown used to the "big room," the circumstantial equivalent of a first-class cabin. Now I found myself in steerage, an enclosure the tininess of which was surpassed only by its squalor. I'd convinced myself, over time, that after this or that gentleman's ejaculations and exudations had besmirched the sheets, they were changed. This belief was now revealed to be the ultimate in airborne pie: I could perceive, in the sour-smelling rag before me, the outlines of countless men— ballprints, ass cheeks, glans-and-shaft combinations of every length and girth—a kind of pornographic, multiple-image version of the Shroud of Turin. The house-cleaning I'd witnessed, moreover, had obviously been an anomaly on the order of Haley's Comet: the carpet held clumps of hair half the size of tumbleweeds, the window sill was crusted with grime.

Perching on the chair in the corner, removing my shoes, I reflected that *the loss of illusion* appeared to be emerging as the night's leitmotif, a theme that had threaded its way through my discovery of the wretchedness of house and whores, my puncturing of Sinclair's control fantasy, and now, as I undressed, my recognition that the regrets I'd expressed to Jessica had been insincere—I had wanted to wound Sinclair, I'd understood the difficulty my disclosure would cause and didn't care. Well, I decided, brushing the pubic filigree off the sheet, settling supine upon it, so be it. I was here to please myself, and "sorry" held no true place in my lexicon.

This acceptance acted upon my anxieties as, formerly, cocaine had: I found myself utterly relaxed, remorse-free. Better still, anticipation had turned my quivering pillar to stone. After countless visits, I'd achieved the condition from which the average john began. At long last, I was good to go.

Heels rapping, Jessica hustled down the hall and came in, her face revealing a greedy anticipation identical to my own. The erotic energy in the room caromed between us.

Then Jessica saw my over-eager erection, the cocaine-free night table, and her eyes lost their glitter. Setting down her bag, she massaged the palm of her left hand with the middle finger of her right. As before, this bespoke acupressure clarified Jessica's thoughts: when again her eyes met mine, the strain within them had been replaced by warmth.

"That was an interesting talk we had," she said.

"It was an interesting session. I got a lot from it."

"Me, too. I sat with what you said for quite some time, some of it."

"What?" I asked. "The part about getting good at a bad situation?"

"About getting sidetracked. Deciding that what you're doing is 'the work' 'cause you're starring in your own little drama. *That* was a revelation."

"Well, but you sort of talked me out of that."

"Did I?"

"You said you can't do what you need to do til you're ready." I stroked myself, watching her. "That you have to play things out before you can change."

"As long as you remember why you're doing it," Jessica said, coming closer. "What you said—how you can get caught up in your fantasy of yourself. It's important to watch that, I think."

This dialogue, unfolding with near-diplomatic formality, I understood to be another of Jessica's adjustments. Realizing that she wasn't going to get what she wanted—that she might get something she *didn't* want—Jessica had chosen to recap the intimacies that had formed our bond, the better to remind me that we were soulmates. To this she added a subtle cautionary overlay: suggesting that, even in the pursuit of transformation, boundaries required respecting.

"Well," Jessica continued, turning saucy. "*You* played something out, it seems."

"What?"

"Cocaine. Or," with a tinge of hope, "are you waiting?"

"I quit," I affirmed cheerfully. Crossing my ankles, I clasped my hands behind my head, two linkings that drove my erection further skyward. "I need to feel my feelings, and I can't with drugs in my system. *Or* alcohol."

"Alcohol, too. Interesting." Jessica returned to the foot of the bed, picked up her bag and turned to face me, holding the little clutch formally with both hands. "Why did you decide that you need to feel your feelings now?" she asked.

"Because I'm ready."

She nodded with slow deliberation, and looked at her bag—deciding, I guessed, whether or not to produce her own coke. Jessica knew instinctively that my desire to remain drug-free as yet remained untested, and that she was my motivation for quitting. Tempting me with her stash might amount to an act of bad faith; yet *not* doing so would be accepting a joyride the direction of which remained unforeseeable. In both directions lay risk.

Jessica was thinking. I, brainlessly, rode the nervous energy of my lust. "Are you going to get undressed?" I said.

Jessica's chin rose, she advanced, looking down at me intently, her clutch bag floating just above my head. Opening it, she removed a tube of K-Y and a condom.

"Were you okay?" she asked. "After last time?"

Last time. I had to smile. This amounted, I knew, to Jessica's hope that, by invoking our past, with its interwoven strands of domination and tenderness, she might cool my ardor's aggression.

I replied, simply, "I was fine."

And waited. Finally, Jessica set down the lubricant and French letter and retreated to the corner of the room. Which is to say, she capitulated.

She stripped overcarefully—heels side by side under the

chair, maillot and fishnets folded over the backrest—bringing a nearly military degree of ritual to the experience. Watching, I again pondered a conundrum over which I myself had come to grief: if Jessica had constantly to redraw her boundaries, how meaningful could any of them be? Was there—for either one of us—a limit?

"Leave it on," I said, standing, as Jessica began to remove her wig.

"I thought you didn't like it."

I smiled, to avoid the answer: it enhanced her resemblance to a love doll.

We stood facing each other, separated only by the length of my erection. Gently, I laid a hand on Jessica's cheek and kissed her lips.

In response, she uncapped the K-Y, lubricated my cock, slid the condom on over it, then lightly lubed the latex—swiftly, and with the preemptive competence of a teacher. I looked at her, very surprised: Jessica had made a wrong move. It was another attempt to draw a line, by demoting me to student; she wanted, moreover, protection, in case a door opened unexpectedly. But this attempt to reassert control, after control had been ceded, was an insult, a whore's trick. And by raising the possibility, she'd opened the door herself.

Inflamed as much by these subdermals as the actuality of her touch, rushing in my insecurity and eagerness, I grasped Jessica's shoulders and faced her toward the mirrored wall. Standing behind her, I studied her reflection, transfixed by the vivid nipples, peeking through the blonde cascade like the eyes of a beast in a painting by Rousseau.

With two fingers, I drew all of the synthetic-smelling sheaf to one side of her neck, exposing her left breast startlingly, completely concealing the other. Then, coming closer, I encircled her waist, her arms beneath my own.

Jessica's eyes narrowed—then opened wide. Before she could react, I picked her up, swung her face-down on the bed, and put myself on top of her.

Without a word—for only the threat of murder caused a

whore to cry out—Jessica broke free and struggled up onto her side; I held on, my right arm around her shoulders, high enough to slip into a choke hold.

"*Easy*," Jessica gasped.

"I'm *being* easy."

She gripped my forearm with both hands as, behind her on my side, I watched our reflection, my free hand roaming Jessica's belly, cunt and thighs. Before, drugs and fear had kept me from this devouring. Now my excitement thundered like a racehorse.

With an electric clarity, even through the latex, I felt the head of my cock tickled by the striations of her anus. Reflexively I pushed, and was in with an ease that startled us both. Alarmed, Jessica clenched. A fireball of pleasure rolled up my spine.

"*Don't*," she said—low, but unmistakably.

"I'm in already."

Again I pushed, inflamed by her clenching, she reached back to push me away. I caught Jessica's wrist and held it. Breathing heavily, we froze, eyes locked in the mirror.

I said it again: "I'm *in* already."

Jessica's tits were thrust forward, her ass upraised. Using my advantage, I turned her downward—the better to observe, in its snug cylinder, the piston of my cock.

But I didn't drive it home. Instead, as Jessica, eyes wide and cheek mashed into the pillow, breathed through her nose, I transferred her wrist to my other hand, laid my free hand atop her head, and peeled off the wig—watching as there emerged, from beneath the fussy tangle, Jessica's pinned and matted, fuscia-colored cap. I threw the thing on the floor and studied her. She had, to me, never looked more naked, more skinned.

And once again Jessica redrew her boundaries, and turned a nonconsensual act into a transit of lovemaking. In incremental calibrations, she gave up the distance within her, I sank into the fire with gratitude and relief; I released her wrist and she reached back for me, pulling me in, moaning with sodden immoderation, my own cries intermingling with hers into a lurid, ringing room tone. I put my hand to her forehead and pulled her flat against me, feeling us fuse and dissolve into one another, watching as Jessica took her hand from my ass and pressed three fingers against her mons, glinting eyes nearly closed. My hands moved to her shoulders and gripped them, so that I could see all of her, and nearly nothing of myself: an intertwined entity, double-headed, single-souled. I pushed in deep and, touching bottom, came, emptying utterly, feeling Jessica, my Jessica, rush into the void, an exchange, not of fluids, but selves. When the spasms ceased, nothing remained of me. I had arrived sober. Now, I was clean.

There was a silence, in which even the ordinarily noisy whorehouse contrived to support my deep sense of peace. Then I withdrew and lay back, my arm loosely around her, wanting to stay close yet entombed within my satisfaction. How seldom anymore did I have sex. And the way in which the experience had combined naked self-expression and an extreme of pleasure with, on Jessica's part, heroism—for how else could I describe her decision to assert her humanity, not by withholding herself, but by being close?—seemed, in my history, unique.

And, thinking this, I thought of my wife. She was not an evil woman; rather, as Jessica and I were united by our need for an environment that enabled us to release and nurture our latent selves, so too were my wife and I identical in our unadmitted refusal to make the accommodations in our natures that would have enabled us to succeed. We had not, I now understood, because we could not. My wife's need to have a child, my belief that her plenitude of good qualities could not be replicated, had made us act, but they had not made us ready. I knew and appreciated my wife in a thousand ways, I would not see the like of our simpatico again, but I would never feel as close to her, in a certain way, as I did to the semi-stranger who lay beside me now. It was sad. But there it was.

I glanced at Jessica, who lay on her back, half against me. Her face was turned so that I could not read its expression, but her body language told a tale, loudly, of ambivalence. Sensing my awareness, she glanced at her watch, then sat up, pushed herself to the end of the bed and stood. Pointedly she plucked a Baby-Wipe from its container and cleaned herself up.

"Okay?" I asked.

She dropped the Baby-Wipe in the trash. "Why did you do that?"

"Are you angry at me?"

"Let's leave me out of it for the moment." Jessica perched on the edge of the chair, crossed her legs and folded her arms, so that she'd achieved a chaste concealment; her face stayed neutral. "What you do is a reflection only on you, and only I can give it enough importance for it to affect me."

"A woman's right to choose."

"That's right."

I'd been snide in response to her canned manifesto. But what she said was true, and I nodded in acknowledgement. Sitting up, I propped myself against the mirror and peeled off the condom. Jessica held out the trash and I tossed it in.

"Two points," she said.

I smiled. Jessica refolded herself and raised her shoulders in an "I'm waiting" gesture.

"I was excited to fuck you. I've been coming here for months, and I've never, believe it or not, once fucked. After last time, I felt something change—I was *ready* to change— and I believed I could do it with you."

"Do what, exactly?"

"Push past myself."

"And did you?"

I leaned my head against the mirror and looked at her. "I think I did. I didn't think about offending *or* satisfying you."

Jessica looked at me with cool bemusement, her thumb stroking the slight cleft in her chin. "Is that going to be your m.o. from here on in?" she said.

"One thing I've learned from my addictions," meeting her small smile with my own. "You only need one perfect experience. After that, it's all repetition."

My answer seemed to activate Jessica's mind, though she still felt a long way away in the tiny room. Unfolding herself, she put her knees together, her elbows atop them, her chin on her hands' heels. "Did you feel like you were getting back some of your own?" she said.

"Own what?"

"Own *ass*hole."

"Ah. No. No, because I didn't lose anything I didn't want to lose, last time. No, I was," I shrugged, "I was incredibly hot for you. I might have been overzealous, because…"

"Afraid you couldn't pull it off."

"Yes—yes. So I was maybe making myself more mindless than I might have been otherwise. And did what I did."

"Which was what?" Jessica said, taking her chin from her hands and canting forward.

"Took us to a place we would have gotten to eventually rather faster than you wanted to go."

"Anally raped me."

I sighed, uncrossing my ankles, I sat up and put one foot on the floor. "Is that the importance you've chosen to give this?"

"Is that what *you* believe you did?"

"You could have stopped me."

There were a variety of disputatious responses Jessica might have made. But she didn't, for the reason that what I'd said was accurate.

"Why," she said, "my ass?"

"I was *in* your ass, it all happened so quickly."

"But you were so *eager*. Was that anxiety about stopping, or…"

I brushed at the filthy sheet. "Maybe it's less intimate," I said. "Than the usual way."

Jessica nodded. "More dramatic, but…"

"But less intimate." I stretched out on my side, fist to temple. Jessica got on the bed and faced me, mirroring my position; it felt good to have her close. "So you weren't trying to humiliate me," Jessica said. "Because I felt aggression that was more than—what did you say? Overzealousness."

Jessica was looking at me straightforwardly, wanting only that her instincts not be denied. "A little," I admitted.

She plucked at the sheet in silence. This straightening out of the record had been elaborate but necessary. Without it, neither of us could have kept the part of our lovemaking that had been momentous.

"A little…" Jessica said, absently but, I sensed, leading me.

"Mostly, I did it to strengthen myself and." She looked at me. "Our connection."

Jessica sighed and fell over onto her back. She sat up quickly and hugged her knees to her chest. "Honey, this is not a relationship. You can't use me this way."

I stayed on my side, looking up at her—unsure whether or not she wanted to be convinced. "Jessica," I said, "why did you fuck *me* in the ass? Not because you hated me."

"Don't be so sure."

I smiled and shook my head. "It was for the same reason I've spent six months here with my face between everyone's legs."

"Oh?"

"You do it to learn, to learn how to create a life for yourself. Let's face it, that's who we are, that's what we're after with all this." I tapped the top of her thigh with a finger. "Buggering men is your way of getting a satisfaction that's your own, that reverses your situation and restores your dignity."

Jessica's head was half-turned toward me, eyes wide and blank as she listened. Now she looked at me.

"*That's* a statement," she said.

I turned up my palms. "It's got nothing to do with hating men, or having a secret desire to be one or, or anything. If you're a sex-change-in-the-making, I'm a Lesbian."

"I think you are a Lesbian," Jessica said. "I think that's

your problem." She again stretched out on her side and faced me. Though the tension had eased, we were still careful not to touch. "You think I do it all the time?" Jessica said, then made a face: "*Bugger men.*"

"No. You did it with me because you knew I'd go for it—because I understood what it meant to you. And that's *precisely* why I could do what I did with you."

"I asked."

"I couldn't. And Jessica"—I reached out and turned her face toward me—"just like I did for *you*, you turned it into a real moment."

She sat up quickly. "I did what I had to do—"

"I know," also sitting up, "I've watched you do it ten times tonight."

"What?"

"Redraw your boundaries—decide the unacceptable's acceptable." We sat cross-legged, facing each other. I could feel my point within my grasp and, as with the sex, I was rushing so as not to lose it. "I've done the same thing with my wife, except that in my case I do it by withholding myself, by...*killing* everything within me that *feels*." I grasped her ankle, then caressed the firm muscle of her calf—unafraid now to touch her. "That's the difference, Jessica. *You* did it by feeling *more*. You—" I broke off, frowning. "What's the line from that play? *The Heiress*. You, you..."

Jessica broke into a broad grin. "I 'enlarged my capacities.'"

"Exactly. You took and gave pleasure and created a real moment between us, and thereby kept your humanity. And that made me love you a little."

I was leaning forward, a finger hooked idly around the thin gold chain encircling her ankle. I felt unable to look Jessica in the eye.

"You don't know what I feel," she replied, editorially rather than in defiance.

"No. But..." I took her hands. "You know, my wife's always talking about wanting to be intimate. '*In*-ti-ma-cy,' she says. Well what *is* intimacy? What we've learned, you and I, to do as individuals—console ourselves—doing it together, and for each other…is intimacy."

Now I was indeed looking at her. When she raised her eyes, I could see the suffering in them. "Where are you going with this?" she asked.

"I could never do this with my wife."

"Have you tried?" I shook my head. "Well, why don't you?"

I rested my forehead on the heels of my hands. "We've missed the boat, my wife and I. I…I don't trust her."

"*She* should trust *you*?"

"Jessica. Give me a break."

She took my hands from my head. Our legs encircled each other's waists, and we held each other. "Honey," she said, "we're *strangers*. You're hot for me. You know how that is."

"How is it?"

"'It clouds men's minds.'"

Our faces were inches apart. It was inevitable, and it was true: kisses never lie. Breaking, we kept our heads together, massaging each other's necks like a pair of exhausted wrestlers.

"We're almost out of time," Jessica said.

We leaned back, and again I took her hands. "We're creeping out on this limb," I said. "And maybe it only goes so far. But…it's not unheard-of for people to meet in this situation and—"

"Mike…," shaking her head, "Mike."

She had used my "john" name. I smiled and looked away. "We can go through the looking glass."

"I have a fiancé."

This stopped me. Jessica's statement pierced through the verbiage I'd been expelling to the heart of the matter.

"Jessica," I said, "I don't want a relationship."

Everything I'd said, I believed. But though I hadn't realized it, I'd been driving my petition forward on the engine of something I did not believe, which was that Jessica and I should be together. This was the most indestructible of the expectations to which I remained susceptible: that my interest in someone had to lead to a conventional connection. If there had been a note of dishonesty in my appeal—if that was what Jessica instinctively resisted—it had come from this.

Our eyes shifted toward the door as a pair of rapping heels hustled down the hall. *Knock-knock.*

"Okay," Jessica called. She looked at me: "What then?"

"Let's be physically intimate. And let's talk to each other. As for the rest of it, as you would say…"

"We're not ready yet."

We looked at one another; and though Jessica was half-distracted by the press of business, our eyes sealed the agreement. Plucking out a Baby-Wipe, I gave myself a going-over as Jessica dressed. She picked the wig up from the floor, shook it violently, then considered me.

"When will you be back?" she said.

"A week or two."

"Can I have your number? Don't worry, I won't—"

"I'm not worried. Let me get dressed and I'll write it down for you."

An aggressive report of approaching heels: that would be Sinclair. Jessica opened the door and stuck her head into the darkness, I heard a sharp exchange of whispers: shots fired without resolution. Jessica leaned back in and closed the flimsy balsa barrier with a bang.

"Go ahead," I said.

I picked up my pants, Jessica opened the door. Leaving, she showed me her cleft chin, green eyes glinting at the prospect of more mayhem.

"Next time?" she said.

"Yeah?"

"*Lady's* choice."

XXXX

It was difficult, in the days that followed, not to view my beatitude with bemusement, given the distance between what I'd done and how I felt about it. Yet pondering this consoling sense of security—a quality, all but unprecedented, of feeling at home in myself—I recognized the source to be particular and profound: I had trusted someone enough to take a reckless gamble, trusted the validity of my desire and the accuracy of my instincts, and the gamble had paid off. Even more: trusting Jessica—seeing the trust hold, deliver truths both erotic and emotional—encouraged me to trust myself. From this derived my peace: the discovery that, when it came to what I wanted, someone else did not, always, know better.

This found an echo of sorts in my marriage. Having learned that, if we resisted our pathology, we might grow closer, my wife and I pursued a campaign to be kind, to not default to our usual hatefulness. Intimacy, however, begetting honesty, increased the chance that difficult truths might tumble out, in particular the ultimate: why it was that, despite all the unhappiness the connection had brought, I remained incapable of leaving it. As had been the case since the start of our troubles, I felt unready to face this.

Instead (and here we see how thin matters may be sliced when we hide from change by pretending to do the opposite) I focused on learning how to help my wife without screaming at her mulishness. As my personal classroom, I chose the several writer's-workshop applications I had, on my own initiative, procured for her.

"List the five professional accomplishments of which you are proudest," I read, as neutrally as possible.

"Oy oy oy," said my wife, head between her knees. We were in my office, I at the desk, she on the rush-seated ladderback. "Does figuring out how to get a bus to an LA audition count?"

"I don't think the dates are important," I lightly lied. "Try…" I gazed thoughtfully at the ceiling, and this bit of bad acting pointed the way. "Try grouping your experiences by category. Theatre: You studied with"—I hesitated:

counting off my wife's acting teachers was like naming the Seven Dwarfs—"Kim, Paul, Stella, Sandra, Barbara, Bobby, and…"

"Geraldine."

I wrote these down. "You worked at—where? The Williamstown festival—"

"In what?"

I stared at her. "How should I know?"

"Nothing!" she declared triumphantly, leaping up. "I had four lines, and at the first rehearsal, the lead threw a hissy fit. 'I refuse to act with this woman,' he said."

"Look," struggling to short-leash the barking dog within, "it doesn't matter, what's important is—"

"I have to stop."

"Finish."

"I appreciate what you're doing—"

"Then finish one, just—"

"I have a meeting."

Silence. Al-Anon, my wife's ace in the hole against the pat hand of change. Once again, I thought as she marched out, we'd failed at maturity. My wife had indeed defaulted to one of her repertoire of evasions, but I was hardly innocent, having designed the exercise to avoid my own feelings. Hearing the door slam, watching my wife head up the path, I reflected that I could not blame her for being unwilling to go where I would not. Resuming my own evasion—passing, as I did a thousand times a day, from honesty to self-deception—I chose to congratulate myself, indeed the both of us, for giving it a try.

But it was self-interest, more than fear, that moved me to keep the marriage on a simmer: my confidence might be profitably applied to reviving my career, and I did not want to be distracted. I was startled to find the itch return, and laid it at first to Martin's interest. But as I began writing again, I found it had to do with a change of feeling: The recognition that I didn't have what it took to be the filmmaker I'd dreamed of being had combined with my well-being to release the talent that I had—to let me accept that this talent, if properly deployed, was enough. I might never do "great" work. But by permitting my imagination to flourish without judging the outcome—one day at a time—I could be better than I'd been.

Relinquishing a certain kind of ambition also made it easier to deal with disappointment, and Martin and his producer Harry, by disappointing me, proved helpful in this regard. Harry's method was the more direct. After I'd enthused over his choice of director, he'd taken the package of Martin, my script and himself to a pair of studios. "What if they both want it?" I asked. "You should live so long," was Harry's reply. As it happened, neither did, after which he instantly lost interest. Martin cushioned his own withdrawal, relating the story of an English actor he'd directed in a hit Broadway play. Night after night, the actor glimpsed movie stars slouching in the house seats—realizing that this had to do, not with his great accomplishment, but the fact that he wasn't going to be reprising it in the film version. "He got more and more upset, more and more depressed, until at last he won a Tony and went back to England a star, while the *mo*-vie came out with someone all wrong for the part and was gone in a week," Martin offered in a purring burst. As I was about to ask how this pertained to me, he appended, "So don't despair because you never know." Martin was proof: A rock 'n' roll band with which he'd worked in TV had produced a miracle, paying his *Vogue*-thick hotel bill, inviting him to London to direct a video. "I'll call you in a few weeks," standing in the Chateau's driveway as a pair of bellhops heaved his desiccated Vuitton trunk into a limo. Newly released from hotel jail, Martin drew in the fumy Strip air benignly and gave me a cigar. "We'll go to dinner when I get back," adding, solemnly, "Someplace we can *smoke*." Yes, I thought, this was the way: Rather than cursing the business, my agent, my stars, I'd use the talents I'd spent decades polishing to have fun and get paid.

First, however, I had to launch my reconsidered career, and settled upon the strategy of a dinner party. As the guest of honor, I had in mind Jason, a mid-level studio executive who'd read several of my scripts and professed to admire them (you never knew). We'd lunched a while back, and over a half-order of Cobb salad, his body switching back and forth like a metronome as he kept track of who in the room was schmoozing whom, Jason confided his interest in a woman we both knew, a bombshell-esque director's assistant. "That," he said, in the cynical, exhausted monotone then in vogue among youngish execs, "is why I've never introduced her to my wife." All he needed was a credible excuse to hook up, and it occurred to me that I might offer it, in the form of an evening chez nous. As Jason could recommend her boss to direct a picture, his presence would attract the bombshell—whose name, impeccably, was Brooke—and I planned also to ask my pal Debbie, a no-less-attractive producer, who'd welcome the chance to expand her power base. Neither woman could help me, but Jason might, if I sent him the right signals.

This last was tricky. If I'd grown tight with Jason the aesthete, I had small acquaintance with his other side, the studio drone bound professionally to support, not just mass-market movies, but industry-friendly personalities. This, I'd come to believe, was the cause of my failure: one could not embrace Dr. Jekyll and eschew Mr. Hyde. As I had changed my attitude toward the business, I decided, so must I do toward those in it, and a fun dinner peopled with sexy babes might show Jason I'd gotten the point. I'd expound on the positive qualities of whatever Hollywood dreck came up, and with luck he'd ring me in a week or so, to request that I look at something in need of a rewrite.

The preliminaries went promisingly. Jason was deadpan-ecstatic, Brooke accepted cheerfully, and Debbie, to whom I confessed my motives, promised to massage compliments about me into the conversation (and to bring her husband, the "eminent cardiologist," to even the sides). A Thursday night was selected, the guests admired our apartment as Cesária Évora pealed from the speakers and cold Sancerre was uncorked. The Chilean sea bass, as Preston Sturges might have put it, was a poem.

It was not until we'd settled back with the coffee, and I'd begun to strum my new tune, that my wife chose to ambush me.

I had, of course, taken pains to prep my wife—given her history of social terrorism, I'd have been foolish not to. I explained that the evening was to be "my reintroduction to the town," and described my own planned posture—fun, no-sweat—by way of encouraging her to play it the same way.

"Just be yourself," I suggested the night before. "Be supportive."

"I thought you wanted me to be myself," replied my wife wittily (I hoped). Wrapped tightly in her own arms, she stared wide-eyed at the living room floor.

"You're always telling me to *play the game*," I parried. "Right? To stop telegraphing my contempt for the business and *be nice*. I'm just following your wise counsel, dear."

"Hee fuckin' hee." My wife continued to stare, arms straightjacketed, resistance rising off her like gas from a swamp. "No cheese," she finally said.

"Excuse me?"

"As an hors d'oeuvre." Then, with grudging acquiescence: "Nuts."

Given this show of magnanimity, I assumed we'd be okay. Later, standing amidst the wreckage, I understood that I'd entered the evening leading with my chin: soaring on the outcome of having trusted Jessica, I had forgotten that trust could be misplaced.

Things began well enough, for which I had the supper-singing women to thank. Jason, I could see, was thrown by Brooke's astonishing logorrhea, which—amplified by her large, inanimate features and barrel chest—was equal to being caught in the path of a rampaging elephant. Yet she specialized in scabrous stories about famous actors, and the unmixed pleasure of this trash talk banished utterly the pain of her yammering. As for Debbie, she had long ago discovered that her obtuseness could be entertaining, as when she threw up her hands, waggled them beside her ears, and cried, "Why go to therapy when you can take drugs? I don't get it. I just don't get it."

Had Jason not been present, the evening would have ended with my wife and I washing up and agreeing that our guests were "good eggs" and the occasion had been "nice enough." But Jason was present indeed—and it was he, indulging his arrogance, who brought out of my wife the dreaded worst.

His manner, I confess, caught me by surprise. I'd always met with him at the studio, and its oppressive omnipotence had subtly bonded us, so that his cynicism regarding the industry became something in which I could participate. In my home, however—now the avatar of that industry rather than its victim—Jason played top dog, he expected to be deferred to and agreed with, and I noticed how quick he was to quash my perception of our equality, pretending upon arrival not to see my outstretched hand, leaving the door for me to close while he shlumped toward Brooke with a sullen toss of his forelock.

Not that I cared, much. Jason was trolling Lake Infidelity, and if Cutting the Screenwriter served the end, in his view, of increasing his attractiveness, well, wasn't I using him, too? He sinned, however, when he extended this behavior to my wife. It was too easy: Naturally curious and effusive, she over-grinned and asked too many questions when nervous; understanding this, Jason treated her with condescension rather than kindness, answering her inquiries about what it was, exactly, that a studio executive did with supercilious aphorisms ("I say no"), the while telegraphing his belief that she wasn't very suitable mate-of-screenwriter material.

At first my wife fell silent, feeling, I could see, humiliated by Jason's treatment; then, as her ego rushed endorphins to her emotional wounds, she began to hate him, clinically, watching Jason with affectless eyes as she dipped each of his qualities in the acid bath of disdain; until, finally, this hostility began to globalize, to become pronounced in my wife's manner and uncomfortably chill the air.

The chill turned to ice about halfway through dinner. My wife emerged from the kitchen carrying a platter, and the "More fish?" she addressed to Jason stopped the conversation. It was an arresting moment. Had my wife been married to someone else—had this not been *my dining room*—I might have regarded the extra-dry blend of boredom and loathing with which she invested "More fish?" as a valuable acting lesson, an example of how a change of mood could be signaled with lethal efficiency. I was, however, not this drama's observer, and so quickly picked up my cue, lobbing Brooke a question, unleashing another verbal fusillade. Not that I kidded myself. Good actress that she was, my wife had committed to her choice, and to my loaded looks she responded with an impenetrable sullenness. We might have an incident or not. It was out of my hands.

When, inevitably, she lost it (one does not depart such moods without receiving satisfaction), the surprise was that my wife attacked, not Jason, but me. And with gusto: she could not, in fact, have beheaded my aspirations more savagely or cleanly.

"I'm sorry, that's a total piece of crap, that movie, and you know it," said my wife.

I'd been praising a potboiler that had just collected a brace of Oscars. All our guests had been waiting for this— the social tension had become excruciating, it would have snatched the aplomb from Proust. Now, relieved that at last the shoe had dropped (and not on them), they turned to look, first, at my wife, and then, attentively, at me.

"Noooo," I said, drawing out the word, looking at her warningly, "I *don't* know it. I think it's a well-made piece of genre filmmaking, in the best American style."

"*You* told *me*," said my wife, leaning forward, planting her fists on either side of her plate, "that *you* thought it was *crude* and predictable."

Hearing this—knowing every word was true—Jason sneered. I could feel something turn in him, away from the snow job I'd been giving the table and toward his original opinion of me, a judgment reinforced by my selection of wife.

Flop sweat filmed my upper lip. The situation, I told myself, might yet be salvaged. But before I could begin to do so, Debbie's husband Newton—who had been scraping icing off his dessert plate with the side of his fork—chose to weigh in.

"If it's such a piece of crap," he said leadingly, in his Jewish parrot's voice, "why did it win so many awards?"

My wife, as we all knew she would, made a short scoffing sound. "Like *winning awards* has anything to do with quality," she said.

Continuing to scrape up his icing with showy meticulousness, he replied, "I guess you're a real expert."

I looked at him like, *Fuck you, man.* Even Debbie shook her head. I don't know why Newton thought he could get away with this dig at my wife's professional malaise. It was an ugly crack, and given the anxiety level in the room, reckless in the extreme. Maybe it was the arrogance of a Cedars-Sinai big shot, known colloquially as Mr. Bypass, who considered that he was slumming in this crowd. Or else—like the rest of us—he'd had it with being on the short, sharp leash of my wife's hostility.

Newton was not, however, prepared for her response: My wife drew in her chin, squinted at him with contempt, and sang out, "Fock *yew.* Don't get shitty with me, you, you *doctor.* You go to the movies, you don't know *what* the fuck you're looking at."

Newton looked at my wife carefully. "My taste is—"

"What? As good as mine? Boy, is *that* the last stand of the ignorant," said my wife, leaning across the table toward him. "You're"—making finger quotes in the air—"'entitled to your opinion.' But it's not *informed*, okay? It just amazes me," said my wife, addressing the very quiet, very uncomfortable assembly, "that every Tom, Dick and Harry thinks his opinion about the movies is worth listening to, because he's *been* to the *movies.*"

"Doesn't seeing a thousand movies inform your opinion?" Brooke said swiftly, thrusting forward her great breasts, as though they leant authority to her observation.

"*Has he studied?*'" said my wife, thrusting her own weapon at Brooke, a face contorted into the visual equivalent of shrillness. "Why don't I go crack someone's chest for him?"

"Let's move on," I said.

"Fock *yew*," came the magic words again, and now my wife brought the drama back home, "*don't* patronize me."

A moment passed in which all of us considered it dangerous to speak. My wife glared at me, grossly offended. I saw nothing in her eyes to suggest that she knew what she'd done.

"Actually," Jason said.

Our heads turned as one. No one, we realized, would venture into this riptide without having figured out how to outwit it.

"Whatever I might think about what you're saying," he continued in his mordant monotone. "In this case, the doctor is correct. It is a matter of taste. Because," leaning forward in his best executive-suite style, "in terms of craft, the movie is of the very highest order." Jason turned his gaze from my wife to Brooke with the deliberation of a tank turret. He curled his lip into a grin. "And I know because...*I've studied.*"

Jason's late-game homer, acknowledged with the raucous laughter of relief, put a period to the evening. "I'll call you," he said, looking me in the eye with a realism that signaled the opposite, then hurried to walk Brooke to her car. I closed the door on the thanks-it-was-lovelys, sat down on the couch, and dropped my head into my hands.

In the kitchen, my wife moved with a mournful slowness as she put away the dregs of dinner.

Implicit in what I heard, I believed, was grievance rather than remorse, my wife's certainty that, not only was it she who'd been victimized, I would shortly compound the injustice by attacking her. This strategic mendacity—which I'd extrapolated from the sound of plates being scraped—helped me decide my feelings. I was *fuming.* Yet I could not decide if my rage was just, or had been inflated to obscure my complicity—my awareness that, while seeming to work on the marriage, I'd been running from its most difficult questions.

I got up and went in, leaning against the cabinetry opposite the stove. My wife remained at the sink with her back to me, shoulders hunched pitiably.

"Things were going so much better," I said—aware, as I spoke, of the truth and the lie in the statement.

My wife turned to face me, her posture put-upon, wide eyes resigned. "Go ahead, yell," she said. "That's what you always do."

"And wouldn't I be a fool to respond to *that*. All I have to say—all there *is* to say—is that I can't trust you."

My own words pierced me—this, I believed: that beneath my rage lay the wreckage of the well-being, based on trust, on which I'd soared since my tryst with Jessica.

"Aren't I allowed to speak?" said my wife, sounding the note of gross offense she'd struck at dinner. "*You* didn't come to my defense."

I felt myself redden. The speed with which she'd dropped her victim's pose, the tack she'd chosen now to take, snuffed the candle of ambivalence in my brain. "You didn't jump on Newton," I said, "not at first. You told *me* I was full of shit and implied that I'd changed my opinion for the purposes of the conversation."

"Which you did."

I grunted with disgust, throwing myself into one of the metal folding chairs at the kitchen table—feeling that, if I had one more conversation like this, I'd die of it, as if from a disease. "Yes, dear," I replied with weary misery, "that was the *point*, that's why Jason was *here*. So he'd see that I was prepared to play by the rules, and give me a job."

"Well why couldn't you just tell him that?" said my wife, whacking her thigh for emphasis. The canny outrage abruptly disappeared, leaving hurt in its place. "Why did you have to do this whole bullshit thing, why did you have to make *me* a part of, of the dishonesty?" She shook an inexpertly made fist. "Why is *my participation* so important?"

Ordinarily, I'd have seen this as more manipulation, my wife resurrecting her aging hippie's contempt for the hypocrisies of business to avoid responsibility. But though she was wrong about my expectation—that she be complicit in a fraud that betrayed her nature—I could feel the depth of her belief. My wife's argument remained a chain mail of strategic dishonesties. Beneath it, however, lay a wound that was genuine.

I might have examined that wound. But my need to win—to be vindicated, even at the expense of a nuanced truth—leapt to the lead of my instincts. "It's business," I said. "It's the way I chose to do it, given my objective and the man involved."

"*Your* choice," said my wife. "But you're forcing me to play this part that's *not me*—it's, it's like you're *denying* me—"

"Oh, please," I brayed, "you're *stuck*, and *un*happy, and *un*productive, and instead of *contributing* who you are—" I flung my arms extravagantly onto the table. "How about *producing* something from your interesting mind? Hah? *For a change*. That, *without* destroying my objectives, moves the conversation along?" Instantly my wife clammed up and retreated to the sink. "So when Jason goes home, he's thinking, *Gee*. Not *only* has that guy changed his *at*titude. He's got that *smart wife*," snarling the last two words. "Hah? Why not that, *ever, once*, why the *fuck* not that?"

Her arms as ever straitjacketed, my wife listened furiously. But this gave me no peace: her silent admission that she might have played a smarter game only raised my anger's temperature. Whether because I'd goosed myself up to win, or out of a terrible bitterness at having my trust betrayed, I could feel myself, as never before, losing control.

"*No*," I said, in a voice hard enough to break bone. "What you did was take *control* of the situation, which *was* what it *was*, with your shitty, *shitty* negativity."

"I'm not always negative," she said. "I really try, you know, and…" My wife sighed shudderingly; I could smell the hen-house aroma of desperation on her breath. "You're so dissatisfied with me. You make so many demands, I don't think you realize. Do that, do this. Do it *this* way. And no matter what I do, it's never good enough. Do you know how demoralizing that is to live with?"

I shot my wife a disgusted glare, the look I used when she'd scored a point and I needed to recoup. I knew perfectly well that I picked on her, and knew why: unwilling to confront the big issue—that I found our life unbearable—I harped on all the little ones.

But I was not about to admit it. "That's not what we're talking about," I said, "and you know it."

"Why isn't it?" she blurted. "You know—" She released a short chuff, her own desire to win converting despair into disgust. "I *cooked* tonight."

"Yeah, and you were so pissed, you had to punish me—"

"You punished *me*," she yelled, "you didn't stick up for me, you just kept kissing his ass! How much do you have to abase yourself? Wasn't it good enough that, you know, you, you were *pimping* for him?" My wife marched across the room, gesturing dramatically; my fingers seemed to sink into the table's soft pine, the floaters in my eyeballs threw off sparks. "I mean, *hey*," she went on, "*believe* me. I wouldn't have people like Jason in my *house* if it weren't for—'

"Blah, blah, *blah*!" I shouted, leaping up, flinging over the table. The ceramic bowl atop it (a souvenir of our Provençal honeymoon) shattered on the floor, the metal chair opposite me hit the wall and bent like a coat hanger. "Don't you see what you've done? Haven't you learned one fucking thing in all these years?" White-faced, my wife stumbled backward, flinching as I rushed at her.

"*Whoah*," in a voice made loud by fear. "Let's get some control here."

Lurching back like the Frankenstein monster, I booted the chair I'd been sitting on into the wall, then stomped it into sculpture.

"Should I leave?" said my wife, suddenly defiant. "Am I in danger?"

Confused by this change in tone, I froze—and then I understood. Aware that I'd never lift a hand to her, my wife had reached for an emergency drill learned in Al-Anon: she was using the pretense of protecting herself from violence to shift the spotlight to me.

This realization, underlain by our history, broke something I'd long struggled to defend: the remnant of my civility. "Fuck you," I brayed with all the contempt I felt, crowding my wife into the right angle of the kitchen counter. "You are the most destructive, dishonest, evil bitch on earth, you will do anything to avoid dealing with what you've done." My wife, who'd drawn as far from me as she could, looked down her nose, gravely surprised at my ugliness. "You have sabotaged, *destroyed*, my entire life and career, what you did tonight's no different from what you've done for years."

"Don't blame me for—"

"Shutup, *shutup*," I snarled, my head trembling as though it were about to explode. Retreating to the cabinetry by the stove, I put my hands behind me and braced against it. "If you had been able," I said, "to set aside your agenda. On those *incredibly* few occasions when I've needed you to. If you'd been able to control your hatefulness and"—I nearly sobbed— "made me feel that you were on *my side*—I might not be in the mess I'm in today."

"I reject that."

"Maybe nothing would be different professionally," I amended. "But at least I wouldn't feel so…beaten from within." As if with the twist of a lens, a half-decade of emotion came sharply into focus. "Everybody's career goes up and down, everybody *loses* in this fucking business," I said. "But I don't think I'd've *felt* like such a loser." I gestured, sharply, at our home. "If I hadn't lost *here*."

"You'd blame me anyway," said my wife. "You'd find some other reason to hate me."

"You're right, *dear*," I replied, with a dazed, sarcastic laugh, "*don't change*. I mean, why bother, if there's nothing in it for you?"

Hearing my own words—bent nearly double—I looked up at my wife abruptly. It was one of those moments when, lashing out reflexively, one pierces the shroud of self-absorption, and a pinpoint of illumination appears. "You're so fucking self-interested," I said. "Did it ever once occur to you that helping me might be in your interest?"

"How?" said my wife, with a child's innocence.

"*How.* If I did well, you'd benefit, that's how. And you wouldn't have a husband who hates you."

We held each other's gaze a moment longer; then looked away. My struggle to preserve a measure of grace between us—to not say things that could never be erased—had been a mistake. I did indeed hate my wife. But in expressing the reasons for that hatred—in pointing out how much better her own LA years might have gone had she helped me with mine—I stumbled over a recognition: my wife's untrustworthiness had to be beyond her control, for the simple reason that it ran so counter to her own welfare. In the silence, I felt a glimmer of that which I'd resisted: the reason why I stayed in the marriage. Our union, seemingly, was in neither of our interests. Yet people did not, in my experience, act against themselves without a reason—usually, the belief that their interests lay elsewhere.

"But not *only* did you not help me," I resumed, tormenting syntax as well as my wife. "I have never had the sense, in *any* situation, that I could just...simply...*trust* you."

Hearing this come out of my mouth depressed me. How much more productive it would have been to share my thoughts! The problem was that I was trying to at once expose the heart of my life's conundrum and win a fight, and these objectives were at odds.

But whereas my wife and I outwardly remained adversaries, something within both of us—catching the scent of possibility—ceased to work at cross-purposes: we were like ideologically opposed regimes that secretly decide to negotiate. Thus did my snipe spark something in my wife that nudged me back toward revelation.

"Well maybe I didn't feel I could trust *you*," she said.

Jessica had said as much. In my mind, my deception was justified, even essential. And yet what had my wife been describing, if not her own sense of betrayal? Were we, in our perfect imperfection, so different?

"I don't think asking you to be nice for a lousy three hours amounts to a betrayal of trust," was my reply.

"So for three hours it can all just cease to exist?" said my wife, her shoulders shooting up to her ears. "Why is that okay?"

"*What* 'ceased to exist'?"

"Us! This!" My wife, I could see, was fanning her own revelatory spark. "You run from our relationship, you run from our, our *values*. Like they were…" She inhaled deeply through her nose. "Like they were a bus stop you were waiting at. Til the bus came to take you where you want to go."

"Is that so."

"Yes!" said my wife, eyes darting wildly. "That's what living with you feels like! These people tonight, it was like they were your bus, they *came* in and you *jumped* aboard and took off—*so relieved* you could leave me!" She put her chin in her palm and shook her head. "That is so painful because *I. Feel. Paralyzed*, I can't get on the bus. It's not handicapped-accessible." My wife laughed grimly and looked sideways, toward the past. "My mom, boy," she said. "Talk about negative. But my father? Would *never* distance himself from her. Certainly not in front of people."

"What would you have had me do?" I said.

"Why can't I be myself?" said my wife, combative again.

"Define 'myself.'"

"Critical, why can't I be critical?" I laughed, she did, too, but quickly broke it off. "It's not funny," she said crossly. "And you *like* that, that I'm feisty. Offbeat."

"Sure."

"Well *I* don't see why *that* can't be part of a night like this," whacking the back of one hand, then the other, on the counter for emphasis. "I don't see why you're practically painting a *sign* on the wall that says, 'I'm Not With Her.'"

Talked out, my wife held herself and caught her breath. I pushed my fingers into the pockets of my jeans and faced her. "It's not what you say," choosing my words with care, "it's where you're coming from. You claim I'm running from our values. All I'm trying to do is have a career."

"I *want* you to—"

"But you *don't*, you *don't*, you *don't*. You don't want me to have anything outside of *this*," gesturing around me. I turned to look at the dining room, the artful disarray of the glasses and plates. "Whenever you see me in, in *action*," I said, considering what had transpired, "when people are responding to me, *listening* to me—the instant I have people's attention, you make a fool of me. You can't stop yourself."

"Why would I do that?" said my wife, defiant, curious.

"Because you're afraid that if the world took at interest, I'd jump on that bus and leave you behind 'cause you're nobody."

"'Well that's how you *treat* me—"

"No," moving toward her. "*No. I'm* not the one who thinks you're nobody. Do you understand?"

My wife stared at me, lips parted.

"That's why 'feisty and offbeat' is always at my expense," I continued, "it's always about my humiliation. You have it just backwards. I wouldn't run away from you if you were on my side. But you think that if anyone else took an interest I'd leave you, because who would stay with a nobody if they had an alternative? So you destroy my chances, you ruin my optimism, my confidence. Over and over and over. To hold on to me." We were very close now. "And *that's* why I want to run away."

Exhaling, I backed off. My wife took her eyes off me; she picked up the least mangled of the two chairs, and righted it. Perching atop the twisted piece of metal, she drew her knees up to her chin and enveloped her legs with her arms, holding herself as if no one else on earth would do so.

"I know what you're saying about your mom and dad," I continued. "But he was a professor—they had to maneuver through academia, a world every bit as political as the film business. I'm sure they accommodated one another as necessary."

"Who they were," said my wife, "didn't have to change in company."

"Your mother wasn't aware of your dad's position, and how her life depended on it?"

The word "depended" sent a wave of vulnerability washing across my wife's eyes. Her parents were as different from one another as we were, but they'd prospered with the help of their marriage. Yet considering my wife's reaction, I was reminded of the special anxiety she'd described as permeating the life of her family. Her father had stuck by her mother through three years in an iron lung, and the four ensuing decades until her death. Still, my wife's mother remained gripped by the fear that, if overburdened, her husband might do as so many other spouses of polio victims had done: leave. Perhaps my wife's mother, famously eccentric and difficult, had indeed been indulged by her husband. But she'd also believed herself to be dependent upon him for survival. And so, according to my wife, there had been a behavioral line in her head that she would never cross.

Watching my wife atop her deformed pedestal, it occurred to me that we had, in Los Angeles, developed a variant of her parents' situation. Until the wheels came off, I had the career and made the money; my wife remained nominally dependent upon me in these respects. But she wasn't a paraplegic, she'd inherited a jackpot in stocks, and these differences had, it seemed, erased whatever mental line my wife might have drawn. Perhaps she had envisioned a marriage not unsimilar to her mother's, only better: one in which her difficulties were accepted, as her mother's had been, yet without the disability that had been her mother's excuse, or the dependence that had restricted her behavior.

Alas, my wife's reaction suggested that, in the most critical respect, her fantasy had not materialized: the essential inheritance—a terror of abandonment—had remained. I wasn't sure what underlay her silence. But I suspected she was considering that it had been her mother's fear, rather than her father's forbearance, that had made that marriage work.

Finally, my wife spoke. "Mom was incredibly difficult. Having guests didn't change that. So far as I can remember, she didn't get shit on after everyone went home."

"Can you imagine her humiliating your father in front of his colleagues?"

After a hesitation, my wife said, "No."

"When the situation demanded it," I said, "they were a team. A marriage can be missing a lot of things. But not that." I considered the spectacle of my wife, her mad hair, the frayed shirt she'd bought in Rome decades ago, faded to a perfect shade of sage, and felt a flash of my first attraction to precisely this eccentricity. "I never expected you to change," I said, again feeling the truth and the lie in my words. "But you haven't been there for me."

"Then why do you put up with it?" she said exhaustedly.

The question that was too painful, that I'd dodged since the start of our troubles. My wife's behavior, which had seemed as self-defeating as my own, had revealed a compelling inner logic. Perhaps my own failure to act served me in ways I did not understand.

"I guess I keep hoping you'll get it," thinking it through. "I have this fantasy that, if I just keep asking you over and over for help and support, one day the fog will lift and"—I shrugged—"things'll be different."

My wife gave no sign that she'd heard; I, too, withdrew, my thoughts lapping across my words like water over stones. There was something about the process I'd described—the asking and the not getting—that was deeply hateful, yet profoundly comforting. Leaving the moment, I went to the whorehouse in my head and studied the faces of the great repeaters I saw there: girls whose expressions revealed precisely my own mixture of loathing and need.

I knew, I believed, what lay behind that look. Bonnie, the most lucid of my paid friends, had observed that every girl she'd met had been abused—"'not all of them sexually, a lot of girls, they had these really controlling parents. Abuse like *that*"—and it had become an article of faith with me that most whores were attempting to redress that primal wrong.

I had often compared my abusive marriage to the girls' traumas. Yet, closing the door to my mental whorehouse, returning to my silent wife, I reflected that I'd never tried to concretize what had been taken by that abuse.

"What's so painful," I said, doing so now, "is that when something like tonight happens, it destroys something fundamental in me. That sense of hopelessness, the *woe* when it's reconfirmed—that, no matter how many times it happens, how many times we *talk* about it…" I trailed off. As was always the case, there seemed to be no place to go with this.

My wife raised her shoulders, then turned the gesture into a shrug. "Do you try and do other things?"

"What, you mean like, *get help?*" I said, ridicule heavy in my voice. I could, of course, have used help. But the belief that she only suggested it to distract me from her treachery had hopelessly tainted the issue.

"*Please* listen to me," said my wife as I gulped air. Her round-eyed gaze was fixed, her voice calm, as though possessed by a commitment to what she wished to say.

I folded my arms and waited.

"If you *need* something, and I can't give it to you, that's *your* responsibility," my wife said with a note of elegy. "Your refusal to take responsibility for your needs—*that's* what's 'sabotaged your life.' Not me."

I stared at my wife dumbly.

"Cutting yourself off from me," she continued, "it's no different from yelling at me, blaming me, trying to get me to do something. It's still *me*, it's *me, me*," her voice incantatory. "What about *you?*"

I turned away bitterly, as though my wife didn't get it and never would. In fact, I was struggling to come to terms with something I had, in my heart, always known: that my wife couldn't be changed in the way I wanted her to be. What I should more properly be looking at was myself, and the very particular scenario I had chosen to repeat: the effort to get something from someone who was incapable of giving it.

My wife remained motionless, looking stricken at her

presumed failure to get through to me. What, I wondered, watching her, did the image of a man endlessly trying to get what could not be gotten reveal to me? Why had this man chosen to form a primary attachment (as the saying goes) to someone who would always betray him?

Abruptly my thoughts stepped out of the forest in which they were lost. "It is," I said, "*childish* to do what I do."

"Childish," said my wife, curling up in the chair, laying her cheek on her knees.

"This scenario," I said, to myself, aloud, "is the one about the disappointed child who hopes that, if he just keeps asking, he'll get what he's not getting. And never does." I cleared my throat. "Excuse me."

I went upstairs to the bathroom and washed my face. Looking at myself in the mirror, I thought: *Do not ask for what you will not get. And everything will be different.*

This was, I thought, precisely the resolution I needed to make—I had in fact made it in regard to Martin when we'd first met, and done so with Wendy before that. Yet my vow filled me with a profound sense of sorrow. I was giving up my oldest, most cherished dream: that of receiving a certain kind of perfect love.

In my twenties, I'd seen a shrink, a fat-faced narcissist who—by raising one eyebrow and sneering at my every utterance—made me feel so stupid, I was certain he was right about everything. Despite my subsequent reevaluation of the work we did, I remained aware that, on one occasion, this man had handed me a key. I was describing one of my unhappy relationships (all of which, to borrow and reverse a phrase, were unhappy in the same way), and my therapist, folding his arms with his usual grandiosity, said, "Kid"—he was about ten years my senior—"you only get one shot at unconditional love, and if you miss it, it's gone for good. There is no such animal," he declared, "as adult-onset unconditional love."

"What's the one shot?" I asked, with my usual unguarded cluelessness.

Up went the eyebrow, out came the sneer. "Childhood," he said.

At the time, my shrink's observation remained nothing more to me than a notion. Now, staring at my dripping face in the mirror, I was able to convert it into belief—and, so doing, found the answer to the question I'd avoided. I had stayed with my wife—I had continued to throw the same bitter tantrum, rather than taking responsibility for my needs—because I could not accept that I had missed the perfect love I wanted, that it was gone for good. This was how the marriage served me: It enabled me to enact, repeatedly, the drama of this insult, until the pain became so great, I could no longer resist its meaning: that no adult woman, with adult expectations, was going to love me the way a mother loves a child.

Accepting the impossibility of this wish, I felt able to give it up—just like that, I gave it up. With this change came another: Whatever might happen in the future, the marriage I had made was over.

My sense of loss felt similar to what I'd experienced upon deciding to give up screenwriting. Yet it was saying goodbye to the movies, I considered, drying my face, starting back down the stairs, that had enabled me to return to them, with an attitude that might let me work in a way that better suited my talent. Perhaps a variant of this could be applied, with equal promise, to my marriage.

Reaching the living room, I switched off the CD player, listening as my wife swept up the shards of the bowl I'd broken. That was appropriate: how often had we cleaned up one mess, so that we might move on to another? My ability to continue in the marriage had depended upon more than my own immaturity: my wife nurtured her own childish desires, her own anger over a primal wrong. The only grownup I knew was Jessica, and her behavior was instructive. When I'd forced myself into her, rather than succumbing to a variant of my tantrum, she had converted what we did into an act of love. This refusal to allow a destructive experience to control her enabled Jessica, not only to strengthen herself, but to help me find my own humanity.

This was what I owed my wife—not the profane screaming that was meant, not for her, but my own ghosts. I had to do what Jessica had done for me: If she and I could turn the evening's betrayal into an act of love, my wife might enjoy the identical sense of well-being I'd experienced. More important: I would no longer be a victim, of her or of myself.

I returned to the kitchen, to find my wife emptying a dustpan full of broken crockery into the trash. "I'm sorry," I said. "That was dumb."

My wife knocked the dustpan against the edge of the can. "It's just a thing," she said.

"Yes. But it was our thing."

My wife went into the laundry room to put away the broom. She emerged holding her running clothes.

"You're not going *running*."

"Putting them back in the bathroom," where they typically hung after my wife's workouts. "I took them out because God forbid His Highness"—meaning Jason—"should have to whiff my stinking shorts while he was taking a leak."

Smiling at this, I saw my opening. "I think it's great, your discipline."

"Yeah, yeah…" My wife held her sweat-stained clothes loosely, her gaze distracted and resigned. "I do have discipline, but it's like." She looked at me. "One of the things I'm disciplined about is being loyal to my mother's negativity."

"What do you mean?"

"It's a way of holding on to her, getting her back."

"I wouldn't think you'd want her back."

"Maybe," she said, "I've gone back to *her*."

This surprised me: my wife's relationship with her mother had been an unrelieved nightmare from beginning to end. I'd heard all about the bind in which my wife, as a child, had found herself: with a mother who, having been struck an unimaginably cruel blow, remained beyond criticism, and so was allowed to inflict her own crippling wound, by blaming her six-year-old for transmitting the disease to her. I'd heard my wife's stories, about her mother's alternation of dissatisfaction ("If you had any spine, any spine at all, you'd be on a bus to Selma now") and ridicule ("You're passing up an orgy to do *homework?*") with abrupt spasms of cruelty, as at the dinner at which, apropos of nothing, she'd thrown a plate of food in my wife's face. Looking at her now as she held her running clothes and stared at the floor, I thought of Bonnie's observation that one didn't have to have been raped or beaten to have been abused. My wife had been a human sacrifice, the one chosen to receive her mother's outrage so that the rest of the family might go on. If that wasn't child abuse, nothing was.

"Have you forgotten," I said, "how you used to go on about your mother?"

"No." She shook her head, looking amused. "But, you know…My relationship with Mom has really turned around since she died."

Hearing this, I released a groan that turned into a barely audible laugh. "I thought the idea was, you cut loose the resentment, you forgave and you moved *on*," I said. "You're not supposed to forgive your mother, then *become the thing you forgave her for being.*"

My wife nodded; she held her cheek sorrowfully. "The last time I went to see her, I was standing by the bed. There was just a little bit of life left, she was really in and out. And I was just, you know, trying to take it in—that *my mom*, who had for so many years struggled to live…That I was witnessing the end of that struggle. There was this long silence; I thought she was asleep. Then—very clearly—she said: 'I never thought I loved you. But now I see I did.'"

My wife's head was lowered. But I could see in her expression a gratitude, at the receipt of a benediction she had long wished for, and long ago given up hope of receiving.

"Well," I said, coughing. "That's great."

A single tear rolled down my wife's cheek. With her usual insistence on doing even the simplest things backwards, she turned her hand upside down and caught the droplet with her pinky.

"I know," said my wife. "But now I'm thinking maybe I made a devil's bargain. For so long, we had this standoff—she was so disapproving, right up to the end. And, boy, I wasn't giving in. And then *she* gave in."

"And?"

"And maybe I just stopped fighting to be myself," said my wife sufferingly. "In exchange for that deathbed confession of love. I mean, it's like you say, you want to forgive and move on, but maybe I feel guilty for winning, and my punishment or my debt is to carry on all those things I spent my life struggling against."

"Like her negativity."

My wife nodded. "It's almost like it's a *relief*, you know? Like, thank God, she's gone, I can stop trying to separate myself from my legacy."

"It's funny you should describe it as a discipline."

"You know how I have to run every day to feel like myself? Well, that negativity is part of what I need to feel every day, to feel like myself."

Listening to this, I felt an anger, a resistance to my wife's words, that was powerfully at odds with my desire to show that she could trust me. I understood: her problems were profound and ingrained, and I did not want to have to deal with them. Without any sense that I was succumbing to false obligation, I reminded myself that I had lived with this woman for many years, no one had put a gun to my head. I thought: *Be a man.*

"How did it manifest itself?" I said. "Your mother's negativity."

"You know what Mom was like. She was very handi-capped, the only way she could have control was by denying everyone their pleasure."

"Yeah, but how, exactly? Give me a for-instance."

"Okay. Her favorite way? *You* would have *loved* this. Was to have people over for dinner and not make enough food."

"Really," I said. "How very interesting."

Dropping her running clothes, my wife took center stage

in the kitchen, hands gesturing beside her vivid face. "She'd sauté a couple of mushrooms—toadstools, right? Not, like, *shitakes* or anything—and put them over brown rice. For ten people!" My wife shrieked with laughter, taking a malicious delight in the memory. "She used to ask me to come in the kitchen? And there'd be this *little tiny plate* with this *little tiny pile* of burnt-to-a-crisp poison mushrooms on it. And she'd say"—my wife thinned her voice into a reedy midwestern twang—"'You don't think that's *too much*, do you?'" Again she cackled, her laughter rattling up and down the do-re-mis. "The guests would get up to pee, then sneak into the kitchen and rifle around for a cracker so they didn't starve. The smart ones brought food!" My wife cocked a hip and shook her head. "And God help you if it was winter."

"Why?"

"She wouldn't put the heat on! Bad for you! So everyone, you know, professors and grad students and, or else these big-shot architects Dad was friends with, they'd all be huddled around the table wrapped in these threadbare shawls Mom crocheted, while they *slowly* ate these *tiny* mounds."

"Was your mother, by any chance, *too cheap* to put the heat on?"

"Hey. You think *I'm* bad. Mom *dreaded* parting with a dime."

"It wasn't *her* money."

"I know, it was Dad's, and boy, she was adamant: not too much pressure on the old man." Leaning against the refrigerator, my wife folded her arms beneath her breasts and looked bitter. "Everybody made such a big fuckin' deal about what a saint my father was, for not abandoning his crippled wife and little children. Uh, ex*cuse* me? Since when is doing what you're supposed to mean you walk on water?"

"Not everyone did, I gather. What they were supposed to."

"Yeah, but, you know, nobody gives Mom any credit, if it wasn't for her toadstool-and-shmatte theme parties, Dad wouldn't have had a social life at all. Everybody liked *her*.

She used to get interested in people she thought had, as she put it, 'star quality,' and bring them into the house." Remembering, my wife's eyes shone. "Into *our lives*—these interesting people! Mom was a, an *appealing oddball*. Not just this cripple who should thank her lucky stars she didn't get thrown out in the street"—she sobbed once, violently—"because who could love someone who couldn't walk."

"Well, but he *did* love her. Your father. He encouraged her, to take the lead in the ways she could."

"What, socially?" said my wife, both pinkies working the tear-trails on her cheeks. "Yeah. Yeah, I guess." Then, with fresh outrage: "Because she was good at it and he wasn't!"

"I'm saying, your father didn't see your mother as helpless," I said. "You're assuming he felt the way the world did—that he was doing her a favor—but he recognized she was a partner with strengths he didn't have, and left those things to her."

"Yeah. Yeah, she was the one with the fears, that's true." My wife snuffled and looked weary. "Mom took a little less, she made everyone else take less. And was negative. Having a full stomach was bad, being warm was bad. Dressing nice, having nice things. Bad, bad, bad."

"Your mom did her best."

"I know she did. It's just so sad"—up came the windshield-wiper pinkies—"it's why, you know," she laughed tiredly, "our relationship's gotten better. Because I see that she did her best. In a way, it was clever. I mean, it wasn't like this woman who had no upper-body strength was going to *cook a meal*. So instead of making something like, you know. *Normal*. Which would have meant people saying, Oh, isn't it wonderful, how this *poor woman* made this tuna casserole? She did things that were extravagantly, outrageously horrible. As a *style*."

"To be special."

"To be special. She was, I gotta hand it to her, she was not going to sit in that chair and be defined."

"So your mother's denial of pleasure wasn't just a way of having control," I said. "It was part of how she found to be a participant."

My wife nodded. "You know how my favorite thing is to be in a group? Of engaged, creative people? I get that from her." She sat in the bent red chair and drew her knees up, playing with her toes as she talked. "My mother desperately, desperately wanted to belong."

"She *did*."

"You mean…"

"All those people she brought into your lives."

My wife nodded minutely, her eyes far away. "I know it's terrible to say. And, you know. There's nothing I ever wished for harder than that Mom could have been able to walk again. But maybe the life she had was the best one for her."

"Well, it's not like she had a choice," I said.

"Yeah, but she was a dissatisfied woman beforehand. She used to say, she and Dad wouldn't have lasted if she hadn't gotten sick."

"Easy enough to say."

"Exactly. It was a fantasy. That, if only she hadn't been stuck in that chair, she'd've found the gumption to change her life." My wife shrugged. "She felt trapped and dissatisfied as a parent and a professor's wife, but maybe the truth was, she didn't have what it took to be an artist. And was afraid." My wife sighed, emotionally. "Crippled or not—afraid."

"Let me ask you something," I said. "If you'd been one of those people eating mushrooms and freezing their asses off. Would you have been charmed?"

My wife made a face. "In small doses."

"Can you be loyal to your mother in that way?"

"You mean, could I embrace the other part, not…"

"Not the part you experienced. The part you witnessed. Because, really, in positive ways, you *are* like your mother. You're a charming eccentric. You're, or you *can* be, encouraging. And you're very lovable. If you could find a way to…*amputate* those things of your mother's that *aren't* good…"

"As you say," with a slight, hard resistance. "Her good

qualities I observed. Her bad ones, I felt."

"Feelings aren't facts," I said with pleasure, as it was one of her favorite Al-Anon nostrums.

"Ha fuckin' ha." Then: "The part of my mother that I've most internalized isn't her negativity."

"What then?"

"Her fear."

"Of not having what it takes?"

"Of being abandoned and not being able to take care of myself," said my wife. "Of being helpless."

"You're not helpless," I said. "And as long as you don't abandon *yourself*, you'll never be alone."

I'd felt inclined to say, simply, "You're not alone," implying that I would never leave her. But just as I'd determined to not ask for what I would not get, neither did I want to say what I didn't believe. Instead, I had told my wife the truth, and while it might have been less reassuring than an avowal of eternal companionship, at least I hadn't violated her trust. Understanding this, something turned in me: I saw the true magnitude of the lies I had been spouting. I wasn't revealing what was in my heart; and the difference between what I said and what my wife surely intuited produced an emotional vertigo that caused her to mistrust herself, to feel more helpless, fearful, alone. Far worse than my secret life of sex and stimulants was the secret life of my feelings. Whether or not I could return to her, as I'd returned to the movies, was an open question. But more than the entire conversation, in which I'd tried to shut up, to listen to my wife and help her come to her own conclusions, the omission of the tiny sentence "You're not alone" was a step toward finding out.

My wife lifted her head. "I'm sorry I spoiled things tonight," she said.

"I'm sorry I made you feel abandoned."

My wife unfolded herself and stood. She shifted her jaw and looked to one side—a look, I knew, of uncertainty.

"I feel, I've been feeling for a long time, that you're not there," she began. "I mean, the way we're talking—this is *sooo* great. I don't want to take away from…"

"I understand."

"You're absolutely right, I can't abandon myself or be helpless. But *are* you abandoning me?" My wife looked at me, closely. "What's going on with you?"

A practiced liar, I returned her look evenly. "I have been unhappy for a long, long time," I said. "And lately, I've been wrestling with what seems to me to be the main question: What is it that keeps me here, when I'm so unhappy?"

My wife turned her eyes aside and nodded, waiting.

"I've been trying to get things from you that you're not capable of giving," I continued. "And I don't mean that critically, like, Why can't you be a better wife?"

"You mean we're both adults."

"Yes," looking at her. "Yes, exactly. And, as you say, if there are things you can't give me, I have to take care of that myself."

"Yes."

"Because everything else gets pushed out, my…"—I saw it clearly—"…my inner life gets pushed out. Anyway. I need to look at those things I need that I'm not getting. And see if they're compatible with the marriage."

My wife tightened her lips and nodded, then blew out her breath. "Well, you're right, obviously," she said. "I just—I mean, you have to decide, but I guess I feel it'd be a shame to throw out the baby with the bathwater. I mean, this is *so nice*—*this* is *in*-ti-ma-cy. And we have all this history, I mean"—my wife bulged her eyes and rocked from foot to foot—"you…knew…*Mom*."

I nodded, I smiled; my wife's mother did not occupy so central a position in my own cosmography. Yet the old woman had made, to my life, a contribution of surpassing significance. "It was meeting your mom that made me think I was in love with you," I said.

"*What?*"

"I thought you were very brave, to have done so well, given what you had to overcome."

"Oh, so, you sentimentalized my unhappy childhood."

I grinned. "Yeah. And look how I've been punished." Then: "There's nothing wrong with loving someone because you're proud of her."

"You know what's interesting?" said my wife.

"What?"

"You know what you said? About how being angry pushes out your inner life?"

"Yes?"

"Well," said my wife, "it doesn't just push out your creative life. It pushes out the inner life of *us*."

"What do you mean?"

"Well, you know, *creatively*, when your mind isn't filled with shit, you make connections. So that when you, like, *have an idea*, behind it is everything you've done that's brought you to that moment."

"Uh-huh." I was very interested in where my wife was going with this.

"Well when we talk to each other without an agenda, that whole history *we* have can be present. The past isn't pushed out. I mean, look at all the things that've been coming up."

"You're absolutely right," I said.

My wife tilted up her chin and batted her eyes, smiling with self-satisfaction.

"It's true," I said, "I don't think I've thought of that moment—that first moment of love—since it happened."

"Huh," said my wife. "I bet you forgot there was a time you ever loved me *period*."

I mimed locking my lips and throwing away the key. In truth, I felt, at that moment, the same love for my wife I'd experienced so many years before, my heart soared in response to the elegance of what she'd said. And as we released the last of our animosity and embraced, I thought, How difficult it is, to know what's in one's heart. I had been certain that, if only I could understand why I'd hung on, I would be able to take my leave. Now I realized that I could not make a decision until I saw what remained when the neurotic tie that bound me to the marriage was eliminated. Just when I felt things would be over, I realized they'd just begun. I held my wife, we put our chins on each other's shoulders, I marveled at what I felt and wondered exhaustedly what it was all about.

"It's funny," said my wife, releasing me. "As difficult as hearing what you've said has been. Knowing that you're not going to attack me makes the hard things easier."

So I had succeeded, I had been able to give my wife a bit of what Jessica had given me. "I'll try and learn how to make accommodations," I said.

My wife made a comic face. "And can we please have more sex, please!"

"Yes. Though not tonight." If I would not ask for what I would not get, nor say what I didn't believe, neither would I do what I did not feel.

Yet as we walked up the stairs to bed, I made the silent admission that my reluctance to make love had as much to do with shyness as depletion of feeling. It it difficult to return to a certain tenderness—to intimacy—once it has been lost: it requires humility, a surrender of pride. But Jessica, I recalled, had helped me to see the benefits of that. And tonight I'd learned another of her lessons: that a willingness to gamble on the humanity of one's intimate destroyer, rather than allowing oneself to be controlled by disappointment, preserved the mind and spirit. As we fell into bed, I thought of Iris Murdoch's observation that "love is the extremely difficult realization that something other than oneself is real." And, too, Beckett's immortal line, "What are you meant to mean?" Perhaps this person, my wife, had never been more to me than a hologram lit by my most intimate longings and sorrows. But she was, in fact, real; and the more I let go of what I'd meant her to mean, the realer she got. Whether that would turn out in the end to be enduring love: we would see.

XXXX

For a while, all my lives were in balance. In each of my inhabitations, I found things to savor, lessons and pleasures that, overlapping their neighbors, amplified and became luminous.

Not that the living was easy. Returning for my third session with Jessica, I envisioned a sexual perpetual motion machine, an organic chain of endless variation. Jessica's imagination, alas, had not similarly taken flight. "Lady's choice," her parting words to me, meant the return of the dildo, and this was an experience I had no need to repeat.

Jessica stood very close to me in the little room. She watched my shoulder with calm attention, as though a fly had alighted on it. "You said, and I quote," she murmured. "'Let's be physically intimate.' What is this resistance?"

"I want to be intimate," I replied in the same neutral murmur, as though we were a pair of spies. "I just don't want to do *that*."

"I thought you liked it."

"It was liberating. Not pleasurable."

Jessica dropped to the edge of the bed, planted her elbows on her knees and let her forearms dangle. "Well I don't know what to do then," she said curtly.

I stared at the top of her head. Jessica's intransigence, the stasis we'd reached so quickly, surprised me.

"I know what to do," I said abruptly.

"What?"

"Let's bring in another girl."

Jessica looked at me. "You want a show?"

I shook my head, sitting on the floor and facing her. "We need to slow down a bit," I said. "Get to know each other *and* ourselves a little better."

"I thought that's what last time was about."

"I did, too. But maybe it was more like, you know. A lucky cast." I thought of the problem I faced with my wife, the difficulty of creating intimacy between people who know each other too well. "We know each other a little too well too quickly," I said aloud.

Jessica nodded, rocking her body gently forward in

rhythm with her rising chin. "That can become a barrier between us," thinking it through. "Or we can use the window we have, between the first attraction and the onset of the status quo. To deepen things."

"Right."

"Where does girl number two fit in?"

I slipped off Jessica's cork-soled sandals and held her perfect white feet in my hands. "I think," I began, "you decided, once upon a time, to be really free about your pursuit of sexual pleasure. And I think as well that, since your experience of that pursuit has been the...*predation* of men, shall we say. You've re-sexed your desire—taken the male thing that was perhaps used against you and turned it around in a way that's restorative. I think that's why it's such a turn-on for you to bugger men."

Beneath her camisole, Jessica's nipples began to harden, the analysis exciting her. I thought: My kind of girl.

"Not," she said in her clotted-cream way, "because I want revenge. I don't, you know."

"I know. You like the *act* because you equate male sexuality with unconstrained pleasure. You like it with *men* because you're not gay."

"So?"

"So girl number two might help you return what you've recast as a male thing to its original gender. *And* get more from it. I mean, do you want to go on buggering men forever?"

Jessica's eyes shifted from side to side; there was the brush of a smile on her lips. "Why, yes," she said.

"Look," changing my tack. "I have a sense that you've not married your sexual aggressiveness to your view of yourself as a woman. You see it as something separate, something male."

"I think I'm pretty female, thank you very much."

"Sure, but I saw that look on your face when you were nailing me. That was completely different from the way you are when you make love as a woman."

"Well, I really get off that way. And"—Jessica hesitated

slightly—"I've never seen a girl get off the way guys get off."

"You're kidding."

Jessica removed her feet from my hands and tucked them defensively against the bed. She'd ventured into an uncomfortable zone, yet felt unable to retreat from it.

"How many women have you actually *seen* get off?" I said.

"Enough. I'm just not connected to the whole female sexuality *thing*. I find it"—she shot her eyes at me—"I find it humiliating."

"Everybody, when they first see someone of their own sex really *get off*? Thinks, 'Is that what *I'm* like?'"

"I suppose."

"So maybe it's easier for you to put distance between yourself and that loss of control. But the fact is, what you've chosen to think of as male is really just the most aggressive aspect of your femininity. And you also have that other female characteristic, that…"

"The intensity that rises to a certain level and sustains itself," with a private smile.

"*Yes*. I'm not telling you *not* to bugger men. I'm just suggesting you unify everything within you. You'll be able to make love with that same passion no matter the circumstances."

"I still don't see what purpose the other girl serves."

"Well." I cleared my throat. "If you only really get off with a dick because you like being a guy. Why not put that dick in a girl, and feel how great it can be when a girl gets off like a girl?" Hearing this mess of words tumble out, like bricks off the back of a truck, I realized how ridiculous was our conversation, and how pleased I was to be having it.

"Boy," Jessica said. "You really overthink this stuff."

"I'm getting better, though."

"If you say so."

I stood, dusting the room's detritus from the seat of my jeans, and sat beside her. Jessica turned to me with amused scorn. "*What* is this supposed to accomplish?"

"What's the ultimate objective? For both of us."

She thought a moment. "Moving on."

"This is about getting a pleasure we can take away."

"What are *you* taking away?"

"Last time," I said, returning Jessica's gaze. "My own aggression. All I could do was ride it. I want that to always be there, so I can control where it goes."

"How will this help?"

"While *you're* getting better acquainted with your female sexuality, by experiencing how much fun a girl can get out of your aggressiveness. *I'll* be sharpening my masculinity by watching you in action. And following suit."

"You're showing me how to be a woman," she said, "and I'm showing you how to be a man?"

Our grins stretched our faces. Jessica put her hands on my shoulders and straddled me, pressing herself into my chest. "Steal my mojo, would you?"

"What are friends for?"

"Hey," her grin loosening, eyes half-closed. "Just because you fucked me doesn't mean we're friends."

Why this wisecrack caused it, I didn't know, but a rush of tenderness flooded my heart. "Haven't you always wanted this?" I blurted.

Jessica's gaze flickered; either she'd had other such connections, or was pondering the possibilities of this one. All she said was, "What if the girl doesn't respond the way you want?"

"But she will, my sweet. Because you'll choose her."

Jessica frowned at herself in the mirror. "Will you smoke a joint?" she said.

"Why?"

"There's this new girl. She's thirty, thirty-two, maybe. Never done this before."

"Actress?"

Jessica nodded. "She's smart—writes a bit. It's still an adventure for her, she hasn't." Jessica glanced at me. "She's not a whore yet."

"What's the weed for?"

"When she gets stoned, she gets horny. Last week, she

came out of an hour and gave me this *look*, you know? Between…surprise and mortification. 'I *came*,' she said."

"Stoned?"

"Stoned. Noelle. She might work."

"Will you supply?" I said.

"Sure. But…"

"What?"

"She's not here tonight."

I had yet to pay. Jessica was still on my lap. We considered each other.

"It's all right," she said. "We've had a nice time."

"Tomorrow?"

"Come at six. I'll make sure we're both free."

Thus it was that, the following evening, I found myself reinstated to the "big" room, sharing a doobie the size of a tailpipe with Jessica and slender, leggy Noelle. I had no idea what manner of persuasion Jessica had used, but Noelle seemed game, if careful. Watching her, I understood what Jessica meant when she said that Noelle had yet to become a whore. When a girl was new to the work, I'd noticed, it could seem for a time like an interesting exercise that taught multiple lessons. Noelle was in this state: with the three of us nude, on our sides, heads propped on our fists and passing a joint, she was leering with anticipation, as though we'd all met at a Laurel Canyon soiree and had decided to adjourn to the hot tub.

"Piggy, piggy," said Noelle, as Jessica sucked the life from the spliff and set it aside.

Jessica crooked a finger at her. The girls got up on their knees, Noelle exhaled and, putting her lips to her sister sex worker's, breathed in deeply as Jessica emptied her lungs.

The sight of two naked girls, rumps thrust out and mouths pressed together, leaked contrails of cannabis smoke hooding them in a fragrant nimbus of sin, was all the encouragement I needed. Taking Noelle by the hand, I drew her away from Jessica and laid her on the mattress so that she bisected it. As my partner made herself comfortable at the bed's foot, I got down on the floor, lowering my head between Noelle's legs as, with a low groan, she released the cloud of smoke.

If I felt, at first, an awkwardness at betraying Jessica beneath her gaze, I quickly forgot myself. Noelle quivered with every stroke of my tongue, emitting a sound like a maraca being rapidly shaken, the heels of her hands pressed to her forehead as though the pleasure proved too much to bear. The girls, in my experience, largely resisted digital insertion, but not Noelle: as I slipped in a finger and began to palpate the terra incognita I found there, her moans became loud, as though a volume control had been incautiously twisted. Encouraged, I sustained my pace until, abruptly, her heels shot skyward, she tilted her pelvis and, connecting a spot within her to my finger's tip, sprayed a jet of fluid that was salty to the taste. Noelle's screams subsided, her legs hung bonelessly down my back; I dried my face on her soft inner thighs. My eyes were on Jessica, on her feet and sliding open the sex-toy drawer, her urgency at odds with her usual reflective state. I understood: she'd never before witnessed female ejaculation—the extremity of Noelle's passion had proven to be, not ridiculous, but transfixing—and Jessica was hurrying to partake.

I eased Noelle's legs off my shoulders and stood, taking her hands and pulling her into a sitting position. Drugs and sex had disoriented her: when, pushing her hair from her face as languidly as a bored memsahib waving off a butterfly, she accidentally bumped my shaft, Noelle began instantly to suck it, eyelids fluttering peacefully.

I was reluctant to stop her, but Jessica was literally in harness, ultra-eager. Placing one hand atop Noelle's head and the other beneath her chin, I withdrew, kissed her swollen mouth lightly, and climbed past her to the head of the bed. I got on my knees, then eased backward, my cock aimed at the seam where the ceiling met the wall.

Semi-stupefied but with her engine racing, Noelle knelt in front of me, gripped my thighs with strong, long-fingered hands, and inhaled me to the root. I watched for a moment, lost in sensation; then looked up. Chin lowered, Jessica was studying Noelle with a researcher's absorption. Concluding, apparently, that it was best just to begin, she separated Noelle's thighs and eased herself in.

Jessica had, for the occasion, strapped on a rather larger appurtenance, as though she'd decided, having committed herself, to indulge every fantasy. But she suffered from a double disadvantage. Used to a shorter dildo, Jessica had not anticipated how much further she'd have to draw back to execute a thrust; and the awkwardness produced by the extra few inches was exacerbated by a reluctance to take Noelle in hand. Wobbling like a wire-walker, unable to manipulate with finesse, Jessica's exertions failed to engage Noelle's interest. This, I thought, required an intervention. Catching her eye, I made my hands into claws and moved them in and out in a pantomime of grasping. I mouthed the words: "Hold her hips."

Gravely, Jessica did so, parted her knees to plant herself more firmly, and tried again. Immediately, the difference was evident: on the third of Jessica's thrusts, Noelle arched her back and took her mouth off me, turning her head to consider Jessica's reflection in the mirror. Jessica met her eyes and repeated what she'd done. Noelle's back humped a bit more, her eyes closed and she huffed near-silently, as though exhaling on an eyeglass lens; she released my thighs and laid both palms flat on the bed. Jessica moved a third time and Noelle moved to meet her, rolling her hips in slow revolutions, extracting everything that could be wrung from what she felt. Discreetly I drew away. For the moment, I was out of the picture.

Jessica's caution been replaced by curiosity. The dildo wasn't a dick, there was no sensation to be had from it; but Noelle had turned the plastic shaft into a divining rod, through which she transmitted to Jessica the full measure of her experience. And Jessica was attuned to it: whereas, with me, she'd been transported by the absoluteness of her power, now she seemed wowed by the reaction she was getting, reminded—as men so often are when they make love—of what infinite creatures women can be.

Jessica being Jessica, her other side began to assert itself; I recognized the familiar abandon and intensity. Yet a difference was apparent: Presented with a partner whose transit depended for its success on nuanced interplay—as opposed to the tortured forbearance of a hetero male—she responded no less aggressively, but with a mixture of feeling and authority that gave that aggression shape. Jessica as she fucked felt not only her private pleasures, but the stream of exquisite intimacies that remained dependent upon her partnership; and the force of her fucking was attuned to that stream's direction, and the objective of driving it forward.

This, I felt with a lurch, was true lovemaking: all me, all you, all us. Here—in a lesson applicable, not only to sex, but all my relations, especially those with my wife—here was power, rather than power's absence, which is force.

Noelle rose up from the bed, spine bowlike and head drifting back; her upper body barely moved as her pelvis rocked and revolved. As she rose and rose, Jessica—with a glance at me, eyes sparkling—slid one hand to Noelle's waist and laid the other on her shoulder, inviting her closer. That was all Noelle needed: she bent her double-jointed arms back and laid her hands on Jessica's ass, her leer registering the fact of that ass's perfection. And Jessica, looking at her openly, with surprise at how far she was going and amazement at what she felt, enveloped Noelle in her arms, holding her at the shoulders, at the waist, their bodies fusing as Noelle came and Jessica watched her and nuzzled her ear and kissed her cheek, and nodded at me with a small, private smile of appreciation.

Thus was I readmitted. A moment, and I was atop Noelle, holding her tightly to me as we balled—that was the word, I thought, that wonderfully rude relic of sixties slang was the ideal description of what we were doing. Raising my head, I discovered Jessica sitting beside me, a naughty grin stretched across her face; I grinned back at her, the two of us sharing the sweet, special pleasure of our partnership. Jessica laid a hand on my madly nodding ass, widening her eyes with mock admiration; she slipped a finger between Noelle's lips and stroked her tongue. As we gazed distractedly at one another, I balling madly, Jessica tracing slow circles in Noelle's purring mouth, I thought, *My God, I have changed, I am very different from what I was.* Right then, I felt it, felt it truly for the first time: the old self not just in abeyance but apart from me. The aged window shade cracked as a breeze flowed in, I felt its caress on my damp back; I listened to the soothing roar on Sunset Boulevard and felt as well a pang of loss riding on the air, for that old self, becoming an increasingly indistinct figure as I balled my way toward my future.

"Something happened," said my wife, "and I'm not sure how I should feel about it."

And with the synchronicity that was the time's hallmark, as it was for me, so it was for my wife: she too was struggling, with how to keep the best of her and leave the rest behind.

"What?" I said. We were in the parking lot behind the Main Street Community Gardens in Santa Monica, fishing in our pockets for quarters.

"A woman was rude to me. In Al-Anon. I don't know, it's—" My wife sighed. "People feel like they can talk to me any way they please, I've noticed."

"Which is how?"

"With contempt." We fed the meter and started down Strand Street toward the ocean. In the clean light, my wife's skin was translucent, her features showed their delicacy. "I borrowed a book from this woman at the Saturday meeting, and she kept asking for it back and I kept forgetting it. So yesterday, it's like, six weeks, and she's *rilly* pissed. So I said to her, will you remind me? Next week, could you call before you leave for the meeting?"

"Yeah?"

"So she says to me, 'I certainly will *not.*'"

We passed under a tangle of power lines and crossed Ocean Avenue. A stairway, damp and slippery, led to a beachside parking lot. I took my wife's hand and said nothing.

"What, she was right?" she said stiffly as we descended. "I have trouble remembering. That's no reason to speak to me that way."

We reached the parking lot, and proceeded along an allee lined with wind-bent saplings toward the beach. "Look," releasing my wife's hand, the familiar frustration overtaking me. "I have no doubt that people dismiss you because I've seen it. But what you're describing is different."

"Why?"

"You see yourself as a good person, with certain harmless difficulties functioning in the world that require understanding—fine. But if you can't see beyond that to the *effect* it has, and have as much respect for other people's feelings as you do for your own, don't be surprised if they get mad."

"Well, I have difficulties."

"Well deal with them."

My wife turned to walk away, I grabbed her arm and stopped her. "These people have lives, okay? They go to Al-Anon to contend with codependency, not to encourage your fascination with the drama of your incompetence." My wife pulled free and strode off, I hurried after her, yelling. "This is the same thing as always, you want to be exactly who you are and loved for it. Grow up!"

My wife darted through the pedestrian traffic filling the paved ribbon between the parking lot and the beach and strode across the sand toward the water's edge. Held in place by a sudden blizzard of cyclists, I had no choice but to watch her, a hunched figure appearing and disappearing in a blur of Spandex.

I caught up with my wife as the ocean foamed around her ankles. We walked for a while without speaking. "I'm sorry I yelled at you," I said finally. "But honey——" I broke off, reaching for clarity. "I hate to put it this way, but frankly you're too *old* to misbehave and expect to be validated for it, it's...*unseemly*. You have to, I don't know. *Move on*."

"I know," she said, looking out to sea. "Old business." The wind caught my wife's hair, pushing it back from her high forehead. Thus exposed, she looked vulnerable, and startlingly young. "So much of what I learned as an actor had to do with understanding behavior, so that I could play a character's actions. You know, and, I mean, I know, as Stella said, 'Hamlet is not a guy like you, *dahling*,' but it's inevitable, isn't it? That you're going to compare a character's longings to your own?" She threw out her arms, palms up. "What does the director always say? 'What do you want to make the other person *do*? What is it that you want to *get*?' Right? Well, how do you *do* these things if you don't understand the effect you have?"

"Sure. But as your teachers would have been quick to remind you. You develop these skills, not for reasons of empty display, but to discover the truth."

"To connect. I know. I know." My wife gazed with wide, blank eyes at the patterns left by the flow of foam in the sand. "My problem…My problem is that I don't have a character to play, except myself. I have immersed myself in the life, and history, and, and *pathology* of this woman. Who is blocked and stuck, and struggling to find the key that will *somehow* release her from the prison of her past. And playing this character, I have completely lost sight of the objective."

"Which is what?"

"*To put on a play*. To be, you know. A person who *functions* in the world."

"I understand," I said, and I did. "Even in the face of"— now I laughed, grimly—"the total, complete destruction of one's life, it is very hard to change the things that satisfy us."

"So what's the answer?"

"I've said it before, but it's all I've got. We can't change ourselves, but we can change the way we see ourselves. And thereby change our lives."

We sat in the sand and snuggled up to one another. "Maybe I need actual transformations for things to sink in," she said. "I was thinking…" My wife shifted her jaw; she sighed emotionally. "When you get your period, a part of you dies."

"What, your innocence?"

"Your independence. When you're a kid, you don't

think with your pussy. You climb a tree. Then you get your period, and it's like, Well, I'm a *voo*-man now, I can find love. But what's the price? Your freedom."

"You have to re-find it."

My wife nodded. "I did. In those early years, in the city." With a shell, she drew a circle in the sand. "You know how, you reach an age, and you're exactly the person you want to be?"

"What do you mean?"

"I mean, when I was twenty-three and studying with all those amazing teachers, and men were falling all over me because I was this diffident artist who was completely available but ultimately not available, blah blah fucking blah. *That* age. I felt like, boy, I have really become myself. And no matter how old I get, in my head, that's who I am. You know?"

"I sure do, baby. When I first came back to New York from LA, and was dreaming my dreams? That was exactly who *I* wanted to be." I looked at her. "I was twenty-three, too."

"Are you still that age in your head?"

"I think," I said carefully, "my life since then has shown me that a lot of the things that underlay that self-image were unsupportable. So I've been trying to leave it behind."

"How?"

We looked at each other; for a dizzying moment, I was tempted to blurt it all out. I said, instead, "By changing the way I see myself."

My wife nodded. "I think for me, the trick is to teach that self to grow old gracefully." She looked away, so that I couldn't see her face. "To *not* misbehave like a twenty-three-year-old with skyward-pointing titties and a fascination with the great drama that is my so-called life. And expect, as you say, to be validated for it."

Something was bothering me. "Why did you mention that, about getting your period?" I said. "What made you think of it?"

My wife picked up a fistful of sand and watched the

grains drain out of her palm. "Because now, I'm *not* getting it."

I looked at her. "Not at all?"

She shook her head. I took her hand.

Then my wife laughed—chortled is more like it. "Well," she said. "Now that *that* self has died. Maybe I can stop looking for love, and get my fuckin' independence back."

It was funny, I thought—as over the ensuing weeks I watched my wife's melancholy deepen—the way life disrupted our efforts to help ourselves. Living in our heads, it was easy to lose sight of the fact that change arose, not only from months or years of inner scrutiny, but from blasts of reality that tore through one's existence with the random, rude irrefutability of an attack of wind. My wife might talk of teaching the 23-year-old within to grow old gracefully, but she had now been physically cut loose from an identity that had defined her for nearly forty years, and the changes *change* produced, she was learning, were much harder to handle than those spooned from the gentle broth of insight.

In another of that time's synchronicities, I was enduring my own version of this—and experiencing my own melancholy. Increasingly, I was able to cultivate healthier habits, I felt more lucid and at home with that lucidity, I even found myself more able to be in the moment as I worked, patiently attentive to the slow-firing Catherine wheel of my talent. But I did not own myself more. Rather, the more I changed, the greater the peculiarly elegant, day-to-day despair, the debonair pessimism, that I came to recognize as a feeling of exile. Like my wife, whose self-image had been set adrift by the death of her menstrual cycle, I'd entered an existential diaspora: the self I had been, however unworkable, was my homeland; and now, driven from that place by a string of internal cataracts and a sober commitment to change, I realized that I could not return. No matter how fully I might come to inhabit another, better self—a self that let me, *par example*, enjoy interludes like the one with Jessica and Noelle—some part of me would always feel, to myself, like a stranger.

Fortunately—contributing his own perfect timing to the moment—Martin returned. The phone rang one afternoon, I picked it up, and there he was. "I'm back, London was fantastic, what are you doing Saturday?" All in a mellifluous, offhand rush.

"What's on?" I asked, my spirit rising like a balloon cut loose from its mooring.

"A barbecue. At my friend Fiona's. Might be fun," he said—vaguely, as if trying to decide if this were true.

"Who's going to be there?"

He offered a partial guest list that included a television comedienne who had lost her career, gotten a face-lift that gave her the look of being electrocuted and become the spokesperson for a chain of enema parlors, and one of the great sixties sex kittens, a very talented, very famous actress who'd beaten a years-long depression but remained, in the aftermath, like a henge monument, standing but skinned to the elemental stones. "Also a lot of Brits," he added, "mostly aged rock stars who go to meetings and drink a great deal of non-alcoholic beer, plus funny, well-bred girls who, oh, maybe did a Ken Russell movie, then danced away too many nights on tabletops and now also drink non-alcoholic beer, only not so much as the boys because it makes them fat." He paused, I heard a match being struck, then a quick succession of puffs. "Is that satisfactory?"

"Yep."

"I mean I think you'll like it, and they'll like you, because you're funny and also drink a great deal of non-alcoholic beer, though it doesn't make you fat, even though you're not a girl. So far as I know."

"Indeed."

"And," he cleared his throat, "you can give me a ride."

"I'd love to go."

"Hm," Martin said. In his catalogue of "Hms," this was his *now*-what-have-I-gotten-into Hm.

"What's wrong?"

"I don't," more puffing, "I don't like to be in a situation in which *too* many people have a higher profile than I do."

"Shouldn't be a problem," I said drolly.

"Well that's bad *too*," whining, "because what am *I* doing there? Amongst the losers."

"You," I said, "are the guest of honor."

"*Ah. Ah. Ah.* There's something else."

"What?"

"In a situation like this, fun, friends, slightly nervous-making, I have to have a drink in my hand. I'm not a drunk, I don't need to *be* drunk to get through it. It's just necessary."

"So?"

"I never drink during the day."

I sighed.

"Am I making this as difficult as I possibly can?" he said, merriment palpable in his voice.

"Can my wife come?"

"Is she fun?"

"She's good company."

"Yeah, sure, bring her. All right," he sighed, "I'll wear a velvet suit or something. Pick up a six or two of your brand of choice. *I'll*," he added, "bring the cigars."

Fiona's house, a midsize Mediterranean Revival fronted by a plenitude of turf, sat half a block south of Sunset in the transitional neighborhood through which I'd passed on my trips to the whorehouse. It was strange but also intriguing to find myself making a right at All-American Burger, a private landmark nearly radioactive with secret meaning, and pulling up, not in front of my usual destination, but at a de facto AA party—with, not only my wife, but a dedicated Rabelaisian (garbed as promised in velveteen and reading aloud from my copy of Gebhard and Winter's *Architectural Guide to Los Angeles*) in the backseat. So extreme were these incongruities that they threatened to distance me from my feelings. But, I realized, being in the situation proved that I'd been taking care of myself. A half-decade earlier, I'd attended my wife's Al-Anon parties, at which bitches in Birkenstocks ate soy burgers while their passive-aggressive husbands ran after their free-range kids, and had wanted to hang myself after every one. Now, I was again a sober man showing up for a largely alcohol-free occasion; but I'd been invited by a pleasure-loving friend to whom life's savor meant everything, and the crowd promised to be, not Stalinist in its anhedonic uniformity, but various and fun. Now, I felt, I had found a balance.

As a hostess, Martin's friend (and ex-squeeze) Fiona showed style. She was in the midst of having a pool dug, a bulldozer took up half the back yard, and Fiona had dealt with this monster by filling its toothed shovel with drinks and ice. We ate like weekend gods—barbecued tuna burgers (my wife had three), jerk chicken marinated in a mixture Fiona discovered in Montego Bay—after which I drew a Hoyo de Monterrey from Martin's proffered case, plucked a Buckler from the bulldozer and, after passing a quarter-hour discussing his forthcoming first feature with a snotty video director, found myself going down, down into the freshly dug pool pit with Fiona. She was classically difficult: compulsively defensive, Fiona found insult in my every utterance; possessive and suspicious, she grilled me about my friendship with Martin, implying that I was a hanger-on draining the great man's vitality; hypercritical, she pissed neatly and with a catholic intelligence on books, films, architecture, photography, and, in passing, a number of her friends. I handled Fiona well, though: resisting an emotionally prophylactic recitation of my credits, talking and listening with the patience of a Zen master. When, after twenty minutes of this jailhouse beating, she turned an inscrutable gaze on her boyfriend, a pest-control magnate decades her junior, and excused herself, I was proud of how well I'd managed (though staggering out of the mulchy hole felt like a resurrection).

Returning to ground level, I saw my wife with the formerly depressed former sex kitten, dazed at finding herself party-intimate with a legend but holding her own with her special forthright empathy; Martin, ten yards away with another director, watched her clinically. Gesturing me over, he introduced me to his friend, who just missed feigning interest when Martin spoke of me as "a very talented screenwriter."

"Did you like Fiona?" Martin purred slyly when we'd been left alone.

"When did you go out with her?"

"In the sixties," he said, pondering his untouched Vouvray. "One must be very young or very old to date a woman like Fiona. Your wife is sweet."

"What did you talk about?"

"All those acting teachers." Martin flicked his gaze at me, then resumed his consideration of my wife, now eliciting a laugh, a sisterly touch on the shoulder, from her new fast friend, the movie star. "She's good at this," Martin said.

I turned to him. "Good at what?"

"LA." He met my eyes. "Isn't she?"

We considered one another. "Her father is a famous academic," I said after a moment. "She comes from money." I returned my gaze to my wife. "She's confident."

As I had when we'd met at the Marmont, I thought of *La Dolce Vita*, Marcello's raffish ease with the Roman rabble, the photographers and publicists and whores, so different from his solemn reverence for the intellectuals, insecurity blinding him to their aridity and pretention. My wife and I had been together for a decade, yet it had never before occurred to me: there was a class difference between us. While I owned a surface élan, I remained at heart a nervous country boy; while she made a style of charming ineptitude, she was a remorseless aristocrat. It was, I realized, a part—perhaps the better part—of my susceptibility to her manipulations: my wife was a predator disguised as a victim. Small wonder LA suited her. Unlike her husband, the Borscht Belt Marcello, my wife had status.

I glanced at Martin, who was observing these recognitions materialize within me. "All that waffling you did on the phone," I said to him. "About what your status would be—that was about making sure you could be yourself in this situation, am I right?"

Martin set down his glass, slipped a hand into his jacket

pocket and cocked his hip. "…Yes," he said, cautiously. "Though I would question the word *status*, which implies that I'm preoccupied with the way in which the 'town' perceives me."

"It seemed to be more about…"

"Keeping oneself close."

"Right. How do you do that?"

"What do you mean? I do it by being difficult."

"Tell you why I ask," I began. "I've been feeling lately like my life has changed, *I've* changed, so much that it's almost like I can't go home again."

"Mm. Hm."

"And what I've been calling my sense of exile from myself has given me a kind of…"

"Not depression," he said quickly. "You get through the day alright but feel vaguely drawn down by a kind of *Weltschmerz*."

I looked at him, surprised by the accuracy of his description. Holding his cigar lightly between his teeth, Martin kept his death's-head gaze on his private abyss.

"After my initial, youthful success," he said, "during which time I was the toast of two continents, I had a long spell in which people would cross the street to avoid having to greet me and everything I attempted fell to pieces. And I guess I got through it—got over that, yes, exile from oneself is a good description—by embracing it."

"How?"

"I decided there would be many lives, and made *that* my self. I would see and do many things, and at times it would seem as if there were no point to any of it. But I would keep that *essential* thing close. And that would be my compass."

"Has it worked?" I asked. I was thinking that I'd banished shame by embracing it, and might do the same with my feelings of loss.

"Mostly," Martin replied. "Sometimes, you have to take anti-depressants"—grinning, as though this were part of the fun. "Look, don't fret about how you feel, feelings are like people and places and things, they change and change. In the end you lose it all." He glanced at my wife, approaching from across the lawn. "But, you know," he said, watching her, "I've discovered that talents I thought I couldn't live without are long gone, and abilities I never imagined I had have risen to take their place."

"Did they all seem to belong to the same man?"

Martin, his eyes far away, didn't reply. Then he looked at me directly. "You have your work," he said, "which is everything you are, and all you own or ever will own. Or need to own, really." Abruptly Martin grinned, with mischief but also genuinely. "Press *that* dried flower between the pages of your Book of Loss. And you'll *always* be at home."

Martin and I considered each other a moment longer. Then he put his arm around my wife as she stepped up. "You were very good with my poor friend Judy."

"Your *friend*?" I said. "Friend" was Martin's code for ex.

"Whoah! Whoo!" said my wife, fanning the air in front of her face.

"Shall we go?" Martin asked, glaring at us. "Or do you two propose to *eat* more?"

It had been, all in, a good afternoon. I had felt comfortable enough with myself to savor the party's every aspect, I'd been nice to my wife and enjoyed the company of my new acquaintance. Most of all, as I air-kissed and clasped hands, I took pride in the fact that I was there, I had propelled myself out of a desperate sump and gotten a purchase on life's cavalcade. From without, it might seem foolish to be offering, as proof of one's resurrection, an overfilled plate, a cigar, and a bunch of B-minus celebrities. But for two hours, I was as appreciative of the world's pleasures as I'd been in half a decade, and had no one to thank but myself.

It was ironic, then, the conclusion the day delivered: that it was time to say goodbye to all that. I had been preoccupied of late with something my wife said after our catastrophic dinner, that I'd effectively been Jason's pimp. It reminded me of my question to Jessica—was whoring really something she *wanted* to get good at? I was grateful, yes, that the ability to write had come back. But despite my resolution to play a smarter game, romancing a tiresome creep like Jason reminded me how much I hated Hollywood—it was why I had gone east, decades earlier, in the first place. The words FADE IN has returned to my literary lexicon, I'd credibly impersonated a showbiz Angeleno at Fiona's. But it was like taking up with an old girlfriend: you could—but, really, did you want to?

No, I admitted, listening to Martin and my wife chat with affectionate familiarity as I swung the Nissan onto Sunset and headed west (into the setting sun). No, I did not. That romance lay beyond rekindling.

Yet I was glad to have an occasion in LA to recall with pleasure, as my years there were, at long last, drawing to a close. Glad, too, to have had a good time with my wife—because, it transpired, we never had another.

XXXX

"As a screenwriter," I said to Jessica, "I was a bad whore."

We lay side by side in the big room, considering ourselves in the gilt mirror as we shared a post-coital cigar. Through the blue haze, our reflection seemed like a snapshot, a frozen moment plucked from a longer narrative.

"What is the screenwriter's version of bad whoring?" she said.

"Same as the whore's version. Trying to win what can't be won." I passed the Montecristo and massaged her temple with my chin. "My scripts were just imperfect enough to not get made, because perfecting them—AKA, giving my employers what they were *paying* for—would have meant accepting that the power lay with them, which of course it did. So the subtext of everything I wrote was, 'I'm smarter than you.'"

"So you quote-unquote won."

"But not ultimately. Because the customers weren't paying me to humiliate them. No surprise, the response of my producers was, you know."

Jessica grinned. "'Send in another girl.'" She put her face close to mine and lowered her eyes. "And were you aggrieved, baby, and bitter? And did you vow to make them see it your way next time?"

"'Bitter' was my middle name. You know, it's interesting—"

"I'm *sure*."

I widened my eyes. We laughed.

"It's *interesting*," I resumed. "When I started out, I wanted to be 'brilliant but flawed,' because the filmmakers I admired were that way. I thought their strengths and weaknesses were inextricable."

"And?"

"And in retrospect, I think the reason I was attracted to those guys was that they had the same in-built sense of grievance that I have. They said to the studios, 'Fuck you, I'm not going to give you a perfect film.' And their stuff was recut, and they got drunk and became unemployable." My reflection and I glanced at one another with disgust, like enemies who pass in the street. "None of my scripts got made," I said, "because what I was writing was not the *story*, but my bitterness at not getting my way."

"Are you saying that a good-whore screenwriter would have sold out?"

"A good-whore screenwriter would have accepted the experience for what it was, and let the rest go. Like a good whore."

Somewhere a door slammed, too violently. Jessica looked toward the sound. "Sinclair," she said, "is the exception that proves the rule."

"The bad whore who's made it work?"

"She's turned this place into her little…eastern-bloc dictatorship," said Jessica with frustrated amazement. "She perverts everyone's humanity. She's brilliant at it."

"Yes. But who would want that kind of death in her soul? Just to be the dictator."

Sinclair's appearance in the conversation was occasioned

by an incident which had occurred shortly after my arrival. I had settled into one of the decrepit chairs, and was about to nod my head in formal acceptance of Jessica's favors, when a moan arose from a corner of the house. Turning, I saw a woman tripping down the hall, in jeans and a sequined tank top, gripping something lacy in both hands. As she was out of uniform, it took a moment for me to recognize her as Michelle.

"*Who did this?*" she boomed in her incongruous baby voice.

Jessica, Wendy and Gloria quickly gathered around her, consoling and curious. Sinclair, however, merely recrossed her legs and got a little comfier on the couch. Whatever was the matter, I had no doubt: Sinclair was the cause.

"What's wrong, honey?" she said. "Did something happen bad?"

"Look!" Michelle held up a body stocking, a rip running from the seat seam all the way up the back. It had been a sexy, if trashy, number, once. Now it was a rag.

"Oh, honey, you *know* you have to be careful when you zip up your duffel," Sinclair said: solicitous, yet with a languid quality to her voice that betrayed—clearly—contempt.

"Guess what?" Michelle replied nastily. "I didn't *take* it out of my *duffel*. It was *here*."

Sinclair squinted with confusion and disbelief. "What, what are you saying? You left your good *thing* here?"

"Behind the Windex and the Panel Magic! Hidden!"

"Well, honey, I gotta say, you know," Sinclair began, the contempt, mixed with pity, overtaking her, "this is *your* fault."

Michelle dropped her extended hands, still clutching the ruined garment. She looked at her watch and sighed.

"Yeah," Sinclair continued, "I mean, only a *stupid* girl leaves her best thing in harm's way. Instead of taking it home."

"What do you mean?" said Michelle, her hot eyes turning sleepy. "*In harm's way.*"

"Well you obviously caught it on a nail or something. When you got it out."

Michelle's sleepy look grew distant. Slowly, she walked past the other girls and stood over Sinclair, who laid a hand on her chest and looked around at us with bemused surprise.

Michelle raised the garment above her head, holding it between thumb and forefinger. "This," she said, staring down at Sinclair, "is *no nail. This* is *spite work.*"

"Get away from me," Sinclair hissed, leaping up and driving Michelle, who was half a head taller, stumbling back. "Are you accusing me?" she said in a raucous voice.

"Yes!" Michelle yelled, with all the pugnacity of her former sex, shaking the stocking at Sinclair. "Fucking bitch!"

Sinclair was too smart for a catfight. Instead, she slapped Michelle's hand—reprovingly, as though the bigger woman were a child who'd misbehaved.

It did the trick. Abruptly Michelle began to bawl, huge tears rolling down her face, her sobs like those of a calf that has lost its mother. It was a shocking, pathetic sound, especially coming from a woman that size, and that masculine.

Sinclair laughed, which only increased the volume and pathos of Michelle's mooing. "Big girls don't cry," she sang, looking at the rest of us, drawing us in. "C'mere," she said to Michelle, taking the body stocking and putting it to the poor girl's nose. Michelle recoiled, but Sinclair just laughed—generously, this time. "Hey, all it's good for now, right?" Miserably, Michelle laughed, too, then blubbered all the harder; the oceans of woe flowing from her, given the minor nature of the tragedy, seemed to reflect how fragile remained her purchase on her new sexuality. I looked at Sinclair, who returned my gaze cooly. She had, of course, understood this, and known precisely what to do.

"Go home," Sinclair said. "You don't got what to wear and, you know. You don't want to do this tonight."

Michelle looked desperate. In a small voice, she said, "I've got Lester in a half hour."

"Ohhhh," Sinclair moaned sympathetically. She grinned

and turned to the others, who watched with rapt unease. "Hey, gang, didja hear?" Sinclair said. "Michelle caught a mouse." That meant, I suspected, a regular, one who might even set Michelle up.

"We know," Gloria answered neutrally. We could all see where this was going—all of us, it seemed, but Michelle. She looked at Sinclair with over-kohled, trusting eyes.

"Can you, like…explain to him," Michelle began.

Jessica opened her mouth to object, but Gloria shot her a glance, and she remained silent. The meaning of the look was clear: if Michelle was going to persist in being, as Sinclair had put it, a stupid girl, they could only care so much. Sinclair, of course, knew this, too. She waved a hypnotic finger before Michelle's face. "Don't you worry about a thing," Sinclair said reassuringly. "*I'll* take care of Lester."

Their eyes met and, for an instant, neither had any illusions. Then Michelle pushed the knowledge away, and embraced the other woman gratefully. It had been chilling, I recalled, to witness the loss of will; to watch someone hand away her opportunity so fatally.

"Death in your soul," said Jessica, echoing my words. "I guess all dictators make that bargain. Turn their backs on the world for a chance to make a world on their terms."

I had been thinking that I didn't want or need to be exposed to this kind of cruelty anymore. Jessica's observation brought me back to the moment.

"How literary," I said.

"The whole incident presented itself as a slice of life, don't you think? Perfect, complete?" Jessica massaged her palm with her middle finger; her voice took on its signature burnished quality. "I could write down a whole series of such things—God knows I've witnessed enough. Don't you think they'd make an interesting book?"

"I do."

"I've even got a title," Jessica said, getting up, taking her maillot from the chair. She ran a finger over the fabric. "*The Rooms*," she said quietly.

Hearing this, I smiled. "What made you think of that?"

"Do you know anything about twelve-step programs?"

"Some," I deadpanned.

Jessica raised her chin slightly, registering my subtext. "You know how, sometimes, when people speak at meetings, they'll talk about the power of *the rooms*, how the alchemy of the program seems somehow to arise from the spaces themselves?"

"I have heard that."

Jessica repositioned herself on the bed's edge, draping the maillot over her shoulder, taking my hand. "Well, I think *these* rooms have a spiritual quality," her gaze moving slowly over the ruin in which we were enclosed. "I'd like to set a story in each, and connect the theme of each incident to the nature of the space in which it unfolds." We considered each other for a moment; then she looked away. "It would seem like such a waste, otherwise. Not to have done something with all this."

"Honey," I said, unable to stop myself. "Why are you here? What happened to you?"

Jessica shook her head, closing and opening her eyes slowly. She withdrew her hand from mine. "Nothing in my history explains this," she said. "My history is your history."

"*My* history explains *my* being here."

"And how many people with your history have never had sex with a whore, and never would? Selling your body for money," Jessica said, "it can be a casual choice or momentous, you can be totally disrupted or barely register what you're doing. You have a pretty good sense of why I'm here, I think. Practically and otherwise."

"I'm just…"

"You're just wondering." She hesitated. "I've had… experiences. But I didn't arrive scarred, and doing this hasn't scarred me—why would it necessarily be any more scarring to *be* a whore than to *go* to one? Do you feel scarred?"

"By this?" It had never occurred to me to ask this question. "I don't have enough distance yet to know."

"I guess I don't, either. But either way, I don't want to live in the past—take bits of it and say, this caused this, that caused that. I want to move on. Do my work as an actress hopefully and maybe write—yes, about this, because this has been such a big part of my existence. And—" She broke off.

"What?"

"Have a man in my life."

Jessica's eyes shifted back and forth unreadably. She sat in silence, hands in her lap.

"Can I ask about your fiancé?"

"You can *ask*."

"What's he do?"

Jessica had been staring at me with a mixture of defiance and uncertainty. Now she released a long, shuddering sigh. "He's a graduate student," she said, rubbing an eye.

"In what?"

"Geology. Earth and Ocean Sciences, as it's now called."

"What's he like?"

"Distracted. Smart—I don't always know *quite* what he's talking about." She shrugged. "He's a bear, a big...loving bearlike guy who, when he looks up and sees me, just smiles."

"Innocent," I said, tight-lipped. I was surprised at how difficult I was finding this.

"Yes. But not helpless—I feel safe with him. Also," giving me an embarrassed glance, "he's got a good mom and dad."

"Do they like you?"

"Yeah, though they're not—" Jessica frowned, looking for words. "They didn't accept me or not accept me. I became one of them. It's hard to explain. It's like, they're interested in my work but don't fantasize about my being a star or ask questions about celebrities."

"They're interested like engineers."

"Yeah," Jessica said and half-smiled slightly. "Yeah, just. The whole thing, you're right, it's like they're specialists and, if I'm on the team, boy, I must know my job or I wouldn't have gotten hired."

"It sounds weirdly appealing."

"Weirdly appealing is just what it is."

I took a deep breath and let it out slowly. I had always thought of Jessica as my therapist, a blank screen. Now, she'd gained a history.

"Do you love him?" I said.

Jessica stared at the floor. "I really, *really* like him. The vibe around him."

"Do you think you're going to go through with it?"

"It's something we've agreed to," returning my look neutrally. "There's no date."

We continued to look at one another. Finally, Jessica cleared her throat.

"So, ah," she said, "what's your wife do?"

"Actress."

Jessica grinned. "Can't escape, can you?" Then: "Why did things go bad? If you don't mind my asking. I'm presuming they were good, once."

I cast my mind back across the years of my marriage, to the time before it, when I'd been delighted by my wife's joie de vivre and entertained (more or less) by her eccentricities.

"Yes," I said. "Things were good. I guess the best way of putting it is that my wife and I were good *and* bad for one another, and because we were so blind to the traps in our personalities, the bad won out."

"And your trap was?"

"I wanted things from my wife that she—that no adult woman could or should have to give. Which I didn't understand."

Jessica considered me. "Are you sorry you got married?"

"I—I regret the waste," I said, exhaling. My lungs hurt, whether from the smoke or the conversation's difficulty I wasn't sure. "On the other hand…" My reflection, watching from the gilt mirror, again appraised me—candidly this time. "On the other hand, being in the marriage forced me to face up to a lot of things. The cost was exorbitant, just…you can't imagine. But I'm changing."

"I can imagine. The cost. You mean we only get the one life."

I glanced at the flimsy door with its drooping knob. The hour was nearly up. Out of the corner of my eye, I saw Jessica start to reach for me, then stop herself. Whatever she wanted to ask, she did not wish to influence me with her touch.

"And now?" she said.

"Well, of course," I said, "things are getting better now."

Again, Jessica gazed at the floor. "Because you're more onto yourself."

In the silence that followed, Jessica breathed steadily through her nose, like a fighter in her corner, awaiting the bell.

"Listen," I said, lurching off my own stool. "I'd like to see you outside of here."

Jessica looked at me, head lowered slightly, breathing still measured. "I thought you didn't want a relationship."

"I don't. But I've always wanted this—to have this kind of freedom with someone. We're friends, Jessica. And I'm good at friendship. I have, apparently, no talent for love. But this—it's like we're, you should forgive me for saying, soulmates. Partners in crime."

"With benefits," Jessica said euphemistically.

"Yeah. Thelma and Louise, with benefits."

We grinned our stretched-out grins.

"Which one are you?" Jessica said as I put my feet on the floor.

"Who was the ditzy one?"

"I forget. *I* think," Jessica said, perching on my knees, "we're *both* Thelma *and* both Louise." She took my face in her hands and studied me fondly. "We were a fair pair of dykes today, I'd say."

This was a reference to our sex. Eschewing conventional penetration yet again, we'd decided to see if we could enjoy the essentially female condition Jessica had described as "that intensity that rises to a certain level and sustains itself." We had decided, in effect, to be two girls, and the erotic tension we'd generated seemed to arise from the texture of our skin, our now-established intimacy with each other's bodies, the way in which we took time to tease each other's private parts, the sweats we raised, the wickedness of the liberties we took and our surprise at how far we could go with each other, the way this made us laugh, the ways in which we soothed each other so that we might raise the flame again, coax out more obscenities of the most extreme and shameless kind.

The memory of all that, as the old song goes, played over Jessica's expression as she studied me. I encircled her waist with my arms and pulled her close.

"Jessica," I said, "I'm not trying to break up your relationship."

"Yeah. Right."

"I'm not. He sounds like a decent guy, I'm not going to tell you that's not the best thing for you. And I'm not using this to catapult myself out of my marriage."

"What then?"

"You make me happy," I said, raising my head and looking at her. "You make me happy like no one's ever made me happy."

"Not even your wife?"

I searched Jessica's expression for signs of malice. Finding only curiosity, I said, "My wife made me happy—she still does—in a way no one else can."

"How?"

"You know how some couples, no matter how bad it goes, they always have great sex? Well no matter how fucking rotten things have gone, my wife and I have still talked about things. With pleasure."

Jessica nodded. "We don't have that, quite."

On came the rapping of the heels, followed by the sharp report of knuckles. Jessica climbed off my lap; we both began to dress. "If I say no," she said, "will I see you again?"

I buckled my belt. "Once more. Money's a big problem." I blew out my breath. "And more than that. Watching Michelle and Sinclair, I was thinking, you know. No more."

Jessica slipped on her cork-soled shoes. We faced each other.

"Can I call you?" she said. "I'll be discreet."

"Whenever you're ready."

Jessica took out a pad and pen and wrote down her number. She tore out the page and handed it over. "The Valley," I said, seeing the area code.

"Take it," she said. "Just in case."

I was, I realized days later, as I sat at my desk surrounded by unpaid (and unpayable) bills, basing my decision to move forward with Jessica, to a degree, on money. But this was not a fact I felt the need to analyze. I was driving myself toward something, grabbing at understanding as it appeared and digesting it, half-chewed, as I rushed on. Now I was in the home stretch, and had developed sufficient faith in this process not to question it. The partisan, my navigator, knew what needed to be done. He, after all, could see the lighthouse, and I could not.

And I was on course: as they had with my dalliance, my financial problems now brought my marriage to a head. I was staring at the Post-Its, scrawled with the names of potential employers, that were stuck to my desk when the front door slammed and my wife stomped in, barking "Fuck! Fuck! Fuck!" as she headed in a fury for the kitchen.

I looked out the window. There, on a branch, sat my squirrel (as I'd come to think of him), gripping a softball-sized avocado and nibbling maniacally as he watched me—expectantly, it seemed, as if waiting to hear the story behind this commotion. Seeing this, I laughed: Whatever the problem might be, I could not muster so much as a squirrel's worth of interest in it. I had been wasteful and stupid, and would now be living with the low smoke of insolvency for a long time to come. Whatever had befallen my wife, I was sure, it was small potatoes compared to this.

I heard the refrigerator door slam, then listened as my wife stomped up the stairs and rattled my door with her knuckles. The squirrel's avid eyes shifted toward the sound. I threw a pencil at him—I was sick of providing food and entertainment for this unambitious rat—it bounced off the screen and he showed me his dustmop of tail.

"Yes?" I said.

My wife jerked open the door, threw herself into the rush-seated ladderback and writhed spasmodically.

"Ooo! Ooo! Ooo!" she gasped, stabbing the air with short, constricted strokes. "*Aaaah!*" My wife put her elbows on her knees and gripped her forehead with both hands.

"What happened?" I said.

"I was talking to some woman at Al-Anon about how painful it is not to have had a kid, and she said, 'You can always adopt.'"

"What did you say?"

"I just lost it." My wife sat up, revealing a loony face, goggle-eyed and slack-mouthed. "'Gee, adopt? I can do *that*? Gee, *I* didn't know I could do *tha*-at.' Ooo!"

"Why did that make you so angry?" I said, with the enthusiasm of a census-taker.

"Because I'm sick and fuckin' tired of feeling judged, you know? Because I couldn't bring myself to adopt. Why does that make me a, a cold, unloving bitch? Hah? Why!"

"I'm sure she didn't mean it that way."

"You know? I don't know. So often," said my wife, "when I try and share this incredible pain I feel. The message I get is, 'Well, you *could* have a kid. You just *won't.*'"

"They don't understand," I said.

"No, and you know what? They don't want to. They can't handle it, so they distance themselves." Getting up, my wife leaned her forehead against the window behind the chair.

"Why did this bother you so much?" I said. "Apart from the obvious."

"You know why?" said my wife, despairing. "Because, on some level, I agree with her. All those horrible traits I had to push aside to, to, you know. Get to the point where I could even *consider* having a family—all those things of my mother's you say I define myself by. I could push 'em aside for my own kid. But I just couldn't do it for a stranger."

"I see."

"So, you know," sitting down again, "even though I think that choosing not to adopt is a legitimate decision, I'm not okay with it, because it's *not clean*. I can't make *peace* with it, because it fits with my known limitations. It fits the profile!"

"Honey," I began.

"Uch! Uch!" said my wife, twisting and writhing and stabbing the air. "I'm so sick and tired of this *thing* in me, I'm missing chance after chance!" My wife turned her palms up and looked wide-eyed at the ceiling. "I'll be like Willy Loman, planting seeds so I've got something to show for my life, even if it's just a fuckin' few petunias." She dropped her hands and gazed with sad bemusement at nothing. "Except I won't even do that."

"Why not?"

"I hate gardening."

I laughed...but I had heard it all before. The nearly clinical lack of interest I felt in my wife's pain and frustration had to do with more than the distractions of money. My wife and I had made a style of analysis, we had passed hundreds of hours admiring the quality of each other's insights, and it had long been an end in itself, a trap. One of us had to break out of it, or neither would.

"Dear," I said, "We need to go back to New York."

Instantly, my wife's sentimental sorrow turned to ice. "Why?" she said sharply.

I heard a discreet rustle outside the window. The squirrel was back.

"In a few months," I said, "if something doesn't happen, I'm going to be broke. And it's not happening for me here. Everyone back east, they keep saying the same thing: 'If you were here, to meet with *clients*, come in and *brain*storm...'"

My wife folded her arms, her mouth was tight. "They *say* they'll give you work—"

"*Ho*-ney..."

"If you have no money, how can you afford to move?"

Hearing this question—which tongued my ear, luring

me into a stupid fight—I grew very still. "Well," I drawled, "*you* could help."

"Why should I?" snapped my wife, her rhythm, in opposition to my own, short and staccato. "I'm happy here. Why should I have to pay to make myself *un*happy?"

I had made a tripod of my thumb, index and middle fingers, and propped my chin on it, so that I might consider my wife objectively. Now I leaned back and folded my arms. "All right," I said, "fair enough. We've got the place in New York. Let's split our year."

"We can't live there, it's not big enough."

"Sure it is," I said, hyper-reasonably, "if it's not full-time. And if we fix it up a bit."

"I won't throw money away on a rental," my wife yelled, braap-braaping the sentence like an actor in an early talkie. "And how can we afford to fix it up if you're broke?"

I was by now smiling faintly at my wife's hermetically self-serving logic. "All right," I continued, "here's *another* possibility. I go back east as necessary, we keep this place, but you split the bills with me." This referenced what remained one of our situation's more astounding facts: I was still paying for everything.

"Why should I?" said my wife. "This is a tax deduction for you."

"Why do I need a tax deduction," I said, "if I have no income?"

"Well you'll make money if you go back east."

I released a sound that was somewhere between a laugh and a groan.

"Look," said my wife, "this *wasn't* my idea, I'm *paying* my fair share"—half the food, half the gasoline—"if you can't take care of yourself, that's not my fault."

"So what you're saying," the sharpness coming into my tone, "is that my problems are mine, they're mine alone, and whatever I might need to do, I should include you out. Correct?"

"Basically."

"You know," I said, feeling my anger, that sleeping

giant, begin to rouse itself, "I cannot be-*lieve* that, after *all these years*, we have not progressed beyond this conversation. We have been in Los Angeles almost *four years longer* than we agreed—"

"*I* didn't *agree* on—"

"For *absolutely* no reason other than that *you won't leave*. And yet despite the fact that everything that was true for you when you came out has *completely* turned around, you are still sitting here and saying, 'This wasn't my idea, why should I have to participate?'"

In response, my wife raised her shoulders to her ears, then let them drop. "I feel you're unstable," she said matter-of-factly. "I'm sorry, there's something off about the way you deal with things."

This caught me off-guard. "Is that so," was the best I could muster.

"You *say* you do your work, but there's no enthusiasm, no *ur*-gen-cy," splitting the word into syllables. "You just get more and more aggrieved that I'm not taking up the slack."

"What are you talking about?" I said—to my own ears, not very convincingly.

"I just think you've created a crisis, to try and get me to do things," my wife said plainly. "Like because I've saved my money, I'm somehow a bad person and should have to pay. You know? No," settling it in her mind, "I *don't* feel it's my responsibility to fix this."

It was amazing, I reflected, how two people with a long, difficult history could braid truth and self-delusion so intricately. My wife could not have been more wrong, it was selfish and treacherous of her to say these things. Yet— considering the months of waste that preceded the moment—could I say with certainty that I hadn't set the house ablaze, just to see if she'd fetch water?

This was not, however, the time for ambivalence. "So," I said, nodding judiciously. "Your total unwillingness to reconsider our life, in the face of impending disaster, has only to do with my failings. Is that correct?"

My wife sat down, laying a hand against her cheek as

though oppressed by a toothache. "No, I have *fears*," abruptly vulnerable again. "You're having a bad patch now, but you'll work—you have a skill, I don't. I'm afraid that if, you know, God forbid something happens, I won't be able to take care of—"

"You know what?" I said, suddenly on my feet. Overwhelmed with anger, I was having trouble getting my breath. "You say to me, 'You have a skill, you can make a living and I can't.' I say to *you*, that's your *choice*—you have made a *conscious choice* not to do, or pursue, *anything* that might make you some money. True?"

My wife made herself smaller in her chair. "Are you through?" she said quietly.

"*No*. You know what your problem is?"

My wife rolled her eyes.

"Don't fucking roll your eyes at me. Your problem, *dear*. Is that your money is doing exactly the opposite of what you think it's doing. It is *not* making you self-supporting, because you *don't* support the life you're living. And it *hasn't* given you security, because you are governed *completely* by your fears. You lead this tiny little existence with nothing in it, and congratulate yourself for being self-sufficient. But one step outside your box, baby, and you need me, and you fucking well know it. And you rationalize the *incredible* dishonesty of living off me by telling yourself, 'Well, I don't want it, so it's not my responsibility.' You have a lot of fucking nerve." I glared at her, furiously, impotently. "*Now* I'm through," I said.

I wasn't, though. How could I be? My argument was a stew of many things—truths, lies, rhetorical constructs, and gratuitous snipes among them—but the dominant ingredient, as always, remained grievance. I wanted redress, and despite my hysterical recitation of "the facts," I hadn't gotten it, I was itching to drag my arguments back out and start screaming all over again. What was this, I thought, if not bad whoring, bad, bad whoring indeed?

And understanding this, I made the final connection, one I had resisted so completely that it had never consciously occurred to me. My wife had humiliated me, and my bad-whore behavior—the hammering and hectoring, my insistence upon defining success or failure by my ability to bend my wife to my will—was an expression of my inability to forgive. This was why, though I vowed repeatedly to treat my wife more humanely, we always ended up having precisely the same fight. I had been watching the scales of the marriage go up and down, but I had not realized what I was looking at. Now, at last, I did. I was waiting to see whether or not I could do the hardest thing, the final thing: accept that what my wife had done could never be redressed, and forgive her.

As if sensing my thoughts, my wife stirred in her chair and raised her head, eyes turned aside and focused on the middle distance. "I think," she began, then sighed. "I think that maybe *you* were that kid I couldn't adopt or...or adopted and couldn't love."

Straightening, I looked at her. "What do you mean?"

"When I think of 'family,' quote-unquote, I think of my mom and dad. You know? Everything I ran away from. And I thought, well, I'll make my own family, but I guess, when you tell me your needs, try and get me to pull my weight in ways I might not want to, the old feelings come back. I think, hey, whoah, this isn't family—it's *family*. I don't mean I don't love you," she added quickly, catching her twin tear-trails with her pinkies, "I just..."

"I understand," I said, and now I did. "We got married to have a baby," remembering the thought I'd had after buggering Jessica. "And when the baby didn't come, we didn't do what was necessary to turn *ourselves* into a family. That's what you mean."

In the silence that followed, my wife and I both stared at the question that she finally voiced.

"Can we do it now?" she said.

We looked at each other. After a little bit, my wife shifted her jaw, and looked away.

"What do you want to do?" she said.

"I don't want to do anything," realizing it as I said it.

"I'm tired of trying to make decisions, and I'm *really* tired of trying to make *you* make decisions. I'm going to go back east for a few weeks, see what's what. Leave this be."

My wife nodded, her eyes, rheumy with the aftereffects of her tears, gazing at nothing. "We both have a lot to think about," she said.

Though I wasn't sure I agreed, I replied, "We do."

XXXX

When I got back to New York, it was spring. The days were fresh and cool, the green of the thickly leaved trees had yet to be blunted by the smoggy depredations of the long, hot summer. I experienced a rush of pleasure at finding myself in a crowd; even the subways moved me with their density of detail, their vivid mix of narratives and lives. My employers welcomed me back, with a satisfaction at my comedown that they took no pains to hide. I didn't mind. I was glad for the work. As long as I got paid, they could think what they liked.

On my third day back, joking with the Egyptian from whom I was buying a newspaper, I abruptly felt a surge of well-being: my fragility had disappeared, owing in part to the certainty that I'd have work, but primarily because I was feeling the old feelings, I was home. This was what had simmered beneath my longing to return: the need to feel like myself again. Flipping through the theatre listings as I walked back to my breakfast, I decided to strengthen this well-being by indulging in one of the principal joys of my first inhabitation. I would go to the half-price ticket window at the World Trade Center, and treat myself to a show.

At one o'clock that afternoon, I walked over to 23rd Street and caught the E train downtown. On the way, I passed a construction site on Eighth Avenue: a supermarket that had lain derelict for decades had been razed, and an apartment tower was going up, the slabs of floorplate stacked to the sky, the ochre faux brick façade—the ubiquitous skin of all the city's new construction—half in place. This, I'd observed, was the story nowadays. Block after block of Manhattan had been bulldozed, scaffolding shrouded countless sidewalks in gloom; the old idiosyncratic city was being replaced, remorselessly, by huge office complexes and anonymous, uniform apartment towers. Boarding the subway, I thought that I did not believe in sentimentalizing an old eyesore that served no function; but I remembered that market, remembered how on wet winter days, when it had become dense with peeling posted bills, the façade could be as arresting as an abstract canvas. The city itself had been such a canvas. Now it was being painted out, and replaced with a faux brick picture plane.

Heading south on the pristine train, surrounded by cheerful tourists in Birkenstocks and fanny packs, I considered that there could be no more pointed example of how much New York had changed than the subways. In the 1970s, when I'd first moved back, I would push my way through a heavy wooden turnstile feeling like a dray horse yoked to a mill, board an aged conveyance the skin of which quivered with graffiti, and take my seat among purveyors of stolen goods, auto-proctologists and other intimate self-examiners, and the occasional armed robber, all to the roar of a dozen ghetto blasters (and for fifty cents plus free rides on weekends, not only the best show in town but the cheapest). Back then, the city had been like the subway, a glorious ruin: one wandered the tourist-free streets of Manhattan as through an archaeological site, pondering fragments of the midcentury civilization of fedoras and ad men and Longchamps lunches; I would walk for hour upon hour, studying the pentimenti of signs painted on the sides of buildings, stopping to read brass letters set into the sidewalk before establishments long departed—reconstructing, out of a thousand clues, the lost paradise of Manhattan. Now, disembarking from a subway car that felt as antiseptic as a well-scrubbed bedpan, walking through the shop-lined lower concourse of the Trade Center—a destination no different from an LA shopping mall—I understood that the New York of my youth might have largely vanished; that, as I had reconstructed that lost civilization twenty years before,

I now faced the prospect of conducting a search for my own time.

I took the escalator up to the TKTS window, where the names of shows that had released half-price tickets for that night's performance were displayed. None of my choices were available. The guy working the window suggested I try the uptown booth, in Times Square; not wanting to get back on the train, drawn outward by the incomparable spring day, I decided that I would walk. I needed to find the city I remembered and recognized, so that I could remember—and recognize—myself.

Ninety minutes later—having traversed, with a flaneur's meditative absorption, half a dozen downtown districts and a decade-plus of personal history—I walked into Washington Square Park, sat down on the edge of the circular fountain, and propped my chin on my hands. For the best years of my life, Greenwich Village had been my home: I had strolled every block, studied the façades, the stonework, the signage, until I knew them with a lover's intimacy; I could describe the shadings of mood that cloaked its corners, knew where the bad smells were, the places the icy winter winds hit hardest. Yet my memory of it, as I walked along Bleecker, up MacDougal and east on Eighth—collectively, the innermost ring of the tree of my New York life—was more emotional than actual: a mental mood that, though suffused with pleasure, remained irretrievable as a set of particulars. Some of the old places remained, most did not; but my invocation of them, I had to admit, had been no more than a recitation of names. The past, irrefutably, was past.

Grimly, I looked around, at the NYU students, the skateboarders, the pot dealers, the fat little cops, the clotted, colliding knots of sightseers and strollers, all of them blabbing their heads off...and felt nothing. For years, I'd told myself I wanted to go back east because I missed the pleasures of a walker's city. But, thinking back to what my wife had said that day on the beach, I realized that I'd been looking for something different: a physical representation of the man I'd been at 23, the man I remained in my head. I had, in LA, increasingly let go of an unworkable identity. But I had assumed I could be a new man in an old life, clung to the fantasy that I could still be happy in the old ways. The problem, I now saw, was not the city's gentrification. It was that I was living in the past, and—existentially as well as physically—the past was no longer available to be lived in. If I was indeed a new man, I had to find a new place to put that self.

To this, I felt violently resistant—I found unbearable the prospect of not being able to embrace the innocent optimism, the unburdened joy in living, I'd experienced a generation ago on these streets. The mix of emotions this inspired—unfairness, shot through with grief—seemed very nearly primal; and, making this connection, I understood my feelings: New York, city of my youth, had been the closest thing to an ideal mother I'd ever had. New York had never broken its promises to me; it had given me every treat for which I'd greedily asked, and none had disappointed; it had never lost patience with me, used my love to manipulate me, punished me for my feelings. Most of all, the city had given me the latitude to learn my own lessons and thereby become—for better, for worse—my own man.

This was not a relationship I cared to lose. And yet, even as I admitted this, my mature side gave me a nudge: I was making, of my town, the same inappropriate demand I'd made of my talent and my wife: asking it to respect my childish wishes, despite the inescapable fact of my adult-hood.

I looked at my watch: 2:30. I'd lost the urge to go to the theatre, but something else seemed to nag at me, something I'd forgotten. All at once it came back: The Whitney Museum had mounted an exhibition of the paintings of Mark Rothko, a show scheduled to close in just a few days. If I got to the Whitney by three, I thought, walking briskly through the crowd toward Fifth Avenue, I would have a few good hours in which to look.

At 3 PM precisely, I strode into the Whitney, Marcel Breuer's Brutalist masterpiece, at the corner of Madison

Avenue and 75th Street. It was—incredibly, given my many previous visits—the first time I realized the building *was* a masterpiece. Buying my ticket, moving through the crowd, I found myself noticing the rows of circular metal light fixtures that covered the ceiling, the way their density made them disappear yet what an elegant, effective choice they were within the lobby's rough-hewn shell; I became aware of the contrast between the concrete walls, the lacquered slate floor, and such carefully designed details as the bronze-and-wood handrail on the stair that led to the café. My God, I thought, what a beautiful building this is, what a privilege to be able to visit it. Mies van der Rohe's famous remark came into my head: God is in the details.

I rode up to the first of the two floors on which the Rothkos had been installed, got off the elevator, and walked into the galleries. Hearing my heels click in the ecclesiastical quiet, I abruptly remembered something else I'd completely forgotten: Twenty years before, I had seen these very same pictures, at *another* Rothko retrospective at the Guggenheim Museum, only a few blocks from where I now stood. That, I realized, had been the first big show I'd attended after arriving in New York, at the magic age of 23. I had been taken by a girl I had just started dating, a colleen with a great mane of chestnut hair, a snorting laugh, and an inexhaustible supply of button-down cashmere sweaters; this girl had been an art history major, and was a great fan of Rothko's pictures, which she described—wonderfully, to my ears—as "windows of contemplation." I'd had a great time at that show. We took the elevator to the museum's top, then gave ourselves to the gravitational pull of Frank Lloyd Wright's great spiral as though it were an amusement park ride, moving down and down, past one canvas after another. About halfway through the exhibition, my girlfriend took my arm as she pointed at something and whispered to me, I turned to listen and glanced over her shoulder at the tiers of paintings across the atrium—a stunning perspective—and thought: Here I am, in the greatest city in the world, in this amazing architectural construction, with this smart, elegant chick, surrounded—literally—by windows of contemplation. Standing in the Whitney twenty years later, I thought back to how I had felt—remembered it sharply and precisely— and realized that it had been the most complete moment of my life.

Returning to the present, I bypassed the galleries featuring Rothko's early work and went directly to those with canvases in the artist's signature style. Positioning myself before the first, a picture entitled *Number 19*, I stared, letting the painting do its work on me, until I felt that I had seen it. Doing so required patience and a suspension of judgment, but it was the only way: If I expected a picture to seize, with its many qualities, my heart and mind, I needed to empty myself of expectations, release the thought that there were fifty more to go and I had better hurry up, and put myself into a meditative state.

I absorbed several paintings this way before an odd realization began to seep through and obstruct my concentration: While I remembered the *experience* of being at the Guggenheim, I had no specific recollection of anything I was seeing now. This disparity of remembrance, moreover, was amplified by the distance between my reaction to the work and the affection with which I usually thought of Rothko's oeuvre—an affection, I realized, that derived from the circumstances under which I had first experienced it.

There was, I thought, planting myself before a large canvas from 1949, a correlative to my response, in the change in critical opinion regarding the artist's work. At the time of that first show, which opened eight years after Rothko's suicide, his paintings *were* in fact largely considered to be expressions of the sublime. "Only that subject matter is valid that is tragic and timeless," the artist had declared; and, presented on the one hand with the tragedy of Rothko's end, the establishment, perhaps inevitably, accepted the judgment of timelessness on the other. This consensus was physicalized by the Guggenheim itself, in which the downward spiral of Rothko's emotional life was reenacted by Wright's architecture, and reinforced by the decision to place the painter's earlier works up top, and his final, doom-laden panels down, down, at the bottom.

I had, at the time, only a general awareness of all this. My girlfriend had given me an interpretive hook on which to hang my hat—"windows of contemplation"—and this had been enough: being young, and knowing nothing, I simply accepted the general view of the pictures' value, and did not really see them.

Now the fog of importance had dissipated, and what were once regarded as transcendental expressions of universal truths had proven to be, *hélas*, mere artworks. Yes, the critics agreed, they were beautiful; but these rectangles of color, endlessly repeated in endless variations, did not support the claims the artist had made for them. The work, the establishment now declared, amounted to an exceptionally refined variant of decoration.

Shaking my head as though to clear it of this—feeling that I had not properly begun—I returned to *Number 19* and started again. What struck me on second viewing was the way in which Rothko had taken different colors and, by varying their intensity and hue, produced the effect of dimension: the yellow shape on the lower right seemed the closest, while the head-like form of washed-out blue inhabited a middle distance; the colors, moreover, seemed to hang in the air of the picture like so many veils, as immaterial as the Aurora Borealis. Returning to *Violet, Black, Orange, Yellow on White and Red*, I experienced this impression of perspective even more strongly, almost as though I were looking at an abstract waterscape: a yellow beach, a placid orange lake, a black band of forest on the horizon beneath a violet sky. In the middle of looking at *Magenta, Black, Green on Orange*, reflecting that the blurry streak of white that divided the painting reminded me of a speeding train, I reminded myself to stop treating the pictures like Rorschach tests and simply take them in. This helped: I felt the paintings become states of feeling I could enter as I looked at them. By the time I reached *Green, Red on Orange*, it was easy to accept the pleasures offered by the violently contrasting colors, to absorb viscerally the inviolate, loudly broadcast purity of their personalities and the ways in which they amplified and subtracted from one another. *Untitled*, for some reason, left me cold, despite the minutes I gave to it; but my delight returned as I beheld the swoony expanse of white in *Number 18*, my spirit lightened and hung above my corporeal self like the shofar-shaped white breath visible on the black field atop *Black, Pink and Yellow over Orange*. At moments I grew tired, felt oppressed by the job of looking; but as the quality of the work ascended, I increasingly experienced the yes yes yes of release, of immersing myself in something wondrous and receiving a satisfying sense of well-being—of peace—in return. *Light, Earth and Blue. Ochre and Red on Red*. Yes. Yes.

The revisionists were right, I supposed, moving upstairs to the next suite of galleries, Rothko's oeuvre didn't amount to an artistic Second Coming. But perhaps the painter had needed to tell himself (and the world) that what he was doing was more "important" than he believed it to be in his secret heart, in order to plunge again and again into the raw waters of color and form and return with so many singular pleasures. With this, I sympathized: having spent half my life gambling on my imagination, I understood the impulse to assign significance to one's endeavors. But I knew also that one's creations had their own lives, they belonged ultimately to themselves, and that what mattered was not what one intended or desired but what one made. The irrefutable *fact* of any artwork, its position as the nexus between the subjective sensibilities of artist and audience, was what made the experience of looking so satisfying: Here was something outside oneself that—because it was a record of the struggle for truth, yet stood apart from that struggle, immutable—could lead one back to oneself. This was, I realized, precisely what was happening to me at the moment. Rothko's work meant something entirely different to me at 43 than it had at 23, the pictures had lost the aura of greatness bestowed on them by youth, ignorance, enthusiasm, most of all by the belief, looking over my girlfriend's shoulder, that I'd at last found happiness. But this diminution of status was not the fault of the paintings—they hadn't changed, I had. And it was this change in myself, I now saw, that was enabling me to meet these old friends, whom I had not properly understood, and to derive the pleasure from them that had always been there to be taken, a pleasure that had awaited me for twenty years, as the frisson of youth evaporated, as self-abuse and suffering deformed my personality and spoiled my nature, as excess led me to wisdom and opened my heart, as my happiness was lost and replaced by something more complex, a state of being that enabled me to appreciate what I was looking at in the moment.

It was with this recognition—that I could not have the experience I was now having if I had not lived the good and bad of the twenty previous years—that I began to feel better. Moving through the rooms, shifting my eyes from one canvas to the next, I offered a silent thank-you to the paintings for their gift—for enabling me, however belatedly, to grow up. If New York had been good mother enough to let me learn my own lessons, I reflected, it had perhaps failed me by not pushing me from the nest. As a corrective, the formulation offered by the Rothkos was simple: I had obtained a rich and various education; but to partake of its benefits—to have experiences, as my wife might have said, that depended upon the simultaneity of the moment and all the history that preceded it—I would have to become an adult. If I clung to the past, I could have no history; and without the resonance of history to inform my days, there could be no future. If I rejected the insight the Rothkos were offering, I would remain a ghost forever, unable to live in a past that no longer existed, unwilling—afraid—to enter the future.

So I did it: stepped into the present, and felt myself become real again, alive and in the world. So doing, I smiled, aware of the irony: I had searched and searched for something that was the same, and when at last I found it— in the form of this exhibition—it showed me that everything was different. The result was a moment as complete as the one I'd experienced twenty years before at the Guggenheim.

I had realized a goal that was no less mine than my wife's: I'd kept hold of the self I had been at the moment I had become myself, and done so with dignity.

Thinking of my wife, I remembered what she'd said about getting, then not getting, her period: that she had been excited about the onset of her menstrual flow because it meant she could find love; but that the need for love had also signaled the end of her freedom, a freedom she hoped would return now that the flow had ceased. I thought of my own fertile years, the time bookended by the two retrospectives, the first nearly simultaneous with my arrival in New York, the second enabling me to accept, indeed embrace, the end of my youth. Was *I* now, I wondered, free?

Passing through the last gallery, looking at Rothko's exhausted final works, I stopped. I had a problem with my wife's formulation. Love, after all, was supposed to *make* you free, not do the opposite. But her perspective struck me so forcefully because it was, of course, my own. I had always defined love as being able to "give" myself freely, yet had felt trapped in every relationship because, once I'd given myself, I invariably placed the needs of my partner above my own. What then, I wondered, *was* love to me? Was there anything, in those fertile years, that had moved me?

The answer, I thought, gazing at the monochrome canvases, lay in my feelings about the city. New York had been the love of my life for a simple reason: it had said *yes*. What excited me—what invariably unleashed, in my fertile years, a frenzy of affection—was permission. Indeed, I recalled (thinking again of my wife, of her barren womb), receiving permission would fill me up to such a degree that I'd feel pregnant with a new life, that life being my own. Permission was the reason I had loved cocaine, loved it with a wild, feral greed: because it said yes, to everything, when nearly everything else said no. I loved cocaine, as I had loved New York, because it made me feel pregnant with myself.

No surprise: my many cocaine-inspired pregnancies had

proven false, for the reason best stated by the fortune in the cookie I'd received with my Chinese take-out two nights earlier: "You alone can give yourself permission." My fertile years had become a prison of false pregnancies induced by my passion for the empty seed of another's good opinion.

Turning slowly, I took a last, long look. And thought: If Iris Murdoch was correct when she observed that love is the extremely difficult recognition that something other than oneself is real, it might equally be said that *self*-love is the recognition—in my case, extremely difficult—that *one* is real, too. My wife had been right, I decided, departing the gallery and moving toward the elevators. My fertile years had concluded with the conviction that I could act, and act, without regret: my life and my desires had become one. The death of my love for permission, the cessation of that flow, had indeed set me free—the proof being that here, after a thousand misfires, I had finally given birth.

Boarding the elevator, I turned back for a final glance. But a platoon of boy-hipped, behemoth-footed Park Avenue gals had followed me onto the car, and their padded Chanel shoulders and peacock fans of hair cut off the view. The door closed; in minutes, I was back on the street. New York had never looked better.

My wife remained silent for a long time after I related this over the phone that night—for so long, in fact, that I thought I'd lost the connection. Then I heard the familiar birdsongs in our courtyard and, distantly, a leaf-blower.

"Rose?" I said.

"That's so amazing," said my wife. "Do you know what happened to me today?"

"What?"

"Well. I'm at the Malibu meeting. And there's this *actress*. *Very* young, *very* pretty. And, like, the time I have invested in *hating* her—I mean, I almost had to stop going to the meeting, because every time she shares, I get *so pissed off*, I fall asleep."

"Is she…?"

"She's nothing, it's totally irrational. I mean, you know—it's so *tough*, she and so-and-so were up for the same *part*, the producers went with the name and all she got was an under-*five*, boo fuckin' *hoo*."

"She's your garden-variety…"

"Exactly. And, and, you know. Always says *hello*, remembers my *name*. It's just, I, I, I just want to kill her."

"So?"

"So today she comes up to me after the meeting and says, 'Will you coach me?'"

"*What?*"

My wife shrieked with laughter. "She says"—again she paused to shriek—"she says, 'You've studied with all those people, you're so smart about acting—you're my *role model*.'"

My wife barely got through the sentence. We were both laughing so hard that all that could be heard by either of us were gasps and shrieks.

"What did she want you to do?" I said.

"She was going up for a play, and wanted me to work with her on a monologue."

"To audition with?"

"Uh-huh."

"Jeez," I said.

"Right? This *twenty*-year-old with titties out to here and teeth like, like, you know. Like *teeth*. And you *know* she's going to get it."

"Not if she's not—"

"She's young, she's blond! She's up for the same shit so-and-so's up for! You think anybody gives the, the flyingest of fucks if she's any good?"

"What happened?"

"So we're standing in the parking lot by her Miata, and I'm fee-*yew*-ming. But, you know, I said to myself, Rose, *don't* be negative, *don't* be bitter. *Appreciate* that this woman has actually been listening to you and is, is, you know. Is *getting* you."

"I can see where this is going," I said abruptly.

"Where?"

"You realized this was something you would find satisfying, if you were willing to let go of the past."

My wife, I could hear, was sniffing, not with laughter but tears. "It was the exact same thing as you," she said. "I mean…" My wife blew her nose. "I said, 'I'll give you an hour, I'll tell you what I think, and that'll be that.' You know? 'It's not what I do but I'll try.'

"So we go to her place, which is this *rilly* cute studio in Santa Monica—*rent*-controlled, some *producer* got it for her because he quote-unquote 'respected her talent.' All 44 Triple D inches of it. She gives me a cup of Yogi Tea and does the monologue."

"How was she?"

"Well? She sucked. She sucked to high heaven, but she had something. Totally artless, plus *she* thinks she's great, but she has something. So she finishes, and she *sits at my feet*, and I realize she, I mean, to this girl I'm as close as she's going to get to the real thing, right? I've *got* the look—you know, wild hair, bad teeth, so *that's* good, *that* says Aging Jewish Acting Guru. And she's sitting there and waiting for me to, to, you know. To *bless* all of this indicating and playing the mood I've just witnessed.

"And I'm *seething*. And *so* bitter. And I just suddenly felt so sad."

"That you hadn't made it?"

"That I *felt* this way. That after all these years of working on myself, I should still have these feelings…" My wife sniffed, and sighed heavily. "And I just thought, you know. Be in the moment. So I said, I put on my hmm-*that*-was-interesting look and said, Do it again."

"And?"

"And she still sucks, but I'm thinking, What would be helpful? She was doing it very sentimentally. What she needed was an *action*. So I said, 'What is this speech going to *get* you?' You know…"

"What does your character hope to get with what she's saying?"

"Right. So she comes up with a few things and—you

would have been very proud—"

"I'm already proud." And I was.

"I let her figure out which action was best on her own. She runs through it a few more times—I gave her some corrections—and sure enough if she didn't get better."

"And how did that make you feel?"

"It was great," my wife said emotionally. "There was a problem that needed to be fixed, and this girl sensed that I could help her fix it. And I did."

"Yes."

"And you know," said my wife, "I realized. It's like you say about New York. The great love of *my* life was groups— being in these situations in which I could be *intensely myself*, and *get down*. Which was great, but…"

"You never grew up."

"I did not put to work what I had learned in an adult way. Because of my loyalty to these things from my past. And I just realized that this *joy*, doing the work and having it come to something, could be mine—as long as I accepted that, more likely than not, it wasn't going to be me on the stage. The work is there. But only if I, you know, like you say."

"Yes."

"*So. Anyway*. She offers to pay me, and I say, no no no, don't be ridiculous, blah blah blah. And *then* she says, can she hire me on an hourly basis to work with her. You know, find monologues, and…"

"What'd you say?"

"Yes. I said yes. We have our first appointment next week."

"Fabulous."

"I'm an acting coach. The one thing on God's green earth I never wanted to be."

"Even if it doesn't work out. With *her*. You have work."

"I have work to do," my wife said simply, gratefully. "I have work."

For a few moments, I listened to my wife breathe. I had never been happier for her; and, I sensed, she'd never been happier for herself.

"I wish I could find work," I finally said.

"Oh, Kerry. You're a writer."

"It doesn't suit me."

"What *does*?"

"Art appreciation. Apparently."

"Can you get paid for that?"

"I don't think so," I said dryly.

"Oh, sweetie."

"What?"

"I'm just thinking, you know. It's an important day in both our lives. I mean, look how long it's taken us to get here."

"Yes."

"And I just feel so blessed that I have someone to share it with. This is soooo great."

"Yes," I said. "No matter what. We have always talked."

There was a silence, in which I sighed, heavily, several times. The blood pounded in my ears.

"What?" my wife said, in a porcelain voice.

"Rose, I'm not coming back."

My wife did not reply.

"For all these years that things have been going bad," I said, "I've been struggling with how to get out—I have wanted, for so long, to be out of this marriage. I've said, if she does *this* one more time, if she does *that*. I've made deals with myself. The one thing I never did is face up to what I'm going to lose."

"What?"

"This. Sharing our day. And in talking, showing each other why life is beautiful. I guess…" I shook my head. "You know, it's funny, it's—*both* our days have been about loss, about accepting things we can *only* get if we let go. And I have to accept that…that though I may very well have a better marriage than this one. I will never have what *we* have with anyone else again. When—" I hesitated. "I was going to say 'this.' When *you* go out of my life, it's gone for good."

My wife clucked her tongue and sighed.

"But, Rose," I said, "we're just not good for each other."

"How can you say that?"

"I used to think it was because we're too far apart. But actually it's the opposite, we're too much alike in this one way—we never grew up."

"Haven't we now?"

I hesitated. Then: "Too much has happened."

My wife exhaled through her nose. As if to say, That's true.

Again, the silence lasted long enough for me to think I'd lost the connection. Until my wife said, "What do you want to do?"

"You want to stay there?"

"Obviously."

"We've got two places. We don't own anything jointly. We can just take back our stuff and go our separate ways."

"Somehow that seems the worst part of it," said my wife, beginning to weep. "Just taking back our things. It's like we were never even here."

"We were here," I said, feeling my own tears, the tightness in my throat. "But it's a measure of *how* we were here that we should end up as two voices."

"Oh shut up. You."

Softly, we shared our last laugh.

"Let me know when you're coming," my wife said, with a trace of the steel that reminded me that she would handle this better than I. "I'll go away, and you can take your things. I don't want to see you."

"Okay."

There was a small pause, in which sat the whole of our time together. Then, with a clarity and simplicity I'd not heard before, my wife said, "Goodbye, Kerry."

"Bye."

My wife hung up and I put down the phone. Now I had lost everything. I could begin.

FOUR

Turns out you *can* get paid for art appreciation. It's called being a curator, and it is my present profession. Back in New York for two years, solvent but bored to enervation by the brochures and annual reports that comprised my literary output, I enrolled in a fine-arts school and took courses in architecture. All the driving and looking I'd done in LA had sparked an interest, and I thought I might write about it if I had an education. I'd completed my courses and was struggling to float my plan when a friend in the school's exhibitions department asked if I'd like to pull together a show. At this entirely unexpected opportunity I lunged ferally—tantalized by the prospect, after decades of gallery-bumming, of having four white-box spaces of my own to fill. I had no idea how or where to begin, but couldn't say no.

Seven months later, the exhibition debuted, and I had found my vocation. Curating used all my talents. Though I worked machine-like and in a way thoughtlessly—each day had its marks to be hit, there was no time for second-guessing—the measure of my mind that remained detached noticed things, for instance the link between my instinct to treat the filling of galleries as a form of storytelling, and my dramatic instincts, the way I'd previously built a script; my subterranean self further noted that, though I could instantly perceive the broad strokes of a spatial story, I'd then struggle to shape the micro-narratives that formed the "scenes" within the rooms. So even as I zoomed forward, through a blinding spray of schedules, decisions, details, some part of me recognized that I was doing the same old things in different circumstances, and began to make adjustments, husbanding the strategies that emerged when I functioned optimally, using them to supplant my inadequacies. Wandering the galleries at the opening, I accepted the surprised congratulations of my colleagues: none of them, they declared, had expected *this*.

Neither had I! I exclaimed modestly. But I was lying. If like the protagonist of *La Dolce Vita* I had once been an insecure provincial, nose pressed to the glass of cultivated society—if I had once pretended to know more than I did—decades of looking, listening, and drawing my own conclusions had led me, incrementally but nonetheless, to the actual transcendence of my origins. Considering the Rothkos that day, I realized to my surprise that I'd developed the discernment to embrace what I loved and appreciated without needing the approbation of nobler minds. Beholding my own exhibition, I felt proud: for trusting that everything I had learned prepared me for the work and would see me through it; for deriving so much from the process; for—at long last—achieving a result.

I parlayed my success into a full-time position, at an institution that mounts regular exhibitions. I have less autonomy, but more money, support, and resources. Finally, I am busy enough. I love my work.

There are, to be sure, difficulties. I think often of what Martin said at Fiona's party, about life being a series of forced self-reinventions, the one constant being work, the consoling homeland one carries through all the inner and outer migrations. As in LA, I experience frequently the isolation of exile: I feel yet like the man who, having taken up residence in a foreign land, scrupulously follows local customs but feels as disengaged as a marionette, awaiting with weary patience the time when, from repetition, his instincts will be rewired permanently. It feels odd that no one knows me as a screenwriter, that the self I was so recently no longer exists. Yet even as I miss that man, it becomes ever harder to recall how it felt to be him. And so I work, and love my work, and wait for the anxiety to evaporate.

There is something else. No matter the beauty of my installations or the quality of my catalogue essays, if I am doing my job properly, I am invisible. The ache of no longer being a creator has to do with more than ego. But as my wife recognized when she swallowed the pain of not doing the work herself, coached her friend and discovered her calling—thereby launching what is a very successful career—a fulfilling life has its price, and sometimes that is the thing we cherish most. It's all a matter of knowing what's good for oneself, and being willing to take the consequences. This, I discovered with Jessica, is no less true in love.

XXXX

Four days after the call that ended my marriage, I went back to Los Angeles, following an exchange of phone messages through which my wife and I set a date for me to move out. "As soon as possible" was the way she put it. In this we were, at long last, in accord.

Greater than my desire to get it over with was my need to be in the arms of Jessica. My appreciation of the strategies that enabled her to keep her soul and imagination alive, the honesty of our understanding, the power of my attraction to her: the effects of these had not been diminished by separation, indeed they struck me even more strongly in my freedom. I wanted to see Jessica most of all, I admitted, gazing out at the wastes of New Jersey from the bus to Newark Airport, because I had begun to be in love with her.

First, however, I had to endure one of the multiple amputations that would make parting from my wife an excruciating ordeal. Returning to my apartment on the appointed day, walking down the sprinkler-dampened concrete path, my arms overburdened with boxes and rolls of tape, I assumed moving out would be sad but easy: I didn't have to face my wife, there were no disputes about who got what—I'd pack up, leave the keys, and be gone with a tired good riddance.

What I discovered, however, in the hours entering what had for nearly six years been my home and pulling shut the door behind me, was that walking away meant the cessation of only one kind of pain. This surprised me completely, for the simple reason that ending the marriage had been so difficult, it seemed inconceivable that there could be anything left to endure. I had not truly understood the stress of staggering on for years with the mountain of the marriage on my back until I'd finally sloughed it off: the tension's release left me limp as a banana skin, for days I had dropped off narcoleptically in movies, coffee shops, conveyances, every moment and location I'd had occasion to sit down.

That exhaustion, I began to understand as I packed, had covered other feelings. As had the abstract quality of the breakup: it was a solitary event, at the end of a silent day, during which I'd been so steeped in memories, observations and discoveries that my wife's voice, arriving in my ear, owned the quality of something invented. Now, feeling the shock of re-entry into LA, surrounded by all my wife's things—all of *our* things—the fact of what I had done struck home, and the hours and days of our connection had never seemed more real to me. As I slogged around the apartment removing pieces from the puzzle that had been our shared life, leaving black voids of regret in their stead, I remembered every layered moment of our years here, replayed both the experiences themselves and the truths beneath them: that no one was to blame, our feelings for one another were and always would be a hopeless jumble of love and hate; that every happiness we shared would hold a particle of disappointment, every lash of anger would be threaded with regret for the tenderness it spoiled; that there was love, that love was not enough, that however good or bad the moment might be, our connection, ultimately, was fugitive.

When the movers had come and gone, I paid a final visit to the dictator's-palace bathroom and went down to the kitchen. There, the paper that would transfer ownership of the car to my wife awaited my signature. Picking up the pen—realizing that this, more than any legal document, was my true divorce decree—I regretted not having our final conversation face to face. We had never dealt with any challenge in a thorough way; now we were ending the marriage in the same half-assed fashion we'd done every other thing. For a moment, I considered waiting for my wife to come back, so that we could at least say goodbye. Instead, I signed the papers, set my key beside them, and left. The car, I thought, pulling shut the door. If I had swallowed my pride and bought another one, I would have been pissed off for a week, and that would have been the end of it. Instead, this.

Of course, I considered, getting into my rental car, my wife could have done the same thing: We might both have looked into ourselves, admitted our faults and made leaps of faith, despite our differences the marriage might have been saved. Well, I decided, making the always-difficult turn from Beverly onto Fairfax, heading south toward the Farmer's Daughter Motel (so help me God that was the name), the past is past. All I can do now is try not to make the same mistakes, to be true to my newfound maturity.

Pulling into the motel parking lot, feeling an oncoming attack of my situational narcolepsy, I considered that I did not feel absolutely equal to the tests of adulthood—and I would shortly be facing a big one. I was, I thought, stumbling toward my room, marching directly from marriage into the embrace of my—what *was* Jessica? My paid partner in self-improvement and truth-seeking? How would she react, I wondered, when I materialized, newly separated, broadcasting my proposals? What *were* my proposals—what did I *want*? Fumbling my keys into the doorknob, pitching face down onto the bedspread and into death-sleep, I made a promise to listen to myself, to follow my instincts wherever they might lead.

Two hours later, I sat up abruptly in the dark room, grabbed my keys, and took off. A choking Santa Ana was blowing down from the canyons, thick with pollen, dust and something like ash, the wind burning with a cindery edge that, allegedly, unhinged animals and people alike. In the past, the Santa Anas would have played a central part in the prologue of the drive, but those nights were over for me. Thinking ahead to what awaited, I took the same attitude:

the dirt and decrepitude, the nerve-wracking dynamics and petty games, none of it could touch me. I was going for a particular purpose, one that would or would not pan out. Whatever went on in the whorehouse wouldn't mean much either way.

Or so I thought. I was, in fact, in for a surprise.

It had seemed, the old lathe-and-stucco clapshack, to be shaking in the wind, but more than the weather was spooking the girls when I arrived. At first I thought the place had been robbed. But why, then, Angel's push-lipped pleasure, Gloria's murmurous sympathy? Why was Wendy brewing tea? I looked quickly around for Jessica, and saw her in a corner of the waiting room, beautiful and fragile, buried beneath her wig. Just as quickly I realized that she was the focus of all this gentling, catty satisfaction, and anxiety.

For a moment, Jessica seemed to look through me; then, recognition hitting her with a jolt, her eyes twitched, she smiled demonically. Rather than waiting for me to make a selection, Jessica sprang up, took my hand, and led me hurriedly down the corridor to the cubicle beside the big room, glancing at the latter apprehensively and, it seemed, increasing the force of her footfalls as we passed.

We went in. Jessica sat on the bed, hands pressed lightly between her thighs.

I stood over her. "What's going on?" I said.

"My fiancé's here," Jessica said, her indented teeth clenched and looking particularly rabbity. She tilted her chin at the paneled wall separating us from the next room.

I stared at her. "You're kidding."

Jessica breathed shallowly and said nothing.

"He found out you work here?"

"He came in as a customer."

"A—…Does he have any history…?"

Jessica shrugged imperceptibly, it was almost like a twitch. If he did, she had no idea.

"Just like that?" I said incredulously. "By coincidence?"

Jessica glanced at me, wide eyes conveying both terror

and amusement, then returned her gaze to the wall. "'Of all the gin joints in all the towns in all the world…'"

I laughed grimly, appreciative of her grace under pressure. *Her fiancé.* It seemed inconceivable, but when the Santa Anas blow, it is said, anything can happen.

"Who's he in with?" I said.

"Sinclair."

"Oh, God," I groaned. Then, catching the look on Jessica's face, I realized it: "She knows who he is, right?"

Jessica nodded.

"How did she find out?" I barked, annoyed that Jessica could have been so stupid.

Jessica made a gesture with one hand and closed her eyes. Meaning, With her genius for divining such things. I could sketch in the particulars myself: the fiancé coming in, Jessica retreating, Sinclair seeing this and teasing it out under the guise of wanting to help. Then—instead of getting rid of him, as might easily have been done—Sinclair had snapped up Jessica's man with the greed of a piranha coming upon a stray finger. She'd have her vengeance now, I thought, considering the bad blood between the women. A famously stingy fuck, Sinclair would give it up for the fiancé like never before, she'd beg for it in the dirt track, throw her great legs to the moon and moan and slobber like a Faulkner loony. I envied him. If ever there was a guy who would testify to the fairness of the value-for-money equation when it came to paid sex, it was Jessica's fiancé. More to the point, I knew, and *Jessica* knew, that when, in the days to come, she'd find him staring off into space with a little smile, he'd not, to borrow a line from Groucho, be thinking of all the years he'd wasted collecting stamps.

"Be right back," Jessica said.

I took off my clothes and sat there, listening like a bat. I had been thinking that the changes in my life would upset the equilibrium between us, but they were nothing compared to this. My brain caromed around my skull. Would Jessica extend to her fiancé the same tolerance she gave herself? Or did their connection depend upon her secret sense of power, a presumption of her fiancé's innocence? Would she be dismayed by the sounds of his lovemaking? Kick down the door and—despite her own culpability—confront him?

Whatever the case, one thing seemed certain: The appearance of her fiancé could not possibly work for us. *This* was now what the night was about. I could not imagine putting it aside even for a moment, let alone long enough to consider our own possible future.

But I had underestimated Jessica. On came the rapping of the heels, with a finality I recognized as the end of this part of my life, the door opened and in she came. Rather than undressing, however, Jessica took me by the hand and led me to the common wall. She took down the mirror that hung there—and revealed, not one, but two bullet-sized peep holes.

I confess that their presence didn't entirely surprise me, I had assumed that something of this nature existed somewhere in the place. What I regretted was that the holes looked into the big room, that volume in which I'd disported so frequently—undoubtedly (on my extra-long, extra-busy nights) for the delectation of my fellow johns.

I turned to Jessica. To my surprise, she was looking at me tenderly, and with eager expectation, as if to suggest that, whereas in the past we'd communicated by having sex with one another, tonight we would do so by observing her fiancé's sex with Sinclair. My heart turned over: Once again, Jessica had distinguished herself, she'd taken an intimate injury and converted it into a potential source of knowledge. I took her hand, drew her to me, and gave her a small, appreciative kiss. I could feel a turn, then, in the decision I had come to make.

Putting our eyes to the peepholes, Jessica and I beheld a not-very-surprising spectacle: Sinclair, orally vacuuming Jessica's fiancé. They were in profile, the fiancé standing, Sinclair kneeling before him, naked but for her red heels, holding up her soupy breasts to improve their appearance, a pillow cushioning her knees. It was a stagy tableau; seeing it,

I realized Sinclair had anticipated that Jessica would be unable to resist watching, and had maneuvered her fiancé into this position, the better to show off his betrayal. Relishing her part, Sinclair sucked his cock with a slow specificity, and his pleasure was in every way obvious, most of all from the leer on his face as he stood looking down at her, hands on hips and feet apart. More interesting to me than the sex was the man himself, my heretofore immaterial rival for Jessica's affections. He was the physical incarnation of the distracted man of science she'd described: very tall, slightly tubby, flat-footed, and covered with a light brown fuzz (though, I had to admit, gifted in the length and girth departments).

I glanced at Jessica apprehensively. She was watching with solemn absorption, the fingertips of both hands touching the wall, the light from the peephole placing a glint in the emerald of her eye. Only a minute trembling betrayed the tumult of her feelings.

I returned my own eye to my peephole, in time to see Jessica's fiancé withdraw himself from Sinclair's mouth and help her to her feet. He slipped his arms around her waist and pulled her close, his huge erection folding upward, rising between Sinclair's breasts. She flashed her eyes and grinned with admiration, but there was, as she laid her hands on his chest, something genuine in her manner.

Jessica whispered, "She's surprised by how big he is."

Again I glanced at her, but she remained riveted to the scene, and so I kept quiet. This was something Jessica had to endure alone.

Peeping, I saw that the fiancé continued to hold Sinclair tight, gazing down into her eyes with authority. Sinclair kissed his palm and looked up at him—still grinning, but with a measure of uncertainty. She was used to having the upper hand, and the fiancé's relaxation—his comfort in what was, typically, an uncomfortable situation—was unbalancing her.

"Look how in control he is," Jessica murmured with a kind of wonder.

I thought of what Jessica had told me about the vaguely needy quality of his affection for her, the security she derived from his solidity. The man on the wall's other side seemed very different from the one Jessica had described, and I sensed from the wonder in her voice that he seemed different to her as well.

"What?" Sinclair blurted, unnerved by his gaze. In response, the fiancé leaned over and whispered in her ear; we were able to observe the surprise, susceptibility, and regard that played through her expression as he suavely explained his game. Sinclair laughed, impressed and willing; the fiancé drew back and looked at her, a loose smile on his face.

Jessica laughed, too, quiet and short—a how-do-you-like-that laugh.

I looked at her, she met my eyes. Our expressions showed an identical observation: given what we knew, Sinclair's pliance in the fiancé's hands was surprising indeed.

Quickly—anxious to see what would happen next—we looked back. Jessica's fiancé put Sinclair face down on the bed and parted her legs. Then he sat down between them and, watching her face with the sly patience of an angler about to hook a fish, slipped in a finger. Whatever he was doing was particular: only the sinews of his forearm seemed to move.

"He *never* did that with…" Jessica whispered, wide-eyed. "Isn't that…interesting."

Sinclair's face, raised up off the bed, was turned toward us. Her eyes were fixed and black, her tongue gathered thickly behind her lower incisors, the progress of her arousal readable by the gill-like pulsing of her nostrils. She had painted herself into a corner: to wound Jessica, Sinclair could refuse the fiancé nothing; yet she'd assumed that he would be on the receiving end of her ministrations, rather than the opposite.

I glanced at Jessica, who was grinning with satisfaction at this reversal. Also, it was amusing, watching Sinclair struggle against the inevitable.

Jessica's fiancé laid his free hand on the base of Sinclair's spine, the better to hold her in position, and made whatever he was doing fatally specific. Her orgasm, a dozen heartbeats later, was startling: Sinclair buried her face in the mattress, put both hands atop her head and, shoulders hunching rhythmically, moaned, "I am. I am. I am."

"Isn't…that…interesting," Jessica said.

Finishing, Sinclair lifted her face from the mattress sharply—as though she'd awakened in a strange bed—looked back at Jessica's fiancé and, covering her mouth with her fingertips, emitted an embarrassed giggle.

He was already turning her over, rolling on a condom he'd brought himself, driving into her. For ten minutes, we watched as, Sinclair lashing and pounding at him, Jessica's fiancé controlled her completely, finally pulling out, removing the latex, and emptying himself into her mouth. Rather that resisting this, Sinclair drew back her head awkwardly and swallowed him, the while palming and palpating his balls.

Jessica sat down on the edge of the bed. I perched on an old, exploded hassock.

"Well," I said.

Jessica turned up her hands, raised them, let them fall atop her thighs. "He was so much better than he is with me."

"Better? Or different?"

Jessica gave me an irritated look. "Don't try and change what it is. I got wet watching him and I barely get wet *fucking* him."

To this, I did not reply.

"I feel bad," she said, her trembling giving way to a down-drawing despair. "I've never been able to get any of that out of him. Obviously, he doesn't feel comfortable with me."

"Maybe you don't have that kind of relationship," I said.

"I guess we're both looking for a kind of comfort and security," she murmured. "That excludes certain aspects of our nature." Jessica's eyes bulged. "*Apparently.*"

"What does he think you do all night, anyway? *What's* his name?"

"Egg." She shrugged. "I'm an actress, I tell him I have straight jobs."

"Doing what?"

"Driving a mobile animal-control unit. Road-grading on the Imperial Highway."

"*What*? Does he actually believe, this guy, that his five-foot-tall bride-to-be is out at four AM, tarring the interstate east of the 405?"

"*Your* wife believes you're in San Luis Obispo with a headache."

We looked at one another and laughed, ashamed.

"It does us no credit," Jessica groused. She turned to me, as upset as I'd ever seen her. "You want to believe in the choices you've made. But the choices don't lie, do they?"

"What do you mean?"

"He *chose* me, okay? Because I was *safe*. A choice *not* to have a certain kind of woman. But he obviously wants a whore—not only because he came to a whorehouse—"

"But because he's engaged to one."

"Right? I mean, how smart are we? Can we ever be as smart as the thing in us that sees the truth? Egg wants *me*, but he can't let himself admit it, because it's too destabilizing."

I nodded. After a silence, Jessica held out a hand to me; I sat beside her. She smiled with apology, knowing that I had returned on other business.

"It's all right," I said. "It's good for us."

"Oh?"

"When I first started coming here," I began, "it was all about, I'm trying to come as close as I can to being intimate without losing myself. And the girls, so many of them, it was about taking something from a man without giving him anything. So much of the experience here, on both sides, is about coming up to a line but not crossing it."

"You mean this is a kind of ultimate example of that,"

Jessica said, glancing at the wall. "How much closer to wanting to change could Egg and I possibly come without changing? It's…" She shuddered. "Boy, it's a real fucking lesson."

"Do you want him?" I said.

Jessica took a breath and let it out slowly. "No," licking her lips as though about to be sick. "I don't want to be with someone who can't be all of himself. It's not a judgment on him—obviously I'm the same way. But I want to change."

"Maybe *he* wants to change. Maybe you could change with him."

"That would mean being honest with each other, about everything," her voice barely audible. "That's not going to happen." Jessica traced a fold in the bedsheet with a finger. "With Egg and me, the lie is part of the choice. Take it away, you lose the connection."

Jessica's observation spoke to my own loss, my wife's and my inability to transcend ourselves for the sake of what we had or might have, an inability that seemed bred into our histories. I thought sorrowfully that my wife and I had spent our lives preparing to undertake a failed marriage—another of the amputations that accompanied my divorce. Abruptly I felt glad for them: one becomes, not inured to pain, but accepting of its necessity.

Jessica was massaging a spot on her chest. I knew that spot. It was where the painful constriction of irredeemable loss lay.

"It's over between you and Egg?"

Jessica nodded, her tears flowing freely. "Something you have said," she began. "That you see in what I do here. My way of converting what has oppressed me into pleasure."

"You mean…"

"'How can you know what you know and not act?' you said."

"Sure."

She gestured at the wall. "Seeing this, I can answer that question. I see how much pain is associated for me with love. And if I have any expectation of using what I've learned…you know. With you."

This was, I saw, Jessica's Rothko Moment. I tightened my grip on her hand. "So you're ready?" I said.

"I'm ready. It hurts to see him here," she said, sobbing, her cheeks mottled and swollen. "It hurts that he *has* to be here. Here we are, two people who *chose* each other. And look."

I had felt the same sense of anguish regarding the choice of Rose, my wife. Goodbye, Rose, I thought, realizing that in a moment our connection would be sealed off in a special part of my memory, one that would get ever smaller, until I put it away forever.

I said, "I've left my wife."

Sentimentally, I saw Rose for the first time, her apartment door opening, the look of disappointment on her funny face; I heard myself laugh, and my remark—"Hey, maybe you'll like me"—that made her smile and got the ball rolling.

Jessica was staring at me. "You did?"

"I moved out this afternoon."

I saw myself, not going through the door into Rose's apartment, but the door closing, her face disappearing, now half there, now a quarter there, now gone.

"I'm sorry," Jessica said.

I saw nothing now but Jessica, her fuscia hair and emerald eyes.

I said, "It was time."

We heard the door to the big room open and close, Sinclair's heels rapping quickly off. Hurrying to the peep holes, we saw Egg, still naked, counting out his cash.

Jessica looked at me with dead eyes. "He's going for the second hour," she said.

"There's no accounting for taste, is there?"

Jessica came to me and, for the first time since I'd arrived, we embraced.

"No, there isn't," she murmured into my shoulder.

Jessica kicked off her shoes, tossed aside the wig, and pulled off her maillot; we got into bed and made love. After a while, Sinclair came back, she and Egg went at it again, even more audibly, their screams and groans could be clearly heard, as I suppose ours could. But rather than being hurtful, Jessica and I seemed reassured by what was happening just beyond the wall. It served as a reminder to us, of how close we were to running from love, lying to ourselves, fearing our own strength. Only the flimsiest of barriers stood between our best and worst selves, they lived side by side in the house of our souls, and the fact that Jessica and I could be together on the good side of that barrier demonstrated that we were indeed our best selves together, we'd earned our love. I had promised that I would listen to what was in my heart, and what I felt as we lost ourselves in one another was that I wanted to be with Jessica, I had made my choice. We made love, and I had never known such certainty.

As for what we actually did—that's personal.

XXXX

Jessica joined me at the Farmer's Daughter the next day. Leaving her fiancé had been difficult but, coming on the heels of his big night, easier than anticipated. Jessica simply told him that, though he was a great guy, she was young and they were rushing things. He was sorry but, undoubtedly thinking of his own mixed feelings, understood. There had been less between them than either realized; less, certainly, than I'd had with my wife.

We hit the road in Jessica's Accord (which engendered our first joint purchase—appropriately, a timing belt), and lived largely on her savings. Eventually, I was able to support us. Technology was on my side: Whereas, at the beginning of my career, my appeal depended upon my appearance at this or that office with my Tales from the Freelance Woods, now no one wanted to see me, the Internet had arrived and all that mattered was that one could receive and return an electronic file. With the advent of the virtual employee, I found myself perfectly situated and was able to make a good living. Better still, we were free.

I was nervous at first, but Jessica made it easy, by having no expectations, exerting no pressures. Cruising around California, we wound up renting a furnished garage apartment near Big Sur, which interested Jessica for its connection to her favorite writer, Henry Miller. I loved her for that: Miller, with his middle-aged flowering and rejection of the norm, was an excellent association for me just then. We spent our days hiking steep trails and exploring narrow bits of beach, struggling with our losses. Withdrawal from prostitution, we discovered, was as anguishing as getting off drugs. For a time, it put Jessica off sex entirely; she'd talk into the night about the hundreds and hundreds of men, raging, bragging, weeping. I have said that every choice comes with its consequences and, for me, this was the first: I found myself cohabiting with an ex-prostitute, and had to live, not only with the pains she inflicted by simply recounting her past, but with my resentments and, I confess, mistrust. But I didn't have to hide my feelings—Jessica and I were skilled at handling difficult impasses—and the lack of concealment that was our hallmark enabled us to get through it.

Eventually we tired of Big Sur, began simply to follow the highway, and I developed an addiction to following my instincts—to acting, and feeling always high. As this became less and less an experiment, more and more my nature, I gained an appreciation of the architect Le Corbusier's maxim, "A successful plan is always based on a problem that has been well stated." For the first time in my life, I made my feelings known, and my actions followed upon them. This led us back to New York, where I returned to school and became the man I am today.

Jessica and I remain together. We live in Rose's old apartment, which is less of a constriction than it might be because, after a lifetime of working from home, I am at an office all day. Jessica goes to auditions and struggles with her writing; and there are times when I am struck by both the strangeness and appropriateness of living in my wife's—now my ex-wife's—old place, with an actress/writer who is not her. To have the old and new intertwined in this way can create jarring juxtapositions; but it is also a materialization of the fact that we live moment to moment with our histories, a reminder of how close I remain to my old self, and of the satisfaction of knowing that, had I not endured, I would not, could not, be here.

It does sometimes distress me that Jessica seems less knowable than did Rose. It reminds me of my experience with the Rothkos: They launched things in my mind, they were exceptionally beautiful, but ultimately two things were in play, object and viewer, thing and perception of thing. The difference is that, while the paintings never changed, Jessica has and continues to do so, we have both changed, separately and together, so that the dialogue between perception and perceived is richer, unifying rather than isolating. And, also, that I can be filled up by Jessica, as I was by the paintings, and not find that I have been displaced. These are the things, I have discovered, that make loving a human being more gratifying than loving a work of art. That's the difference in my life—that I can be happy with Jessica but that my happiness does not depend upon her, or hers on me. Neither of us needs permission.

Now I have confessed, and have, I think, confessed it all. Except for one thing I never expected to find in life and love, a condition best described by something Jessica said the other day, when we were walking beside the river, past the piers in the West Village. We saw something that made us both smile; Jessica and I caught each other's eyes. When the rush of gratitude, of joy that bordered on the sacred, had passed, she shook her head.

"Huh," she said. "This is easy."

Acknowledgments

It would be hard to overstate my gratitude to Nick Courtright for selecting *Permission* for publication; Kyle McCord, whose wisdom, tact and forbearance as my editor improved the manuscript substantially; art director Ronaldo Alves, for his good humor, inexhaustible patience and sharp eye; and Alex Kale and Erin Larson, who applied their imagination, judgment and taste to perfecting the book's jacket text and interior design.

To paraphrase Tennessee Williams, I have always depended on the kindness of friends, especially those who generously gave me the space and solitude in which to write: Barbara and Sidney Cheresh, Wendy Dozoretz and Fred Woocher, and Mary Anne and Michael Tanner. My gratitude as well to the MacDowell Colony, where this book first took shape, and the New York Society Library, where it was completed.

Finally, a very special thank you to Scott Flander, for his discerning literary judgment, and for nearly half a century of the most sublime and immaculate friendship; and to Elaine Chekich, to whom *Permission* owes its life.

About Atmosphere Press

Atmosphere Press is an independent, full-service publisher for excellent books in all genres and for all audiences. Learn more about what we do at atmospherepress.com.

We encourage you to check out some of Atmosphere's latest releases, which are available at Amazon.com and via order from your local bookstore:

Twisted Silver Spoons, a novel by Karen M. Wicks
Queen of Crows, a novel by S.L. Wilton
The Summer Festival is Murder, a novel by Jill M. Lyon
The Past We Step Into, stories by Richard Scharine
The Museum of an Extinct Race, a novel by Jonathan Hale Rosen
Swimming with the Angels, a novel by Colin Kersey
Island of Dead Gods, a novel by Verena Mahlow
Cloakers, a novel by Alexandra Lapointe
Twins Daze, a novel by Jerry Petersen
Embargo on Hope, a novel by Justin Doyle
Abaddon Illusion, a novel by Lindsey Bakken
Blackland: A Utopian Novel, by Richard A. Jones
The Jesus Nut, a novel by John Prather
The Embers of Tradition, a novel by Chukwudum Okeke
Saints and Martyrs: A Novel, by Aaron Roe
When I Am Ashes, a novel by Amber Rose
Melancholy Vision: A Revolution Series Novel, by L.C. Hamilton
The Recoleta Stories, by Bryon Esmond Butler
Voodoo Hideaway, a novel by Vance Cariaga
Hart Street and Main, a novel by Tabitha Sprunger
The Weed Lady, a novel by Shea R. Embry
A Book of Life, a novel by David Ellis
It Was Called a Home, a novel by Brian Nisun

About the Author

Marc Kristal has authored, co-written or contributed to more than forty books, notably *Re:Crafted: Interpretations of Craft in Contemporary Architecture and Interiors*, *Immaterial World: Transparency in Architecture*, and *The New Old House: Historic and Modern Architecture Combined*. His journalism has appeared in numerous publications, including the *New York Times*, *Architectural Digest*, *Wallpaper*, *Metropolis*, and *Dwell*. Also a screenwriter, Kristal wrote the 1990 feature *Torn Apart*, and created the script for *Saigon '68*, which received the 2013 Best Documentary award at the L.A. Shorts Fest and the CINE Special Jury award. He is presently at work on a biography of the British Pop artist Pauline Boty.